Ethical Vegetarianism

From Pythagoras to Peter Singer

edited by

Kerry S. Walters
and
Lisa Portmess

State University of New York Press

Cover illustration is *Peaceable Kingdom*, by Edward Hicks, Gift of Edgar William and Bernice Chrysler Garbisch, © 1998 Board of Trustees, National Gallery of Art, Washington, D.C., © 1834, canvas, .745 x .901 (29 3/8 x 35 1/2).

Production by Ruth Fisher
Marketing by Fran Keneston

Published by
State University of New York Press, Albany

For information, address State University of New York Press, State University Plaza, Albany, NY 12246

Library of Congress Cataloging-in-Publication Data

Ethical vegetarianism : from Pythagoras to Peter Singer
  / edited by Kerry S. Walters and Lisa Portmess.
      p.   cm.
    Includes bibliographical references and index.
    ISBN 0-7914-4043-5 (alk. paper). — ISBN 0-7914-4044-3 (pbk. :
alk. paper)
      1. Vegetarianism. 2. Vegetarianism—Moral and ethical aspects.
I. Walters, Kerry S. II. Portmess, Lisa, 1950–
TX392.E84 1999
613.2'62—dc21   98-14897
                                                                     CIP

10   9   8   7   6   5   4   3   2

Prefatory Note

When the idea of an anthology devoted to vegetarianism was originally conceived, we (the editors) innocently planned to include readings that offered religious as well as ethical perspectives. But we quickly discovered that the literature in both arenas is so vast and rich that we couldn't do justice to either between the covers of a single volume. Consequently, we took the obvious decision to dedicate one volume—this one—to ethical vegetarianism and a second one to religious vegetarianism. The latter, entitled *Religious Vegetarianism: From Hesiod to the Dalai Lama*, serves as a companion volume to this one, although the two may, of course, be read separately.

We would like to thank the librarians of Musselman Library, Gettysburg College, for their patient and expert help in tracking down frequently obscure works on ethical vegetarianism; Ms. Chrissy Matthies, PETA, for her generous legwork; and Ms. Sandra Martin and Ms. Cynthia Gibbon, for their help in preparing the manuscript.

For
Jonah and Kim
K. S. W.

For
my mother
Jane Rafferty Portmess
L. P.

Contents

Introduction: Cruel Fatalities

If there are any marks at all of special design in cre-
ation, one of the things most evidently designed is
that a large proportion of all animals should pass
their existence in tormenting and devouring other
animals. They have been lavishly fitted out with the
instruments necessary for that purpose; their
strongest instincts impel them to it and many of
them seem to have been constructed incapable of
supporting themselves by any other food. . . . The
scheme of Nature regarded in its whole extent, can-
not have had, for its sole or even principal object, the
good of human or other sentient beings. Whatsoever,
in nature, gives indication of beneficent design,
proves beneficence to be armed only with limited
power; and the duty of man is to co-operate with the
beneficent powers, not by imitating but by perpetu-
ally striving to amend the course of nature—and
bringing that part of it over which we can exercise
control, more nearly into conformity with a high
standard of justice and goodness.

—John Stuart Mill

In his "Essay on Nature," John Stuart Mill confesses his wonder
at those who would see perfection and beneficent design in
nature. He observes darkly that "everything . . . which the worst

men commit either against life or property is perpetrated on a larger scale by natural agents." With callous indifference, "a single hurricane destroys the hopes of a season; a flight of locusts, or any inundation, desolates a district; a trifling chemical change in an edible root, starves a million people."

Mill, like many of the writers in this anthology, contemplates the cruelty of nature and the suffering of sentient beings in light of the metaphysical and moral questions that reflection on nature gives rise to: Is there beneficent design in nature, "a more excellent nature in the universe" as Porphyry declares? How are we to view "devourers and the devoured," predators and prey? Is our own purpose to follow or to amend nature? Do we kill for food as tigers kill or do we resist such violence toward animals that may be natural to us? Is the suffering that nature ordains ultimately good in its provision for the renewal of life?

In confronting the specific cruelty human beings impose on animals killed for food, these same philosophical questions about nature and about human nature arise even when such suffering is believed justified. Such animal suffering, carried out by the human hand and not by the impersonal forces of disease, wind, or fire, has the peculiar power to turn our gaze at once both inward and outward. When the jaguar pounces, when tidal waters flood, when nightingales fall in the nighttime hunt, our gaze turns outward, like Mill's, to a world perplexing in its seeming "redemptionless suffering," its "cruel fatalities." How is the world constituted that this is its being? But when we contemplate the violence of our own hand, the remorseless rituals of the slaughterhouse, "the death-set eyes of beasts," our gaze turns inward to questions about human nature, human violence, and the human relationship to other animals. Is the killing of animals for food a pardonable crime? Is it a crime at all? Is remorse futile? Is the disavowal of violence to animals requisite to any striving for moral goodness?

In all the traditional arguments in defense of killing animals for food—that animals have no soul, that they feel no pain, that they lack rational capacity and moral standing, that they exist for human need, that as brutes their suffering is without moral significance— much importance is given to the "naturalness" of such killing. We too are jaguars. We too prey on the weak. Life is harsh and cruel even to us. And yet, as the selections in this anthology indicate, a fainter but persistent strain of protest can be heard throughout the centuries, beginning with Pythagoras and resounding in nineteenth- and twentieth-century vegetarian literature on animal rights, animal suffering, global ecology, and modern factory farming. Plutarch's caustic observation that "no one eats . . . flesh just as it is; men boil it and roast it, altering it by fire and drugs, recasting and diverting and smothering with condiments the taste of gore so that the palate may be deceived" reverberates in the outrage Harriet Schleifer feels today at a McDonald's television commercial which speaks of hamburgers that "grow in little hamburger patches." The faint yet persistent history of such protest literature affirms certain themes with constancy: that animal suffering matters, that the brutalization of animals brutalizes the human soul, that moral goodness, in whatever form it is attainable, cannot be achieved without renouncing violence to animals—that, as Porphyry puts it, "the more excellent nature in the universe is entirely innoxious," just, restrained in passion, "possessing a power which preserves and benefits all things."

Moral concern over the suffering caused to animals by humans, faint yet persistent as it has been, is one thing; confidence in the hope that it can be eliminated is another. Some ethical vegetarians are optimistic that the worse excesses eventually will be ameliorated, others are not. Writers such as Percy Shelley, Anna Kingsford, and Henry Salt believe our relationship to animals can be made just and harmonious. Even the less sanguine John Stuart Mill implies that human efforts to "amend the course" of cruel nature can mitigate suffering. But in the minds of others, our brutality to animals is evidence of a world irretrievably broken. Such a gloomy appraisal led William Alcott in the nineteenth century to write that "the world is a mighty slaughterhouse—one grand school for the suppression of every kind, and tender, brotherly feeling— one grand process of education to the entire destitution of all moral principle—one vast scene of destruction to all moral sensibility, and all sympathy with the woes of those around us." The figure of Jean-Christophe in Romain Rolland's eponymous novel echoes Alcott's sense that to contemplate the wretchedness suffered and inflicted by humans is to contemplate "the tragedy of the universe." But he also rages against it as an unpardonable crime that cries vengeance upon the Creator: "If God is good only to the strong, if there is no justice for the weak and lowly, for the poor creatures who are offered up as a sacrifice to humanity, then there is no such thing as goodness, no such thing as justice. . . ."

Out of this deepest of metaphysical and religious question—
Can things be made right? Can they be made better?—comes the
moral complexity of the writings of this anthology.

"Animal Life, Somber Mystery": What is Human Duty?

Whatever the metaphysical, cosmological, or religious meditations
occasioned by human cruelty to animals, moral conviction itself is
everywhere entwined with it. Here is one such example, taken from
Ovid's account of Pythagoras' thought, all the more interesting for
how alien its cosmology is to that of much contemporary vegetarian
literature:

> Remember this:
> The heavens and all below them, earth and her creatures,
> All change, and we, part of creation, also
> Must suffer change. We are not bodies only,
> But winged spirits, with the power to enter
> Animal forms, house in the bodies of cattle.
> Therefore, we should respect those dwelling-places
> Which may have given shelter to the spirit
> Of fathers, brothers, cousins, human beings
> At least, and we should never do them damage. . . .
>
> Let the bull plow
> And let him owe his death to length of days;
> Let the sheep give you armor for rough weather,
> The she-goats bring full udders to the milking. . . .
>
> Kill, if you must, the beasts that do you harm,
> But, even so, let killing be enough;
> Let appetite refrain from flesh, take only
> A gentler nourishment.

In this evocation of soul-transmigration, the ethical imperative
derives not only from disgust at befouling the dwelling place of
ancestors, though that is without doubt one of Pythagoras's main
tenets, but also from a sense of the wrongness itself of consuming
animal flesh. Ovid writes in the spirit of Pythagoras:

> Oh what a wicked thing it is for flesh
> To be the tomb of flesh, for the body's craving
> To fatten on the body of another,
> For one live creature to continue living
> Through one live creature's death.

Elsewhere he associates animal eating with fear, treachery, and cunning, a destruction of all that was once peaceful. An intricate conjoining of both cosmological and moral reasons for abstinence, Pythagoras's vegetarianism springs from a sense that we do justice both to ourselves and to our ancestors, as well as to animals themselves, when we abstain from eating their flesh. Especially fascinating in the Pythagorean records, as well as in more recent vegetarian literature, are the allusions to a golden age, a Garden of Eden, a time when flesh eating was unthinkable, when earth's generosity with her provisions was sufficient for human life. Shining through dark worries about pridefulness, arrogance, and bloodlust is the hope that our brutality to animals is not fixed and immutable, that humans can somehow recapture the innocence they enjoyed before the Fall. This is the lighter counterpart to the dark pessimism of an Alcott or Rolland.

Alien as it now seems, the Pythagorean cosmology of a living, breathing universe, eternal, divine, and unitary, affirms a kindredness of spirit among all living things. If our souls transmigrate to animals, we "winged spirits are evermore the same, though passing always to ever-changing bodies." Thus from a cosmology strange to us today springs a declaration of the unity of life that in various forms is expressed by many writers of this collection—Albert Schweitzer, for one, Howard Moore for another. Rolland describes Jean-Christophe looking into the eyes of the beasts and seeing "a soul like his own, a soul which could not speak." Out of this sense of kindredness comes the ethical conviction that "the continual endeavor of man should be to lessen the sum of suffering and cruelty" even if we cannot eliminate it.

Human duty is more obscure when no golden age casts its glow on the darker present. In his nineteenth-century *La bible de l'humanité*, Jules Michelet, who saw no escape from the killing of animals for food, nonetheless insisted that "the animals below us have also their rights before God. Animal life, somber mystery!

Immense world of thoughts and of dumb sufferings! All nature protests against the barbarity of man, who misapprehends, who humiliates, who tortures his inferior brethren. Life—Death! . . . Let us hope that there may be another globe in which the base, the cruel fatalities of this may be spared to us." In this pained witness to animal suffering, Michelet implores us at least to forego the pretense of justification for slaughter. If we cannot refrain from killing for food, we can at least cease defending the act, a diminished ethical duty certainly, but an ethical duty nonetheless.

In Richard Wagner's letter to Mathilde Wesendonck another stark sense of ethical obligation emerges. As he reflects on the fate of the lower animals, who are denied the ability to transcend their suffering and achieve that stoical resignation attainable at least in principle by human beings, Wagner remarks that "all I see—with a sense of my own tormented despair—is their absolute, redemptionless suffering without any higher purpose, their only release being death. . . . And so, if this suffering can have a purpose, it is simply to awaken a sense of fellow-suffering in man, who thereby absorbs the animal's defective existence, and becomes the redeemer of the world by recognizing the error of all existence." A gloomy ethical imperative, indeed, but profound in the moral burden it places upon humankind. To shake people out of their complacency, their ignorance—"to make them feel life's great anguish"—this is what is morally required, if there is no hope of eliminating such suffering.

"The Lamb is Fat"

Alphonse De Lamartine describes in his autobiographical *Confidences* his first realization that butchers kill. As a child he was once given a pet lamb and grew to love it "with that first fondness which little children and young animals naturally have for one another." But one fateful day the family cook announced to his mother: "Madam, the lamb is fat, and the butcher has come for it; must I give it to him?" Spared by the child's anguish, the lamb remained alive. Lamartine's mother later took him through the yard of a slaughterhouse, trusting that his instinctive revulsion would reinforce the horror of the "shameful human infirmity" of carnivorism. Horror and pity he indeed felt, "a repugnance, based on reason, to cooked flesh," along with a sober sense of lost innocence. This theme of first awakening to violence, of lost innocence, like first awakenings to sexual knowledge, haunts vegetarian literature. Not only Lamartine, but Mandeville, William Alcott, and Tolstoy, among others, all dwell on the metamorphosis of vision caused by witnessing animal slaughter. "It is such as *you* makes such as *us*"—so Henry Salt has the butcher say. Primal and terrifying, the slaughterhouse becomes indelibly inscribed upon consciousness and the source of deepest moral protest in vegetarian literature. Tolstoy, in his vivid descriptions of visiting a slaughterhouse, concentrates as much on the slaughterer as the slaughtered when he protests not only the cruelty and pain experienced by animals, but also the dreadful suppression in humans of "the highest spiritual capacity—that of sympathy and pity toward living creatures. . . ." We are kindred enough to animals to empathize with their helplessness and pain, yet capable of withholding all pity. The dissonance between these responses reveals, especially for witnesses of animal slaughter, the paradox of our violence toward animals: are we the slaughterer or the slaughtered? Terrifying in the absolute power the slaughterer represents and the absolute powerlessness of the animal awaiting slaughter, the slaughterhouse reveals a larger, unbearable truth about life itself—that we too are subject to such power, not just at moments of violent crime and accident, but in the remorseless movement of all living things toward death. The animal suffers and in that suffering embodies more than its own destiny. Thus the slaughterhouse instructs.

"Disciplined Passion"

Instead of focusing on questions of virtue and moral purity, contemporary philosophical defenses of ethical vegetarianism wrestle, with "disciplined passion," over the more formal question of just what the wrongness is in our killing of animals for food. Is it the denial it represents of the inherent value of animal life? Is it the suffering it causes to kindred creatures? Is it the way in which modern agribusiness mass-produces animals for consumption, the way in which it masks suffering with "smiling cows, dancing pigs, and laughing chickens"? Is it the ecological damage done by factory farming, its despoliation of land and squandering of natural resources? Each of these interpretations has been argued for by recent proponents of ethical vegetarianism.

Such diverse contemporary positions seem far removed from more traditional questions about moral purity and the good life asked by earlier writers. Yet although these modern queries focus on considerations of animal rights and interests, concerns about global ecology, and claims that the slaughter of animals reflects wider forms of political and gender oppression, much of their moral force stems from the same commitment to living justly and well evident in the writings of a Plutarch, Goldsmith, or Tolstoy.

A case in point is the work of Tom Regan. His defense of vegetarianism, based on the rigorously argued premise that animals possess a right to life analogous to the one claimed by humans, carries with it a call both for justice toward animals and moral reformation on our part. He believes that reason, not sentiment or emotion, compels this conclusion. Yet the very rationality of Regan's approach is infused with what he describes as "disciplined passion," a fervent conviction that "the whole creation groans under the weight of the evil we humans visit upon these mute, powerless creatures." This combination of rigorous analysis and disciplined passion is characteristic of other recent arguments for vegetarianism as well, from Peter Singer's thesis that their ability to suffer shows that animals deserve moral consideration, to Carol Adams' linkage of women's oppression with the oppression of livestock.

Contemporary defenders of ethical vegetarianism not only share with earlier writers a passion for justice and the moral life. In the company of ancient proponents of vegetarianism such as Plutarch and Porphyry, they likewise tend to reject the claim that there are essential moral differences between humans and animals—although contemporary writers do so more on the basis of a formal egalitarianism than a Pythagorean sense of the unity of all creation. They accordingly attack what traditionally has been the source of most defenses of our use of animals for food—that in some key characteristic human beings differ from animals in a way that justifies human exploitation of animals.

Regardless of the specific lines of argumentation taken by the authors in this volume, no perceptive reader can fail to see that the ultimate concern which inspires them is animal suffering. Their deep-seated moral ideal of nonviolence rebels against the slaughter of animals for food. Their fundamental intuition that suffering is an evil protests against the perpetuation of panicked death in the slaughterhouse so that human appetite can be pleased. Their horror at the natural cruelty that "makes the whole creation groan" is too fierce for them to tolerate the additional needless cruelties of factory farming. Compassion for animal suffering, revulsion at human violence: without these abiding themes in the literature of ethical vegetarianism, arguments from justice and virtue would have considerably less force.

"The waves of the sea, like banditti seize"

The suffering of animals at human hands, for all its cruelty and callousness, is dwarfed by the suffering that all living creatures endure from life itself. "The waves of the sea, like banditti seize and appropriate . . . with the same accompaniments of stripping, wounding, and killing as their human antitypes," Mill writes. Life is profligate, destruction prevalent. Species are extinguished by forces of nature, disease and predation diminish animal life even further by painful death, and chance and accident prevail in the struggle of every creature to survive. Michelet is right to remind us of the inevitability—the "cruel fatality"—of this spectacle of death in life.

But there is no reason to conclude that our destiny is to collaborate with nature's cruelty. Surely Mill's claim to the contrary that we ought perpetually to strive to amend the course of nature, even if in the end our accomplishment is small, better resonates with our deepest sensibilities. From these sensibilities are born ethical reflection and the determination to seek through argument, metaphor, and regimens of purification a different way to coexist with animals and to rise above that which, natural or not, has long been human habit. To ponder human violence and "animal life, somber mysteries" is to ponder the mystery of life itself and to seek ways to live well amidst nature's harshness, our own nature, and animal suffering. The writings here gathered are as much reflections on life's history and meaning as they are on how and why we ought to live a life of ethical vegetarianism.

Part I

Antiquity

The Kinship of Humans and Animals

Vegetarianism has been a religious lifestyle, particularly in the east, for thousands of years. But the first primarily ethical defense of abstention from food animals appears in the sixth century BCE with the philosopher Pythagoras. Even so, Pythagoras's moral objections to flesh eating appear to be intimately tied to his religious conviction that human souls transmigrate, or reincarnate, after physical death. Consequently, Pythagoras warns, the consumption of a food animal may in fact be the devouring of a human soul. It's for this reason, he concludes, that humans must regard all living things as kindred and bestow on them equal moral consideration. Failure to obey this principle results in actions that sully the moral purity of a person's life and prevent him or her from realizing full spiritual potential.

This theme, which Porphyry tells us was first introduced to Greece by Pythagoras, becomes a steady reference point for all ancient defenses of ethical vegetarianism. Proponents of a vegetable diet after Pythagoras tended not to take his doctrine of soul transmigration as seriously as he evidently did. (An apparent exception to this rule is the cryptic Empedocles of Acragas, c. 450 BCE, whose fragments suggest an endorsement of Pythagorean transmigration.) But they agreed that the consumption of animal flesh renders humans spiritually coarse by desensitizing them to the suffering of

11

animals. Moreover, the habituation to cruelty that a carnivorous diet breeds inevitably extends to a disregard for the suffering of humans as well because there is no clear-cut line of separation between human and animal existence. Animals, like humans, display sentience, intelligence, and emotions. The enterprise of achieving the ethically good life, then, must extend to consideration for animals.

Seneca, although not a lifelong vegetarian, was so impressed by the ancient world's assumption of kinship between humans and animals that he advocated, even if he himself failed to follow, a noncarnivorous lifestyle. Plutarch continues the theme, insisting that animals possess characteristics such as intelligence and sentience that entitle them to moral consideration. Although he does not adopt Pythagoras's doctrine of transmigration, he clearly agrees with the latter's claim that humans and animals are properly seen as belonging to the same moral community. Porphyry agrees that carnivorism is unsuited to a morally pure life, likewise choosing to focus many of his arguments on the kinship of animals and humans that so impressed Pythagoras and Plutarch. His defense of the rationality of animals, and hence of their moral standing, is one of the most eloquent defenses of ethical vegetarianism to emerge from antiquity.

The advent first of neo-Platonism and then of Christianity, both of which insisted on a radical metaphysical and hence moral distinction between humans and animals, gradually eliminated Pythagorean-inspired ethical reservations about flesh consumption. From the time of Porphyry to the eighteenth century, vegetarianism as an ethical choice was almost completely eclipsed.

The Kinship of All Life

Pythagoras

Of all the pre-Socratic philosophers, none is more enig-matic, and few more influential, than Pythagoras (c. 570–490). Like Socrates, he appears to have written noth-ing. Consequently, his teachings come to us from his disci-ples and subsequent commentators. But in spite of the absence of primary texts, as well as the often sketchy nature of secondary ones, the outlines of the Pythagorean doctrine can be pieced together fairly well. A good synopsis is pro-vided by Porphyry, a fourth-century (CE) follower: "What he said to his disciples no man can tell for certain, since they preserved such an exceptional silence. However, the follow-ing facts in particular became universally known: first, that he held the soul to be immortal, next that it migrates into other kinds of animals, further that past events repeat themselves in a cyclic process and nothing is new in an absolute sense, and finally that one must regard all living things as kindred. These are the beliefs which Pythagoras is said to have been the first to introduce into Greece."

Pythagoras's belief in the kinship of all living crea-tures and the transmigration of souls served as the basis for his ethical condemnation of carnivorism. This posi-tion exerted a colossal influence on subsequent defenses of vegetarianism. "Pythagoreanism" or the "Pythagorean diet" were synonyms for vegetarianism, in fact, well into the nineteenth century.

13

*The three selections here shed light on the Pytha-
gorean notions of transmigration, biological kinship, and
vegetarianism. The first is taken from Iamblichus's (c.
250–325)* On the Pythagorean Life, *the second from Diogenes Laertius's (third century BCE)* Life of Pythagoras,
*and the final selection is from book 15 of Ovid's (c. 43
BCE–18 CE)* Metamorphosis.

On the Pythagorean Life

Iamblichus

Since food, used properly and regularly, greatly contributes to the
best discipline, it may be interesting to consider Pythagoras' precepts
on the subject. Forbidden was generally all food causing flatulence or
indigestion, while he recommended the contrary kinds of food that
preserve and are astringent. Wherefrom he recommended the nutritious qualities of millet. Rejected was all food foreign to the Gods, as
withdrawing us from communion with them. On the other hand, he
forbade to his disciples all food that was sacred, as too honorable to
subserve common utility. He exhorted his disciples to abstain from
such things as are an impediment to prophecy, or to the purity and
chastity of the soul, or to the habit of temperance, and virtue. Lastly,
he rejected all things that are an impediment to sanctity, and disturb
or obscure the other purities of the soul, and the phantasms which
occur in sleep. Such were the general regulations about food.

Specially, however, the most contemplative of the philosophers, who had arrived at the summit of philosophic attainments,
were forbidden superfluous food such as wine, or unjustifiable food,
such as was animated, and not to sacrifice animals to the Gods, nor
by any means to injure animals, but to observe most solicitous justice towards them. He himself lived after this manner, abstaining
from animal food, and adoring altars undefiled with blood. He was
likewise careful to prevent others from destroying animals of a
nature kindred to ours, and rather corrected and instructed savage
animals, than injuring them as punishment. Further, he ordered
abstaining from animal food even to politicians; for as they desired
to act justly to the highest degree, they must certainly not injure
any kindred animals. How indeed could they persuade others to act
justly, if they themselves were detected in an insatiable avidity in

devouring animals allied to us? These are conjoined to us by a fraternal alliance through the communion of life, and the same elements, and the co-mingling of these. Eating of the flesh of certain animals was, however, permitted to those whose lives were not entirely purified, philosophic and sacred; but even for these was appointed a definite time of abstinence. Besides, these were not to eat the heart, nor the brain, which was entirely forbidden to all Pythagoreans. For these organs are predominant, and are as it were ladders and seats of wisdom and life.

Food other than animal was by him also considered sacred, due to the nature of divine reason. Thus his disciples were to abstain from mallows, because this plant is the first messenger and signal of the sympathy of celestial with terrestrial Gods. Moreover, the fish *melanurus* because it was sacred to the terrestrial Gods. Likewise, the *erythinus*. Beans also were interdicted, due to many causes, physical, psychic and sacred.

Many other similar precepts were enjoined, in the attempt to lead men to virtue through their food. . . .

Life of Pythagoras

Diogenes Laertius

He is said to have been the first man who trained athletes on meat. Eurymenes was the first man, according to the statement of Favorinus, in the third book of his *Commentaries,* who ever did submit to this diet, as before that time men used to train themselves on dry figs, and moist cheese and wheaten bread, as the same Favorinus informs us in the eighth book of his *Miscellaneous History.* But some authors state that a trainer of the name of Pythagoras certainly did train his athletes on this system, but that it was not our philosopher, for as he even forbade men to kill animals at all, much less could he have allowed his disciples to eat them, since they have a right to live in common with mankind. And this was his pretext, but in reality he prohibited the eating of animals because he wished to train and accustom men to simplicity of life, so that all their food should be easily procurable, as it would be if they ate only such things as required no fire to cook them, and if they drank plain water; for from this diet they would derive health of body and acuteness of intellect.

The only altar at which he worshipped was that of Apollo the Giver of Life, at Delos, which is at the back of the Altar of Horns, because wheat and barley, and cheese cakes are the only offerings laid upon it, as it is not dressed by fire, and no victim is ever slain there, as Aristotle tells us, in his *Constitution of the Delians*. It is also said that he was the first person who asserted that the soul, revolving around the circle of necessity, is transformed and confined at different times in different bodies.

The Teachings of Pythagoras

Ovid

There was a man here, Samian born, but he
Had fled from Samos, for he hated tyrants
And chose, instead, an exile's lot. His thought
Reached far aloft, to the great gods in Heaven,
And his imagination looked on visions
Beyond his moral sight. All things he studied
With watchful eager mind, and he brought home
What he had learned and sat among the people
Teaching them what was worthy, and they listened
In silence, wondering at the revelations
How the great world began, the primal cause,
The nature of things, what God is, whence the snows
Come down, where lightning breaks from, whether wind
Or Jove speaks in the thunder from the clouds,
The cause of earthquakes, by what law the stars
Wheel in their course, all the secrets hidden
From man's imperfect knowledge. He was first
To say that animal food should not be eaten,
And learned as he was, men did not always
Believe him when he preached "Forbear, O mortals,
To spoil your bodies with such impious food!
There is corn for you, apples, whose weight bears down
The bending branches; there are grapes that swell
On the green vines, and pleasant herbs, and greens
Made mellow and soft with cooking; there is milk
And clover-honey. Earth is generous
With her provision, and her sustenance
Is very kind; she offers, for your tables,
Food that requires no bloodshed and no slaughter.

Meat is for beasts to feed on, yet not all
Are carnivores, for horses, sheep, and cattle
Subsist on grass, but those whose disposition
Is fierce and cruel, tigers, raging lions,
And bears and wolves delight in bloody feasting.
Oh, what a wicked thing it is for flesh
To be the tomb of flesh, for the body's craving
To fatten on the body of another,
For one live creature to continue living
Through one live creature's death. In all the richness
That Earth, the best of mothers, tenders to us,
Does nothing please except to chew and mangle
The flesh of slaughtered animals? The Cyclops
Could do no worse! Must you destroy another
To satiate your greedy-gutted cravings?
There was a time, the Golden Age, we call it,
Happy in fruits and herbs, when no men tainted
Their lips with blood, and birds went flying safely
Through air, and in the fields the rabbits wandered
Unfrightened, and no little fish was ever
Hooked by its own credulity: all things
Were free from treachery and fear and cunning,
And all was peaceful. But some innovator,
A good-for-nothing, whoever he was, decided,
In envy, that what lions ate was better,
Stuffed meat into his belly like a furnace,
And paved the way for crime. It may have been
That steel was warmed and dyed with blood through killing
Dangerous beasts, and that could be forgiven
On grounds of self-defense; to kill wild beasts
Is lawful, but they never should be eaten.

One crime leads to another: first the swine
Were slaughtered, since they rooted up the seeds
And spoiled the season's crop; then goats were punished
On vengeful altars for nibbling at the grape-vines.
These both deserved their fate, but the poor sheep,
What had they ever done, born for man's service,
But bring us milk, so sweet to drink, and clothe us
With their soft wool, who give us more while living
Than ever they could in death? And what had oxen,
Incapable of fraud or trick or cunning,
Simple and harmless, born to a life of labor,

What had they ever done? None but an ingrate,
Unworthy of the gift of grain, could ever
Take off the weight of the yoke, and with the axe
Strike at the neck that bore it, kill his fellow
Who helped him break the soil and raise the harvest.
It is bad enough to do these things; we make
The gods our partners in the abomination,
Saying they love the blood of bulls in Heaven.
So there he stands, the victim at the altars,
Without a blemish, perfect (and his beauty
Proves his own doom), in sacrificial garlands,
Horns tipped with gold, and hears the priest intoning:
Not knowing what he means, watches the barley
Sprinkled between his horns, the very barley
He helped make grow, and then is struck
And with his blood he stains the knife whose flashing
He may have seen reflected in clear water.
Then they tear out his entrails, peer, examine,
Search for the will of Heaven, seeking omens.
And then, so great man's appetite for food
Forbidden, then, O human race, you feed,
You feast, upon your kill. Do not do this,
I pray you, but remember: when you taste
The flesh of slaughtered cattle, you are eating
Your fellow-workers.
                                Now, since the god inspires me,
I follow where he leads, to open Delphi,
The very heavens, bring you revelation
Of mysteries, great matters never traced
By any mind before, and matters lost
Or hidden and forgotten, these I sing.
There is no greater wonder than to range
The starry heights, to leave the earth's dull regions,
To ride the clouds, to stand on Atlas' shoulders,
And see, far off, far down, the little figures
Wandering here and there, devoid of reason,
Anxious, in fear of death, and so advise them,
And so make fate an open book.
                        O mortals,
Dumb in cold fear of death, why do you tremble
At Stygian rivers, shadows, empty names,
The lying stock of poets, and the terrors
Of a false world? I tell you that your bodies

Can never suffer evil, whether fire
Consumes them, or the waste of time. Our souls
Are deathless; always, when they leave our bodies,
They find new dwelling-places. I myself,
I well remember, in the Trojan War
Was Panthous' son, Euphorbus, and my breast
Once knew the heavy spear of Menelaus.
Not long ago, in Argos, Abas' city,
In Juno's temple, I saw the shield I carried
On my left arm. All things are always changing,
But nothing dies. The spirit comes and goes,
Is housed wherever it wills, shifts residence
From beasts to men, from men to beasts, but always
It keeps on living. As the pliant wax
Is stamped with new designs, and is no longer
What once it was, but changes form, and still
Is pliant wax, so do I teach that spirit
Is evermore the same, though passing always
To ever-changing bodies. So I warn you,
Lest appetite murder brotherhood, I warn you
By all the priesthood in me, do not exile
What may be kindred souls by evil slaughter.
Blood should not nourish blood.

        Full sail, I voyage
Over the boundless ocean, and I tell you
Nothing is permanent in all the world.
All things are fluid; every image forms,
Wandering through change. Time is itself a river
In constant movement, and the hours flow by
Like water, wave on wave, pursued, pursuing,
Forever fugitive, forever new.
That which has been, is not; that which was not,
Begins to be; motion and moment always
In process of renewal. Look, the night,
Worn out, aims toward the brightness, and sun's glory
Succeeds the dark. The color of the sky
Is different at midnight, when tired things
Lie all at rest, from what it is at morning
When Lucifer rides his snowy horse, before
Aurora paints the sky for Phoebus' coming.
The shield of the god reddens at early morning,
Reddens at evening, but is white at noonday
In purer air, farther from earth's contagion.

And the Moon-goddess changes in the nightime,
Lesser today than yesterday, if waning,
Greater tomorrow than today, when crescent.

Notice the year's four seasons: they resemble
Our lives. Spring is a nursling, a young child,
Tender and young, and the grass shines and buds
Swell with new life, not yet full-grown nor hardy,
But promising much to husbandmen, with blossom
Bright in the fertile fields. And then comes summer
When the year is a strong young man, no better time
Than this, no richer, no more passionate vigor.
Then comes the prime of Autumn, a little sober,
But ripe and mellow, moderate of mood,
Halfway from youth to age, with just a showing
Of gray around the temples. And then Winter,
Tottering, shivering, bald or gray, and aged.

Our bodies also change. What we have been,
What we now are, we shall not be tomorrow.
There was a time when we were only seed,
Only the hope of men, housed in the womb,
Where Nature shaped us, brought us forth, exposed us
To the void air, and there in light we lay,
Feeble and infant, and were quadrupeds
Before too long, and after a little wobbled
And pulled ourselves upright, holding a chair,
The side of the crib, and strength grew into us,
And swiftness; youth and middle age went swiftly
Down the long hill toward age, and all our vigor
Came to decline, so Milon, the old wrestler,
Weeps when he sees his arms whose bulging muscles
Were once like Hercules', and Helen weeps
To see her wrinkles in the looking glass:
Could this old woman ever have been ravished,
Taken twice over? Time devours all things
With envious Age, together. The slow gnawing
Consumes all things, and very, very slowly.

Not even the so-called elements are constant.
Listen, and I will tell you of their changes.
There are four of them, and two, the earth and water,
Are heavy, and their own weight bears them downward,
And two, the air and fire (and fire is purer

Even than air) are light, rise upward
If nothing holds them down. These elements
Are separate in space, yet all things come
From them and into them, and they can change
Into each other. Earth can be dissolved
To flowing water, water can thin to air,
And air can thin to fire, and fire can thicken
To air again, and air condense to water,
And water be compressed to solid earth.
Nothing remains the same: the great renewer,
Nature, makes form from form, and, oh, believe me
That nothing ever dies. What we call birth
Is the beginning of a difference,
No more than that, and death is only ceasing
Of what had been before. The parts may vary,
Shifting from here to there, hither and yon,
And back again, but the great sum is constant.

Nothing, I am convinced, can be the same
Forever. There was once an Age of God,
Later, an Age of Iron. Every place
Submits to Fortune's wheel. I have seen oceans
That once were solid land, and I have seen
Lands made from ocean. Often sea-shells lie
Far from the beach, and men have found old anchors
On mountain-tops. Plateaus have turned to valleys,
Hills washed away, marshes become dry desert,
Deserts made pools. Here Nature brings forth fountains,
There shuts them in; when the earth quakes, new rivers
Are born and old ones sink and dry and vanish.
Lycus, for instance, swallowed by the earth
Emerges far away, a different stream
And Erasinus disappears, goes under
The ground, and comes to light again in Argos,
And Mysus, so the story goes, was tired
Of his old source and banks and went elsewhere
And now is called Caicus. The Anigrus
Was good to drink from once, but now rolls down
A flood that you had better leave alone,
Unless the poets lie, because the Centaurs
Used it to wash their wounds from Hercules' arrows.
And Hypanis, rising from Scythian mountains,
Once fresh and sweet to the taste, is salty and brackish. . . .

We must not wander far and wide, forgetting
The goal of our discourse. Remember this:
The heavens and all below them, earth and her creatures,
All change, and we, part of creation, also
Must suffer change. We are not bodies only,
But winged spirits, with the power to enter
Animal forms, house in the bodies of cattle.
Therefore, we should respect those dwelling-places
Which may have given shelter to the spirit
Of fathers, brothers, cousins, human beings
At least, and we should never do them damage,
Not stuff ourselves like the cannibal Thyestes.
An evil habit, impious preparation,
Wicked as human bloodshed, to draw the knife
Across the throat of the calf, and hear its anguish
Cry to deaf ears! And who could slay
The little goat whose cry is like a baby's.
Or eat a bird he has himself just fed?
One might as well do murder; he is only
The shortest step away. Let the bull plow
And let him owe his death to length of days;
Let the sheep give you armor for rough weather,
The she-goats bring full udders to the milking.
Have done with nets and traps and snares and springs,
Bird-lime and forest-beaters, lines and fish-hooks.
Kill, if you must, the beasts that do you harm,
But, even so, let killing be enough;
Let appetite refrain from flesh, take only
A gentler nourishment.

Abstinence and the Philosophical Life

Seneca

*Lucius Annaeus Seneca (4 BCE [?]–65 CE), tutor and vic-
tim of the Emperor Nero, was the leading Roman Stoic of
his time. Like so many other well-meaning officials
caught up in the splendor of the Imperial court, Seneca
appears to have at least partially succumbed to the allure
of fortune and power his position made available. But he
never completely foresook his philosophical calling, nor
the Stoic ideal of the simple life that inspired him as a
youth. In this selection, taken from his* Epistolae ad Lucilium, *Seneca recounts his early experiments with diet.
Influenced by the Pythagorean tradition as well as the
belief that abstention from flesh purifies the spirit and
hence prepares the individual for the philosophical life,
the young Seneca swore off meat for a year. Even though
he confesses to bowing to custom at the end of this period
by returning to a carnivorous lifestyle, he concludes his
recollection by regretfully suggesting that students of philosophy—and would-be abstainers from flesh—often sacrifice deed for high-sounding rhetoric.*

I nasmuch as I have begun to explain to you how much greater
was my impulse to approach philosophy in my youth than to continue it in my old age, I shall not be ashamed to tell you what

ardent zeal Pythagoras inspired in me. Sotion [a Pythagorean, one of Seneca's tutors] used to tell me why Pythagoras abstained from animal food, and why, in later times, Sextius did also. In each case, the reason was different, but it was in each case a noble reason. Sextius believed that man had enough sustenance without resorting to blood, and that a habit of cruelty is formed whenever butchery is practised for pleasure. Moreover, he thought we should curtail the sources of our luxury; he argued that a varied diet was contrary to the laws of health, and was unsuited to our constitutions. Pythagoras, on the other hand, held that all beings were interrelated, and that there was a system of exchange between souls which transmigrated from one bodily shape into another. If one may believe him, no soul perishes or ceases from its functions at all, except for a tiny interval—when it is being poured from one body into another. We may question at what time and after what seasons of change the soul returns to man, when it has wandered through many a dwelling-place; but meantime, he made men fearful of guilt and parricide, since they might be, without knowing it, attacking the soul of a parent and injuring it with knife or with teeth—if, as is possible, the related spirit be dwelling temporarily in this bit of flesh! When Sotion had set forth this doctrine, supplementing it with his own proofs, he would say: "You do not believe that souls are assigned, first to one body and then to another, and that our so-called death is merely a change of abode? You do not believe that in cattle, or in wild beasts, or in creatures of the deep, the soul of him who was once a man may linger? You do not believe that nothing on this earth is annihilated, but only changes its haunts? And that animals also have cycles of progress and, so to speak, an orbit for their souls, no less than the heavenly bodies, which revolve in fixed circuits? Great men have put faith in this idea; therefore, while holding to your own view, keep the whole question in abeyance in your mind. If the theory is true, it is a mark of purity to refrain from eating flesh; if it be false, it is economy. And what harm does it do to you to give such credence? I am merely depriving you of food which sustains lions and vultures."

I was imbued with this teaching, and began to abstain from animal food; at the end of the year the habit was as pleasant as it was easy. I was beginning to feel that my mind was more active; though I would not today positively state whether it really was or not. Do you ask how I came to abandon the practice? It was this way: the days of my youth coincided with the early part of the reign of Tiberius Caesar. Some foreign rites were at that time being inaugurated, and abstinence from certain kinds of animal food was set down as a proof of interest in the strange cult. So at the request of my father, who did not fear gossip, but who detested philosophy, I returned to my previous habits; and it was no very hard matter to induce me to dine more comfortably.

I have mentioned all this in order to show you how zealous neophytes are with regard to their first impulses towards the highest ideals, provided that some one does his part in exhorting them and in kindling their ardour. There are indeed mistakes made, through the fault of our advisers, who teach us how to debate and not how to live; there are also mistakes made by the pupils, who come to their teachers to develop, not their souls, but their wits. Thus the study of wisdom has become the study of words.

On the Eating of Flesh

Plutarch

The Roman essayist Plutarch (c. 56–120) is best remembered today for his Parallel Lives, *biographical studies of Greek and Latin statesmen and philosophers. But he was also the author of a number of influential ethical treatises dealing with topics ranging from education to marriage to religious observance. Several of these pieces discuss the moral status of animals, the presence of reason in nonhuman creatures, and ethical vegetarianism. Especially noteworthy is the essay "On the Eating of Animal Flesh," excerpted here. In it, Plutarch denies that humans are naturally carnivorous and argues that indulgence in a flesh diet "makes us spiritually coarse and gross by reason of satiety and surfeit." In addition, the cruelty with which food animals are treated brutalizes the human character, rendering it callous to the suffering of people and animals alike. Plutarch does not build his case on the Pythagorean / Empedoclean doctrine of soul transmigration, but instead holds that animals deserve moral consideration because of their possession of attributes that indicate intelligence and sentience. There is little doubt that Plutarch, like Porphyry after him, accepted the claim that animals are rational and hence fall within the moral community, but unfortunately his treatise breaks off at the point where he introduces this theme.*

I

Can you really ask what reason Pythagoras had for abstaining from flesh? For my part I rather wonder both by what accident and in what state of soul or mind the first man who did so, touched his mouth to gore and brought his lips to the flesh of a dead creature, he who set forth tables of dead, stale bodies and ventured to call food and nourishment the parts that had a little before bellowed and cried, moved and lived. How could his eyes endure the slaughter when throats were slit and hides flayed and limbs torn from limb? How could his nose endure the stench? How was it that the pollution did not turn away his taste, which made contact with the sores of others and sucked juices and serums from mortal wounds? . . . It is the man who first began these practices that one should seek out, not him who all too late desisted.

Or would everyone declare that the reason for those who first instituted flesh-eating was the necessity of their poverty? It was not while they passed their time in unlawful desires nor when they had necessaries in abundance that after indulgence in unnatural and antisocial pleasures they resorted to such a practice. . . . But you who live now, what madness, what frenzy drives you to the pollution of shedding blood, you who have such a superfluity of necessities? Why slander the earth by implying that she cannot support you? Why impiously offend law-giving Demeter and bring shame upon Dionysus, lord of the cultivated vine, the gracious one, as if you did not receive enough from their hands? Are you not ashamed to mingle domestic crops with blood and gore? You call serpents and panthers and lions savage, but you yourselves, by your own foul slaughter, leave them no room to outdo you in cruelty; for their slaughter is their living, yours is a mere appetizer.

It is certainly not lions and wolves that we eat out of self-defence; on the contrary, we ignore these and slaughter harmless, tame creatures without stings or teeth to harm us, creatures that, I swear, Nature appears to have produced for the sake of their beauty and grace. . . .

But nothing abashes us, not the flower-like tinting of the flesh, not the cleanliness of their habits or the unusual intelligence that may be found in the poor wretches. No, for the sake of a little flesh we deprive them of sun, of light, of the duration of life to which they are entitled by birth and being. Then we go on to assume that when they utter cries and squeaks their speech is inarticulate, that they do not, begging for mercy, entreating, seeking justice, each one of them say, "I do not ask to be spared in case of necessity; only spare me your arrogance! Kill me to eat, but not to please your palate!" Oh, the cruelty of it! What a terrible thing it is to look on when the tables of the rich are spread, men who employ cooks and spicers to groom the dead! And it is even more terrible to look on when they are taken away, for more is left than has been eaten. So the beasts died for nothing! There are others who refuse when the dishes are already set before them and will not have them cut into or sliced. Though they bid spare the dead, they did not spare the living.

We declare, then, that it is absurd for them to say that the practice of flesh-eating is based on Nature. For that man is not naturally carnivorous is, in the first place, obvious from the structure of his body. A man's frame is in no way similar to those creatures who were made for flesh-eating: he has no hooked beak or sharp nails or jagged teeth, no strong stomach or warmth of vital fluids able to digest and assimilate a heavy diet of flesh. It is from this very fact, the evenness of our teeth, the smallness of our mouths, the softness of our tongues, our possession of vital fluids too inert to digest meat that Nature disavows our eating of flesh. If you declare that you are naturally designed for such a diet, then first kill for yourself what you want to eat. Do it, however, only through your own resources, unaided by cleaver or cudgel of any kind or axe. Rather, just as wolves and bears and lions themselves slay what they eat, so you are to fell an ox with your fangs or a boar with your jaws, or tear a lamb or hare to bits. Fall upon it and eat it still living, as animals do. But if you wait for what you eat to be dead, if you have qualms about enjoying the flesh while life is still present, why do you continue, contrary to nature, to eat what possesses life? Even when it is lifeless and dead, however, no one eats the flesh just as it is; men boil it and roast it, altering it by fire and drugs, recasting and diverting and smothering with countless condiments the taste of gore so that the palate may be deceived and accept what is foreign to it.

It was, indeed, a witty remark of the Spartan who bought a little fish in an inn and gave it to the innkeeper to prepare. When the latter asked for cheese and vinegar and oil, the Spartan said, "If I had those, I should not have bought a fish." But we are so refined in our blood-letting that we term flesh a supplementary food; and then we need "supplements" for the flesh itself, mixing oil, wine, honey, fish paste, vinegar, with Syrian and Arabian spices, as though we were really embalming a corpse for burial. The fact is that meat is so softened and dissolved and, in a way, predigested that it is hard for digestion to cope with it; and if digestion loses the battle, the meats affect us with dreadful pains and malignant forms of indigestion.

Diogenes ventured to eat a raw octopus in order to put an end to the inconvenience of preparing cooked food. In the midst of a large throng he veiled his head and, as he brought the flesh to his mouth, said, "It is for you that I am risking my life." Good heavens, a wondrous fine risk! . . . the philosopher risked his life struggling with a raw octopus—in order to brutalize our lives!

Note that the eating of flesh is not only physically against nature, but it also makes us spiritually coarse and gross by reason of satiety and surfeit. "For wine and indulgence in meat make the body strong and vigorous, but the soul weak." [From the Greek physician Androcydes] . . . Empty jars make a noise when struck, but full ones do not resound to blows. Thin bronze objects will pass the sounds from one to another in a circle until you dampen and deaden the noise with your hand as the beat goes round. The eye when it is flooded by an excess of moisture grows dim and weakened for its proper task. When we examine the sun through dank atmosphere and a fog of gross vapors, we do not see it clear and bright, but submerged and misty, with elusive rays. In just the same way, then, when the body is turbulent and surfeited and burdened with improper food, the lustre and light of the soul inevitably come through it blurred and confused, aberrant and inconstant, since the soul lacks the brilliance and intensity to penetrate to the minute and obscure issues of active life.

But apart from these considerations, do you not find here a wonderful means of training in social responsibility? Who could wrong a human being when he found himself so gently and humanely disposed toward other nonhuman creatures? Two days ago in a discussion I quoted the remark of Xenocrates, that the Athenians punished the man who had flayed a ram while it was still alive; yet, as I think, he who tortures a living creature is no worse than he who slaughters it outright. But it seems that we are more observant of acts contrary to convention than of those that are contrary to nature. In that place, then, I made my remarks in a popular vein. I still hesitate, however, to attempt a discussion of the principle underlying my opinion, great as it is, and mysterious and incredible, as Plato says, with merely clever men of mortal opinions, just as a steersman hesitates to shift his course in the midst of a storm, or a playwright to raise his god from the machine in the midst of a play. Yet perhaps it is not unsuitable to set the pitch and announce the theme by quoting some verses of Empedocles. [The Empedoclean verses are missing.] By these lines he means, though he does not say so directly, that human souls are imprisoned in mortal bodies as a punishment for murder, the eating of animal flesh, and cannibalism. This doctrine, however, seems to be even colder, for the stories told about the sufferings and dismemberment of Dionysius and the outrageous assaults of the Titans upon him, and their punishment and blasting by thunderbolt after they had tasted his blood—all this is a myth which in its inner meaning has to do with rebirth. For to that faculty in us which is unreasonable and disordered and violent, and does not come from the gods, but from evil spirits, the ancients gave the name "Titans," that is to say, those that are punished and subjected to correction.

II

Reason urges us with fresh ideas and fresh zeal to attack again our yesterday's discourse on the eating of the flesh. It is indeed difficult, as Cato remarked, to talk to bellies which have no ears. . . . Like the Egyptians who extract the viscera of the dead and cut them open in view of the sun, then throw them away as being the cause of every single sin that the man had committed, it would be well for us to excise our own gluttony and lust to kill and become pure for the remainder of our lives, since it is not so much our belly that drives us to the pollution of slaughter; it is itself polluted by our incontinence. Yet if, for heaven's sake, it is really impossible for us to be free from error because we are on such terms of familiarity with it, let us at least be ashamed of our ill doing and resort to it only in reason. We shall eat flesh, but from hunger, not as a luxury. We shall kill an animal, but in pity and sorrow, not degrading or torturing it—which is the current practice in many cases, some thrusting red-hot spits into the throats of swine so that by the plunging of the iron the blood may be emulsified and, as it circulates through the body, may make the flesh tender and delicate. Others jump upon the udders of sows about to give birth and kick them so that, when they have blended together blood and milk and gore (Zeus the Purifier!) and the unborn young have at the same time been destroyed at the moment of birth, they may eat the most inflamed part of the creature. Still others sew up the eyes of cranes and swans, shut them up in darkness and fatten them, making the flesh appetizing with strange compounds and spicy mixtures.

From these practices it is perfectly evident that it is not for nourishment or need or necessity, but out of satiety and insolence and luxury that they have turned this lawless custom into a pleasure. . . . Their lust tries everything, goes astray, and explores the gamut of profligacy until at last it ends in unspeakable practices; so intemperance in eating passes beyond the necessary ends of nature and resorts to cruelty and lawlessness to give variety to appetite. For it is in their own company that organs of sense are infected and won over and become licentious when they do not keep to natural standards. Just so the art of hearing has fallen sick, corrupting musical taste. From this our luxury and debauchery conceives a desire for shameful caresses and effeminate titillations. These taught the sight not to take pleasure in warlike exercises or gesticulations or refined dances or statues and paintings, but to regard the slaughter and death of men, their wounds and combats, as the most precious sort of spectacle. Just so intemperate intercourse follows a lawless meal, inharmonious music follows a shameful debauch, barbarous spectacles follow shameless songs and sounds, insensitivity and cruelty toward human kind follow savage exhibitions in the theatre. . . .

For what sort of dinner is not costly for which a living creature loses its life? Do we hold a life cheap? I do not yet go so far as to say that it may well be the life of your mother or father or some friend or child, as Empedocles declared. Yet it does, at least, possess some perception, hearing, seeing, imagination, intelligence, which every last creature receives from Nature to enable it to acquire what is proper for it and to evade what is not. Do but consider which are the philosophers who serve the better to humanize us: those who bid us eat our children and friends and fathers and wives after their death, or Pythagoras and Empedocles who try to accustom us to act justly toward other creatures also? You ridicule a man who abstains from eating mutton. But are we, they will say, to refrain from laughter when we see you slicing off portions from a dead father or mother and sending them to absent friends and inviting those who are at hand, heaping their plates with flesh?

[E]ven if the argument of the migration of souls from body to body is not demonstrated to the point of complete belief, there is enough doubt to make us quite cautious and fearful. It is as though in a clash of armies by night you had drawn your sword and were rushing at a man whose fallen body was hidden by his armor and should hear someone remarking that he wasn't quite sure, but that he thought and believed that the prostrate figure was that of your son or brother or father or tentmate—which would be the better course: to approve a false suspicion and spare your enemy as a friend, or to disregard an uncertain authority and kill your friend as a foe? The latter course you will declare to be shocking. Consider also Merope in the play raising her axe against her son himself because she believes him to be that son's murderer and saying, "This blow I give you is more costly yet"—what a stir she rouses in the theatre as she brings them to their feet in terror lest she wound the youth before the old man can stop her! Now suppose one old man stood beside her saying, "Hit him! He's your enemy," and another who said, "Don't strike! He is your son!": which would be the greater misdeed, to omit the punishment of an enemy because of the son, or to slay a child under the impulse of anger against an enemy? In a case, then, where it is not hate or anger or self-defence or fear for ourselves that induces us to murder, but the motive of pleasure, and the victim stands there under our power with its head bent back and one of our philosophers says, "Kill it! It's only a brute beast!"; but the other says, "Stop! What if the soul of some relative or friend has found its way into this body?"—Good God! Of course the risk is equal or much the same in the two cases—if I refuse to eat flesh, or if I, disbelieving, kill my child or some other relative!

There remains yet another contention with the Stoics about flesh-eating. . . . "Of course," they say, "we human beings have no compact of justice with irrational animals." Nor, one might reply, have you with perfume or exotic sweetmeats either. Refrain from animals also, if you are expelling the useless and unnecessary element in pleasure from all its lurking places.

Let us, however, now examine the point whether we really have no compact of justice with animals; and let us do so in no artificial or sophistical manner, but fixing our attention on our own emotions and conversing like human beings with ourselves and weighing. . . . [The manuscript breaks off here.]

On Abstinence from Animal Food

Porphyry

Along with Plutarch's On the Eating of Flesh, *Porphyry's neo-Platonic* On Abstinence *is the second major work to come down from Greek antiquity specifically devoted to a defense of ethical vegetarianism. Porphyry, a student of Plotinus and admirer of Pythagoras and Empedocles, wrote the book as an appeal to one Firmus Castricius, who had left the Plotinian school, joined the Christians, and renounced a vegetable diet. Porphyry tries to dissuade Firmus from his apostasy by arguing four points in* On Abstinence: *that carnivorism is intemperate and hence unsuitable for the philosophical life (book 1), that animal sacrifices are impious (book 2), that animals deserve just treatment (book 3), and that a distinguished host of past sages condemned flesh eating (book 4). The selections here are from the third book.*

For Porphyry and the neo-Platonic school to which he belonged, justice consists in two elements: "in not [needlessly] injuring any [sentient] thing" and "in the rational [faculty] ruling over the irrational [passions]." Humans, he claims, have traditionally justified the slaughter of animals for food by insisting that they are members of inferior species because lacking in rationality, and hence have no legitimate claims for just treatment by humans. But, Porphyry argues, animals display reason, both "internal" (memory, prudence, fellow-feeling, sensa-

*tion) and "external" (speech), even though the former is
less acute than its human counterpart and the latter is
not understandable except by animals. This, however, is
no reason to disenfranchise animals from the moral community. After all, many humans are rationally defective,
but justice is extended to them. Similarly, the Greek cannot comprehend the Indian's language, but nonetheless
regards him as a being worthy of ethical consideration.*

*Having established to his satisfaction the claim that
animals possess reason, Porphyry continues by arguing
against the carnivorous mistreatment of them. Such acts
are unjust for several reasons: first, because they arro-
gantly exclude animals from the set of rational creatures;
second, because they inflict needless pain and death upon
them. Except in extreme circumstances, humans do not
need to eat meat to survive or prosper; third, because the
human craving for meat and its attendant slaughter of
animals is an irrational enslavement to the desire for
frivolous pleasure at the expense of sentient creatures;
finally, because "innoxious" treatment of animals encourages unjust treatment of humans.*

*It is interesting to note that although Porphyry
clearly admires Pythagoras and indeed mentions him on
several occasions in* On Abstinence, *the latter's theory of
transmigration is not invoked by Porphyry in his defence
of vegetarianism. Instead, he bases his case upon the
claim of "alliance," or kinship, between humans and animals. This notion of brotherhood obviously smacks of
Pythagoreanism, but without relying on its more mystical
elements.*

The Rationality of Animals

In the two preceding books, O Firmus Castricius, we have demonstrated that animal food does not contribute either to temperance
and frugality, or to the piety which especially gives completion to
the theoretic life, but is rather hostile to it. Since, however, the
most beautiful part of justice consists in piety to the Gods, and this
is principally acquired through abstinence, there is no occasion to

fear that we shall violate justice towards men, while we preserve piety towards the Gods. Socrates therefore says, in opposition to those who contend that pleasure is the supreme good, that though all swine and goats should accord in this opinion, yet he should never be persuaded that our felicity was placed in the enjoyment of corporeal delight, as long as intellect has dominion over all things. And we also say, that though all wolves and vultures should praise the eating of flesh, we should not admit that they spoke justly, as long as man is by nature innoxious, and ought to abstain from procuring pleasure for himself by injuring others. We shall pass on, therefore, to the discussion of justice; and since our opponents say that this ought only to be extended to those of similar species, and on this account deny that irrational animals can be injured by men, let us exhibit the true, and at the same time Pythagoric opinion, and demonstrate that every soul which participates of sense and memory is rational. For this being demonstrated, we may extend, as our opponents will also admit, justice to every animal. . . .

Since, however, with respect to reason, one kind, according to the doctrine of the Stoics, is internal, but the other external, and again, one kind being right, but the other erroneous, it is requisite to explain of which of these two, animals, according to them, are deprived. Are they therefore deprived of right reason alone? Or are they entirely destitute both of internal and externally proceeding reason? They appear, indeed, to ascribe to brutes an entire privation of reason, and not a privation of right reason alone. For if they merely denied that brutes possess right reason, animals would not be irrational, but rational beings, in the same manner as nearly all men are according to them. For, according to their opinion, one or two wise men may be found in whom alone right reason prevails, but all the rest of mankind are depraved; though some of these make a certain proficiency, but others are profoundly depraved, and yet, at the same time, all of them are similarly rational. . . . If, however, it be requisite to speak the truth, not only reason may plainly be perceived in all animals, but in many of them it is so great as to approximate to perfection.

Since, therefore, reason is twofold, one kind consisting in external speech, but the other in the disposition of the soul, we shall begin from that which is external, and which is arranged according to the voice. But if external reason is voice, which through the tongue is significant of the internal passions of the soul . . . —if this be the case, in what pertaining to this are such animals as have a voice deficient? Do they not discursively perceive the manner in which they are inwardly affected, before it is vocally enunciated by them? By a discursive perception, however, I mean the perception produced by the silent discourse which takes place in the soul. Since, therefore, that which is vocally expressed by the tongue is reason, in whatever manner it may be expressed, whether in a barbarous or a Grecian, a canine or a bovine mode, other animals also participate of it that are vocal; men, indeed, speaking conformably to the human laws, but other animals conformably to the laws which they received from the Gods and nature. But if we do not understand what they say, what is this to the purpose? For the Greeks do not understand what is said by the Indians, nor those who are educated in Attica the language of the Scythians, or Thracians, or Syrians; but the sound of the one falls on the ears of the other like the clangor of cranes, though by others their vocal sounds can be written and articulated, in the same manner as ours can by us. . . . The like also takes place in the vocal sounds of other animals. For the several species of these understand the language which is adapted to them, but we only hear a sound, of the signification of which we are ignorant, because no one who has learnt our language is able to teach us through ours the meaning of what is said by brutes. . . .

But it is now requisite to show that brutes have internal reason. The difference, indeed, between our reason and theirs, appears to consist, as Aristotle somewhere says, not in essence, but in the more and the less; just as many are of opinion, that the difference between the Gods and us is not essential, but consists in this, that in them there is a greater, and in us a less accuracy, of the reasoning power. And, indeed, so far as pertains to sense and the remaining organization, according to the sensoria and the flesh, every one nearly will grant that these are similarly disposed in us, as they are in brutes. For they not only similarly participate with us of natural passions, and the motions produced through these, but we may also survey in them such affections as are preternatural and morbid. No one, however, of a sound mind, will say that brutes are unreceptive of the reasoning power, on account of the difference between their habit of body and ours, when he sees that there is a great variety of habit in man, according to their race, and the nations to which they belong and yet, at the same time, it is granted that all of them are rational. . . .

It does not follow, if we have more intelligence than other animals, that on this account they are to be deprived of intelligence; as neither must it be said, that partridges do not fly, because hawks fly higher. . . . Some one, therefore, may admit that the soul is copassive with the body, and that the former suffers something from the latter . . .

It must be demonstrated, therefore, that there is a rational power in animals, and that they are not deprived of prudence. And in the first place, indeed, each of them knows whether it is imbecile or strong, and, in consequence of this, it defends some parts of itself, but attacks with others. Thus the panther uses its teeth, the lion its nails and teeth, the horse its hoofs, the ox its horns, the cock its spurs, and the scorpion its sting; but the serpents in Egypt use their spittle (whence also they are called *ptuades,* i.e. spitters), and with this they blind the eyes of those that approach them: and thus a different animal uses a different part of itself for attack, in order to save itself. . . . They likewise change their places of abode at certain times, and know every thing which contributes to their advantage. In a similar manner, in fishes and in birds, a reasoning energy of this kind may be perceived. . . .

But he who says that these things are naturally present with animals is ignorant in asserting this, that they are by nature rational; or, if this is not admitted, neither does reason subsist in us naturally, nor with the perfection of it receive an increase, so far as we are naturally adapted to receive it. A divine nature, indeed, does not become rational through learning, for there never was a time in which he was irrational; but rationality is consubsistent with his existence, and he is not prevented from being rational, because he did not receive reason through discipline: though, with respect to other animals, in the same manner as with respect to men, many things are taught them by nature, and some things are imparted by discipline. Brutes, however, learn some things from each other, but are taught others . . . by men. They also have memory, which is a most principal thing in the resumption of reasoning and prudence. They likewise have vices, and are envious; though their bad qualities are not so widely extended as in men: for their vices are of a lighter nature than those of men. This, indeed, is evident; for the builder of a house will never be able to lay the foundation of it, unless he is sober; nor can a shipwright properly place the keel of a ship, unless he is in health; nor a husbandman plant a vine, unless

he applies his mind to it; yet nearly all men, when they are intoxi-
cated, can beget children. This, however, is not the case with other
animals; for they propagate for the sake of offspring, and for the
most part, when the males have made the female pregnant, they no
longer attempt to be connected with her; nor, if they should attempt
it, would the female permit them. But the magnitude of the lasciv-
ious insolence and intemperance of men in these things, is evident. . . .

Who likewise is ignorant how much gregarious animals preserve justice towards each other? For this is preserved by ants, by
bees, and by other animals of the like kind. And who is ignorant of
the chastity of female ring-doves towards the males with whom
they associate? For they destroy those who are found by them to
have committed adultery. Or who has not heard of the justice of
storks towards their parents? For in the several species of animals,
a peculiar virtue is eminent, to which all species is naturally
adapted; nor because this virtue is natural and stable, is it fit to
deny that they are rational? For it might be requisite to deprive
them of rationality, if their works were not the proper effects of
virtue and rational sagacity; but if we do not understand how these
works are effected, because we are unable to penetrate into the reasoning which they use, we are not on this account to accuse them of
irrationality; for neither is anyone able to penetrate into the intellect of that divinity the sun, but from his works we assent to those
who demonstrate him to be an intellectual and rational essence.

But someone may very properly wonder at those who admit
that justice derives its subsistence from the rational part, and who
call those animals that have no association with men, savage and
unjust, and yet do not extend justice as far as to those that do associate with us; and which, in the same manner as men, would be
deprived of life, if they were deprived of human society. Birds,
therefore, and dogs, and many quadrupeds, such as goats, horses,
sheep, asses, and mules, would perish, if deprived of an association
with mankind. Nature, also, the fabricator of their frame, constituted them so as to be in want of men, and fashioned men so as to
require their assistance; thus producing an innate justice in them
towards us, and in us towards them. But it is not at all wonderful,
if some of them are savage towards men; for what Aristotle says is
true, that if all animals had an abundance of nutriment, they would
not act ferociously, either towards each other, or towards men. For

on account of food, though necessary and slender, enmities and friendships are produced among animals, and also on account of the places which they occupy; but if men were reduced to such straits as brutes are, how much more savage would they become than those animals that appear to be wild. War and famine are indications of the truth of this; for then men do not abstain from eating each other; and even without war and famine, they eat animals that are nurtured with them, and are perfectly tame. . . .

The Injustice of Carnivorism

Through these arguments, therefore . . . , it is demonstrated that brutes are rational animals, reason in most of them being indeed imperfect, of which, nevertheless, they are not entirely deprived. Since, however, justice pertains to rational beings, as our opponents say, how is it possible not to admit, that we should also act justly towards brutes? For we do not extend justice to plants, because there appears to be much in them which is unconnected with reason; though of these, we are accustomed to use the fruits, but not together with the fruits to cut off the trunks. We collect, however, corn and leguminous substances, when, being efflorescent, they have fallen on the earth, and are dead. But no one uses for food the flesh of dead animals, that of fish being excepted, unless they have been destroyed by violence. So that in these things there is much injustice. As Plutarch also says, it does not follow that because our nature is indigent of certain things, and we use these, we should therefore act unjustly towards all things. For we are allowed to injure other things to a certain extent, in order to procure the necessary means of subsistence (if to take any thing from plants, even while they are living, is an injury to them); but to destroy other things through luxury, and for the enjoyment of pleasure, is perfectly savage and unjust. And the abstinence from these neither diminishes our life nor our living happily. For it, indeed, the destruction of animals and the eating of flesh were as requisite as air and water, plants and fruits, without which it is impossible to live, this injustice would be necessarily connected with our nature. But if many priests of the Gods, and many kings of the barbarians, being attentive to purity, and if, likewise, infinite species of animals never taste food of this kind, yet live, and obtain their proper end according to nature, is not he absurd who orders us, because we are compelled to wage war with certain animals, not to live peaceably with those with whom it is possible to do so, but thinks, either that we ought to live without exercising justice towards any thing, or that, by exercising it towards all things, we should not continue in existence? As, therefore, among men, he who, for the sake of his own safety, or that of his children or country, either seizes the wealth of certain persons, or oppresses some region of city, has necessity for the pretext of his injustice; but he who acts in this manner through the acquisition of wealth, or through satiety or luxurious pleasure, and for the purpose of satisfying desires which are not necessary, appears to be inhospitable, intemperate, and depraved;—thus too, divinity pardons the injuries which are done to plants, the consumption of fire and water, the shearing of sheep, the milking of cows, and the taming of oxen, and subjugating them to the yoke, for the safety and continuance in life of those that use them. But to deliver animals to be slaughtered and cooked, and thus be filled with murder, not for the sake of nutriment and satisfying the wants of nature, but making pleasure and gluttony the end of such conduct, is transcendently iniquitous and dire. For it is sufficient that we use, for laborious purposes, though they have no occasion to labor themselves, the progeny of horses, and asses, and bulls, as Aeschylus says, as our substitutes who, by being tamed and subjugated to the yoke, alleviate our toil.

[T]o compare plants, however, with animals, is doing violence to the order of things. For the latter are naturally sensitive, and adapted to feel pain, to be terrified and hurt; on which account also they may be injured. But the former are entirely destitute of sensation, and in consequence of this, nothing foreign, or evil, or hurtful, or injurious, can befall them. . . . And is it not absurd, since we see that many of our own species live from sense alone, but do not possess intellect and reason, and since we also see, that many of them surpass the most terrible of wild beasts in cruelty, anger, and rapine, being murderous of their children and their parents, and also being tyrants, and the tools of kings, to fancy that we ought to act justly towards these, but that no justice is due from us to the ox that ploughs, the dog that is fed with us, and the animals that nourish us with their milk, and adorn our bodies with their wool? Is not such an opinion most irrational and absurd?

But, by Jupiter, the assertion of Chrysippus is considered by our opponents to be very probable, that the Gods made us for the sake of themselves, and for the sake of each other, and that they made animals for the sake of us. . . . Let him, however, to whom [this assertion appears] to possess a certain probability, and to participate in something worthy of deity, consider what he will reply to the saying of Carneades, that every thing which is produced by nature, is benefited when it obtains the end to which it is adapted, and for which it was generated. But benefit is to be understood in a more general way, as signifying what the Stoics call useful. The hog, however, [says Carneades] was produced by nature for the purpose of being slaughtered and used for food; and when it suffers this, it obtains the end for which it is adapted, and is benefited. But if God fashioned animals for the use of men, in what do we use flies, lice, bats, beetles, scorpions, and vipers? Of which some are odious to the sight, defile the touch, are intolerable to the smell, and in their voice dire and unpleasant; and others, on the contrary, are destructive to those that meet with them. . . . And if our opponents should admit that all things are not generated for us, and with a view to our advantage, in addition to the distinction which they make being very confused and obscure, we shall not avoid acting unjustly, in attacking and noxiously using those animals which were not produced for our sake. . . . I omit to mention, that if we define, by utility, things which pertain to us, we shall not be prevented from admitting, that we were generated for the sake of the most destructive animals, such as crocodiles . . . and dragons. For we are not in the least benefited by them; but they seize and destroy men that fall in their way, and use them for food; in so doing acting not at all more cruelly than we do, excepting that they commit this injustice through want and hunger, but we through insolent wantonness, and for the sake of luxury, frequently sporting in theatres, and in hunting slaughter the greater part of animals. And by thus acting, indeed, a murderous disposition and a brutal nature become strengthened in us, and render us insensible to pity: to which we may add, that those who first dared to do this, blunted the greatest part of lenity, and rendered it inefficacious. The Pythagoreans, however, made lenity towards beasts to be an exercise of philanthropy and commiseration. So that, how is it possible they should not in a greater degree excite us to justice, than those who assert that, by not slaughtering animals, the justice which is usually exercised towards men will be corrupted? For custom is most powerful

in increasing those passions in man which were gradually introduced into his nature. . . .

Hence, since animals are allied to us, if it should appear,
according to Pythagoras, that they are allotted the same soul that
we are, he may justly be considered as impious who does not
abstain from acting unjustly towards his kindred. Nor because
some animals are savage, is their alliance to us to be on this
account abscinded. For some men may be found who are no less,
and even more malefic than savage animals to their neighbors, and
who are impelled to injure any one they may meet with, as if they
were driven by a certain blast of their own nature and depravity.
Hence, also, we destroy such men; yet we do not cut them off from
an alliance to animals of a mild nature. Thus, therefore, if likewise
some animals are savage, these, as such, are to be destroyed, in the
same manner as men that are savage; but our habitude or alliance
to other and wilder animals is not on this account to be abandoned.
But neither tame nor savage animals are to be eaten; as neither are
unjust men. Now, however, we act most unjustly, destroying,
indeed, and feeding on such as are tame. With respect to tame animals, however, we act with a twofold injustice, because though they
are tame, we slay them, and also, because we eat them. And, in
short, the death of these has a reference to the assumption of them
for food.

To these, also, such arguments as the following may be added.
For he who says that the man who extends the just as far as to
brutes, corrupts the just, is ignorant that he does not himself preserve justice, but increases pleasure, which is hostile to justice. By
admitting, therefore, that pleasure is the end, justice is evidently
destroyed. For to whom is it not manifest that justice is increased
through abstinence? For he who abstains from every thing animated, though he may abstain from such animals as do not contribute to the benefit of society, will be much more careful not to
injure those of his own species. For he who loves the genus, will not
hate any species of animals; and by how much the greater his love
of the genus is, by so much the more will he preserve justice
towards a part of the genus, and that to which he is allied. He,
therefore, who admits that he is allied to all animals, will not injure
any animal. But he who confines justice to man alone, is prepared,
like one enclosed in a narrow space, to hurl from him the prohibi-
tion of injustice. . . . Hence, therefore, since justice consists in not

injuring any thing, it must be extended as far as to every animated nature. On this account, also, the essence of justice consists in the rational ruling over the irrational, and in the irrational being obedient to the rational part. For when reason governs, and the irrational part is obedient to its mandates, it follows, by the greatest necessity, that man will be innoxious towards every thing. For the passions being restrained, and desire and anger wasting away, but reason possessing its proper empire, a similitude to a more excellent nature immediately follows. But the more excellent nature in the universe is entirely innoxious, and, through possessing a power which preserves and benefits all things, is itself not in want of any thing. . . .

Do you therefore ask, O man, what we should do? We should imitate those that lived in the golden age, we should imitate those of that period who were free. For with them modesty, Nemesis, and Justice associated, because they were satisfied with the fruits of the earth.

Part II

❧ ❧

The Eighteenth Century

Diet and Human Character

Interest in ethical vegetarianism diminished in the west from the late Hellenistic period through the middle ages and renaissance. A number of Christian thinkers, beginning with St. Benedict in the sixth century, defended a largely noncarnivorous diet, but their advocacy was primarily based on religious rather than ethical reasons, and their influence was by and large limited to monastic circles. An occasional nonclerical author during this period raised cursory concerns about flesh eating. Sir Thomas More, for example, worries in his Utopia *(1516) that the sanguinary butchery of food animals sets a bad example for the residents of his mythical land. But interest in vegetarianism as a moral position was in the main dormant until the advent of the eighteenth century. There are doubtlessly many reasons for this reawakening of interest. Probably one of the most obvious explanations is the general repugnance that greeted Rene Descartes's claim in his* Discourse on Method *(1637) that animals are nothing more than animated machines, utterly incapable of pain, and his subsequent defense of experimental vivisection. The implications of Descartes's position were so distasteful that even Voltaire, hardly a proponent of vegetarianism, felt compelled to attack them in his* Philosophical Dictionary *(1764).*

The eighteenth century's rediscovery of ethical vegetarianism tended to revolve around the assumption that flesh eating, along with its concomitant slaughter of food animals, was detrimental to the formation of virtuous human character. Bernard Mandeville argues that it encourages the chauvinistic belief that humans are innately superior to other forms of life (a position Peter Singer will later dub "speciesism"). David Hartley and William Paley both worry that the butchery of animals legitimizes human patterns of cruelty and insensitivity to suffering. The two men, both clerics, ultimately conclude that there is no scriptural injunction against the eating of flesh, but it is clear they are uncomfortable with this position. In a bitingly satirical fable, Oliver Goldsmith underscores the hypocrisy of those who claim to "love" animals and yet acquiesce in the slaughter of them merely to please their palates. And the poet Shelley condemns carnivorism as an impediment both to physical health and the moral perfection of humanity.

The Carnivorous Custom and Human Vanity

Bernard Mandeville

In his 1723 The Fable of the Bees, *from which this selection is taken, the Dutch-born satirist Mandeville (1670–1733) mercilessly and sometimes hilariously pokes fun at the received wisdom of his day. In this piece, the target of his wit is the cruelty that the slaughter of animals for food entails. Mandeville argues that it is the "tyranny of custom" which blinds humans to the horrors of butchery by reinforcing the orthodox belief that humans are unquestionably superior to other species and hence can do with them what they will. The emptiness of this vain pretension is illustrated by the imaginative fable with which Mandeville concludes his discussion.*

In what concerns the fashions and manners of the ages men live in, they never examine into the real worth or merit of the cause, and generally judge of things not as their reason, but custom directs them. Time was when the funeral rites in the disposing of the dead were performed by fire, and the cadavers of the greatest emperors were burnt to ashes. Then burying the corpse in the ground was a funeral for slaves, or made a punishment for the worst of malefactors. Now nothing is decent or honorable but interring, and burning the body is reserved for crimes of the blackest dye. At some times we look upon trifles with horror, at other times we can behold enormities without concern. If we see a man walk with his hat on in a church, though out of service time, it shocks us, but if on a Sunday night we meet half a dozen fellows drunk in the street, the sight makes little or no impression upon us. If a woman at a merry-making dresses in man's clothes, it is reckoned a frolic amongst friends, and he that finds too much fault with it is counted censorious: upon the stage it is done without reproach, and the most virtuous ladies will dispense with it in an actress, though everybody has a full view of her legs and thighs; but if the same woman, as soon as she has petticoats on again, should show her leg to a man as high as her knee, it would be a very immodest action, and everybody will call her impudent for it.

I have often thought, if it was not for this tyranny which custom usurps over us, that men of any tolerable good nature could never be reconciled to the killing of so many animals for their daily food, as long as the bountiful earth so plentifully provides them with varieties of vegetable dainties. I know that reason excites our compassion but faintly, and therefore I would not wonder how men should so little commiserate such imperfect creatures as crayfish, oysters, cockles, and indeed all fish in general: as they are mute, and their inward formation, as well as outward figure, vastly different from ours, they express themselves unintelligibly to us, and therefore 'tis not strange that their grief should not affect our understanding which it cannot reach; for nothing stirs us to pity so effectually, as when the symptoms of misery strike immediately upon our senses, and I have seen people moved at the noise a live lobster makes upon the spit, that could have killed half a dozen fowls with pleasure. But in such perfect animals as sheep and oxen, in whom the heart, the brain and nerves differ so little from ours, and in whom the separation of the spirits from the blood, the organs of sense, and consequently feeling itself, are the same as they are in human creatures; I can't imagine how a man not hardened in blood and massacre, is able to see a violent death, and the pangs of it, without concern.

In answer to this, most people will think it sufficient to say, that all things being allowed to be made for the service of man, there can be no cruelty in putting creatures to the use they were designed for; but I have heard men make this reply, while their nature within them has reproached them with the falsehood of the assertion. There is of all the multitude not one man in ten but what will own (if he was not brought up in a slaughter house) that of all trades he could never have been a butcher; and I question whether ever anybody so much as killed a chicken without reluctancy the first time. Some people are not to be persuaded to taste of any creatures they have daily seen and been acquainted with, while they were alive; others extend their scruple no further than to their own poultry, and refuse to eat what they fed and took care of themselves; yet all of them will feed heartily and without remorse on beef, mutton and fowls when they are bought in the market. In this behavior, methinks, there appears something like a consciousness of guilt, it looks as if they endeavored to save themselves from the imputation of a crime (which they know sticks somewhere) by removing the cause of it as far as they can from themselves; and I can discover in it some strong remains of primitive pity and innocence, which all the arbitrary power of custom, and the violence of luxury, have not yet been able to conquer.

What I build upon I shall be told is a folly, that wise men are not guilty of: I own it; but while it proceeds from a real passion inherent in our nature, it is sufficient to demonstrate that we are born with a repugnancy to the killing, and consequently the eating of animals; for it is impossible that a natural appetite should ever prompt us to act, or desire others to do, what we have an aversion to, be it as foolish as it will.

Everybody knows, that surgeons in the cure of dangerous wounds and fractures, the extirpations of limbs, and other dreadful operations, are often compelled to put their patients to extraordinary torments, and that the more desperate and calamitous cases occur to them, the more the outcries and bodily sufferings of others must become familiar to them; for this reason, our English law, out of a most affectionate regard to the lives of the subject, allows them not to be of any jury upon life and death, as supposing that their practice itself is sufficient to harden and extinguish in them that tenderness, without which no man is capable of setting a true value upon the lives of his fellow-creatures. Now if we ought to have no concern for what we do to brute beasts, and there was not imagined to be any cruelty in killing them, why should of all callings butchers, and only they jointly with surgeons, be excluded from being jurymen by the same law?

I shall urge nothing of what Pythagoras and many other wise men have said concerning this barbarity of eating flesh; I have gone too much out of my way already, and shall therefore beg the reader, if he would have any more of this, to run over the following fable, or else, if he be tired, to let it alone, with an assurance that in doing of either he shall equally oblige me.

A Roman merchant in one of the Carthaginian Wars was cast away upon the coast of Africk: himself and his slave with great difficulty got safe ashore; but going in quest of relief, were met by a lion of a mighty size. It happened to be one of the breed that ranged in Aesop's days, and one that could not only speak several languages, but seemed moreover very well acquainted with human affairs. The slave got upon a tree, but his master not thinking himself safe there, and having heard much of the generosity of lions, fell down prostrate before him, with all the signs of fear and submission. The lion, who had lately filled his belly, bids him rise, and for a while lay by his fears, assuring him withal, that he should not be touched, if he could give him any tolerable reasons why he should not be devoured. The merchant obeyed; and having now received some glimmering hopes of safety, gave a dismal account of the shipwreck he had suffered, and endeavoring from thence to raise the lion's pity, pleaded his cause with abundance of good rhetoric; but observing by the countenance of the beast that flattery and fine words made very little impression, he betook himself to arguments of greater solidity, and reasoning from the excellency of man's nature and abilities, remonstrated how improbable it was that the gods should not have designed him for a better use than to be eaten by savage beasts. Upon this the lion became more attentive, and vouchsafed now and then a reply, till at last the following dialogue ensued between them.

Oh vain and covetous animal (said the lion), whose pride and avarice can make him leave his native soil, where his natural wants might be plentifully supplied, and try rough seas and dangerous mountains to find out superfluities, why should you esteem your species above ours? And if the gods have given you a superiority over all creatures, then why beg you of an inferior? *Our superiority* (answered the merchant) *consists not in bodily force but strength of understanding; the gods have endued us with a rational soul, which, though invisible, is much the better part of us.* I desire to touch nothing of you but what is good to eat; but why do you value your self so much upon that part which is invisible? *Because it is immortal, and shall meet with rewards after death for the*

*actions of this life, and the just shall enjoy eternal bliss and tran-
quillity with the heroes and demi-gods in the Elysian Fields.* What
life had you led? *I have honored the gods, and studied to be beneficial to man.* Then why do you fear death, if you think the gods as
just as you have been? *I have a wife and five small children that
must come to want if they lose me.* I have two whelps that are not
big enough to shift for themselves, that are in want now, and must
actually be starved if I can provide nothing for them: your children
will be provided for one way or another; at least as well when I have
eaten you as if you had been drowned.

As to the excellency of either species, the value of things
among you has ever increased with the scarcity of them, and to a
million of men there is hardly one lion; besides that, in the great
veneration man pretends to have for his kind, there is little sincer-
ity farther than it concerns the share which everyone's pride has in
it for himself; 'tis a folly to boast of the tenderness shewn and atten-
dance given to your young ones, or the excessive and lasting trouble bestowed in the education of them: man being born the most
necessitous and most helpless animal, this is only an instinct of
nature, which in all creatures has ever proportioned the care of the
parents to the wants and imbecilities of the offspring. But if a man
had a real value for his kind, how is it possible that often ten thousand of them, and sometimes ten times as many, should be
destroyed in few hours for the caprice of two? All degrees of men
despise those that are inferior to them, and if you could enter into
the hearts of kings and princes, you would hardly find any but what
have less value for the greatest part of the multitudes they rule
over, than those have for the cattle that belong to them. Why should
so many pretend to derive their race, though but spuriously, from
the immortal gods; why should all of them suffer others to kneel
down before them, and more or less take delight in having divine
honors paid them, but to insinuate that themselves are of a more
exalted nature, and a species superior to that of their subjects?

Savage I am, but no creature can be called cruel but what
either by malice or insensibility extinguishes his natural pity: the
lion was born without compassion; we follow the instinct of our
nature; the gods have appointed us to live upon the waste and spoil
of other animals, and as long as we can meet with dead ones, we
never hunt after the living. 'Tis only man, mischievous man, that
can make death a sport. Nature taught your stomach to crave noth-

ing but vegetables; but your violent fondness to change, and greater eagerness after novelties, have prompted you to the destruction of animals without justice or necessity, perverted your nature and warped your appetites which way soever your pride or luxury have called them. The lion has a ferment within him that consumes the toughest skin and hardest bones as well as the flesh of all animals without exception: your squeamish stomach, in which the digestive heat is weak and inconsiderable, won't so much as admit of the most tender parts of them, unless above half the concoction has been performed by artificial fire beforehand; and yet what animal have you spared to satisfy the caprices of a languid appetite? Languid I say; for what is man's hunger if compared to the lion's? Yours, when it is at the worst, makes you faint, mine makes me mad: oft have I tried with roots and herbs to allay the violence of it, but in vain; nothing but large quantities of flesh can any ways appease it.

Yet the fierceness of our hunger notwithstanding, lions have often requited benefits received; but ungrateful and perfidious man feeds on the sheep that clothes him, and spares not her innocent young ones, whom he has taken into his care and custody. If you tell me the gods made man master over all other creatures, what tyranny was it then to destroy them out of wantonness? No, fickle timorous animal, the gods have made you for society, and designed that millions of you, when well joined together, should compose the strong Leviathan. A single lion bears some sway in the creation, but what is a single man? A small and inconsiderable part, a trifling atom of one great beast. What nature designs she executes, and 'tis not safe to judge of what she proposed, but from the effects she shews: if she had intended that man, as man from a superiority of species, should lord it over all other animals, the tiger, nay, the whale and the eagle, would have obeyed his voice.

But if your wit and understanding exceeds ours, ought not the lion in deference to that superiority to follow the maxims of men, with whom nothing is more sacred than that the reason of the strongest is ever the most prevalent? Whole multitudes of you have conspired and compassed the destruction of one, after they had owned the gods had made him their superior; and one has often ruined and cut off whole multitudes, whom by the same gods he had sworn to defend and maintain. Man never acknowledged superiority without power, and why should I? The excellence I boast of is visible, all animals tremble at the sight of the lion, not out of panic fear. The gods have given me swiftness to overtake, and strength to conquer whatever comes near me. Where is there a creature that has teeth and claws like mine; behold the thickness of these massy jaw bones, consider the width of them, and feel the firmness of this brawny neck. The nimblest deer, the wildest boar, the stoutest horse, and strongest bull are my prey wherever I meet them. Thus spoke the lion, and the merchant fainted away.

The lion, in my opinion, has stretched the point too far; yet when to soften the flesh of male animals, we have by castration prevented the firmness their tendons and every fibre would have come to without it, I confess, I think it ought to move a human creature when he reflects upon the cruel care with which they are fattened for destruction. When a large and gentle bullock, after having resisted a ten times greater force of blows than would have killed his murderer, falls stunned at last, and his armed head is fastened to the ground with cords; as soon as the wide wound is made, and the jugulars are cut asunder, what mortal can without compassion hear the painful bellowings intercepted by his blood, the bitter sighs that speak the sharpness of his anguish, and the deep sounding groans with loud anxiety fetched from the bottom of his strong and palpitating heart; look on the trembling and violent convulsions of his limbs; see, while his reeking gore streams from him, his eyes become dim and languid, and behold his strugglings, gasps and last efforts for life, the certain signs of his approach fate? When a creature has given such convincing and undeniable proofs of the terrors upon him, and the pains and agonies he feels, is there a follower of Descartes so inured to blood, as not to refute, by his commiseration, the philosophy of that vain reasoner?

Carnivorous Callousness

David Hartley

In this piece, taken from his 1748 Observations on Man: His Frame, His Duties, and His Expectations, *David Hartley (1705–1757), a British utilitarian whose thought subsequently influenced David Hume, Jeremy Bentham, and John Stuart Mill, argues that animal slaughter does violence to the moral principles of benevolence and compassion by rendering humans callous to suffering. Animals share enough characteristics with humans to warrant the supposition that they possess intelligence as well as emotional attributes such as "nascent benevolence" and fear and they are clearly sentient. Hartley even takes seriously the possibility that they may be immortal. To inflict pain and death upon animals is to indulge in cruelty harmful to both their well-being and our own moral sensitivity. Hartley ultimately does not condemn carnivorism, but urges moderation as an inducement to "piety, benevolence, and the moral sense."*

With respect to animal diet, let it be considered, that taking away the lives of animals, in order to convert them into food, does great violence to the principles of benevolence and compassion. This appears from the frequent hard-heartedness and cruelty found amongst those persons, whose occupations engage them in destroying animal life, as well as from the uneasiness which others feel in beholding the butchery of animals. It is most evident, in respect of the larger animals, and those with whom mankind have a familiar intercourse, such as oxen, sheep, domestic fowls, etc., so as to distinguish, love, and compassionate individuals. These creatures resemble us greatly in the make of the body in general, and in that of the particular organs of circulation, respiration, digestion, etc., also in the formation of their intellects, memories, and passions, and in the signs of distress, fear, pain, and death. They often likewise win our affections by the marks of peculiar sagacity, by their instincts, helplessness, innocence, nascent benevolence, etc. And if there be any glimmering of hope of an hereafter for them, if they should prove to be our brethren and sisters in this higher sense, in immortality as well as mortality, in the permanent principle of our minds, as well as the frail dust of our bodies, if they should be partakers of the same redemption as well as of our fall, and be members of the same mystical body, this would have a particular tendency to increase our tenderness for them. At the same time the present circumstances of things seem to require, that no very great alteration should be made in this matter: we ourselves are under the same law of death, and of becoming food to our fellow animals; and philosophy has of late discovered such numberless orders of small animals in parts of diet formerly esteemed to be void of life, and such an extension of life into the vegetable kingdom, that we seem under the perpetual necessity, either of destroying the lives of some of the creatures, or of perishing ourselves, and suffering many others to perish. This therefore seems to be no more than an argument to stop us in our career, to make us sparing and tender in this article, and put us upon consulting experience more faithfully and impartially, in order to determine what is most suitable to the purposes of life and health, our compassion being made by the foregoing considerations, in some measure, a balance to our impetuous bodily appetites. At least, abstinence from flesh meats seems left to each person's choice, and not necessary, unless in peculiar circumstances.

The doctrine of the scriptures on this head appears very agreeable to these dictates of sympathy. For Noah, and we in him, received a permission from God to eat flesh; and that this was no more than a permission, may be concluded from its not being given to Adam, from the shortening of human life after the flood, from the strict command concerning blood, from the Israelites being restrained from animal food for forty years during their purification and institution in religion in the wilderness, from the distinction of animals into clean and unclean, from the burning of part in sacrifice, and sometimes the whole, from the practice of many Jews and Christians particularly eminent for piety, etc. All these may be considered as hints and admonitions to us, as checks and restraints upon unbridled carnal appetites and lusts: at the same time that our Saviour's partaking in meats with all kinds of men, and many express instances and testimonies both in the Old and New Testament, as particularly the command to eat the paschal lamb, and other sacrifices, remove all scruple from those persons who eat with moderation, and in conformity to the rules of piety, benevolence, and the moral sense.

They Pity, and Eat the Objects of Their Compassion

Oliver Goldsmith

In his series The Citizen of the World, *the British poet and essayist Oliver Goldsmith (1728–1774) satirically scrutinized the norms of eighteenth-century England through the eyes of "Lien Chi Altangi," a fictional Chinese visitor to the West who regales his Pekin correspondents with sometimes bewildered accounts of British customs. In this selection, Lien Chi Altangi describes the curious British habit of flesh consumption, claiming that it betokens a fall from the state of "innocence and simplicity" originally enjoyed by humankind. Lien Chi Altangi's primary objection to European carnivorism is the "exquisite torture" inflicted upon animals for the sake of human gluttony. In a move reminiscent of Mandeville, the Chinese traveller concludes his description of British dietary customs by reminding his readers of the "Zendevesta" tale of Kabul, in which a voracious epicurean is judged after his death by a tribunal comprised of the scores of animals slaughtered to please his palate.*

From Lien Chi Altangi, to Fum Hoam, first president of the Ceremonial Academy at Pekin, in China.

The better sort here pretend to the utmost compassion for animals of every kind: to hear them speak, a stranger would be apt to imagine they could hardly hurt the gnat that stung them; they seem so tender and so full of pity, that one would take them for the harmless friends of the whole creation; the protectors of the meanest insect or reptile that was privileged with existence. And yet (would you believe it?) I have seen the very men who have thus boasted of their tenderness, at the same time devouring the flesh of six different animals tossed up in a fricassee. Strange contrariety of conduct! They pity, and they eat the objects of their compassion! The lion roars with terror over its captive; the tiger sends forth its hideous shriek to intimidate its prey; no creature shows any fondness for its short-lived prisoner, except a man and a cat.

Man was born to live with innocence and simplicity, but he has deviated from nature; he was born to share the bounties of heaven, but he has monopolized them; he was born to govern the brute creation, but he is become their tyrant. If an epicure now shall happen to surfeit on his last night's feast, twenty animals the next day are to undergo the most exquisite tortures, in order to provoke his appetite to another guilty meal. Hail, O ye simple, honest brahmins of the East; ye inoffensive friends of all that were born to happiness as well as you; you never sought a short-lived pleasure from the miseries of other creatures! You never studied the tormenting arts of ingenious refinement; you never surfeited upon a guilty meal! How much more purified and refined are your sensations than ours! You distinguish every element with the utmost precision; a stream untasted before is new luxury, a change of air is a new banquet, too refined for Western imaginations to conceive.

Though the Europeans do not hold the transmigration of souls, yet one of their doctors has, with great force of argument, and great plausibility of reasoning, endeavoured to prove, that the bodies of animals are the habitations of demons and wicked spirits, which are obliged to reside in these prisons till the resurrection pronounces their everlasting punishment; but are previously condemned to suffer all the pains and hardships inflicted upon them by man, or by each other, here. If this be the case, it may frequently happen, that while we whip pigs to death, or boil live lobsters, we are putting some old acquaintance, some near relation, to excruciating tortures, and are serving him up to the very table where he was once the most welcome companion.

"Kabul," says the Zendevesta, "was born on the rushy banks of the river Mawra; his possessions were great, and his luxuries kept pace with the affluence of his fortune; he hated the harmless brahmins, and despised their holy religion; every day his table was decked out with the flesh of a hundred different animals, and his cooks had a hundred different ways of dressing it, to solicit even satiety.

"Notwithstanding all his eating, he did not arrive at old age; he died of a surfeit, caused by intemperance: upon this, his soul was carried off, in order to take its trial before a select assembly of the souls of those animals which his gluttony had caused to be slain, and who were now appointed his judges.

"He trembled before a tribunal, to every member of which he had formerly acted as an unmerciful tyrant; he sought for pity, but found none disposed to grant it. Does he not remember, cries the angry boar, to what agonies I was put, not to satisfy his hunger, but his vanity? I was first hunted to death, and my flesh scarce thought worthy of coming once to his table. Were my advice followed, he should do penance in the shape of a hog, which in life he most resembled.

"I am rather, cries a sheep upon the bench, for having him suffer under the appearance of a lamb; we may then send him through four or five transmigrations in the space of a month. Were my voice of any weight in the assembly, cries a calf, he should rather assume such a form as mine; I was bled every day, in order to make my flesh white, and at last killed without mercy. Would it not be wiser, cries a hen, to cram him in the shape of a fowl, and then smother him in his own blood, as I was served? The majority of the assembly were pleased with this punishment, and were going to condemn him without further delay, when the ox rose up to give his opinion: I am informed, says this counsellor, that the prisoner at the bar has left a wife with child behind him. By my knowledge in divination, I foresee that this child will be a son, decrepit, feeble, sick, a plague to himself, and all about him. What say you, then, my companions, if we condemn the father to animate the body of his own son; and by this means make him feel in himself those miseries his intemperance must otherwise have entailed upon his posterity? The whole court applauded the ingenuity of his torture; they thanked him for his advice. Kabul was driven once more to revisit the earth; and his soul in the body of his own son, passed a period of thirty years, loaded with misery, anxiety, and disease."

The Dubious Right to Eat Flesh

William Paley

In this selection from his Principles of Moral and Political Philosophy, *the British divine William Paley (1743–1805) concludes that there is no argument afforded by "the light and order of nature" to justify the claim that humans possess a right to the flesh of animals. The painful slaughter of animals is not necessary for the perpetuation of the human species, nor is it true that the animal realm, if left unchecked, would unduely "interfere" with human affairs by overrunning the earth. Still, Paley somewhat awkwardly claims, there is a general right to consume meat granted by scripture. But even this revealed—as opposed to rational—right does not condone "wanton, and, what is worse, studied cruelty to beasts." Like David Hartley before him, Paley's ultimate appeal to scripture as a justification for moderate carnivorism has a somewhat embarrassed tone to it.*

By the General Rights of Mankind, I mean the rights which belong to the species collectively, the original stock, as I may say, which they have since distributed among themselves. These are,

I. A right to the fruits or vegetable produce of the earth.

The insensible parts of the creation are incapable of injury; and it is nugatory to inquire into the right, where the use can be attended with no injury. But it may be worth observing, for the sake of an inference which will appear below, that, as God has created us with a want and desire of food, and provided things suited by their nature to sustain and satisfy us, we may fairly presume, that he intended we should apply them to that purpose.

II. A right to the flesh of animals.

This is a very different claim from the former. Some excuse seems necessary for the pain and loss which we occasion to brutes, by restraining them of their liberty, mutilating their bodies, and at last putting an end to their lives, which we suppose to be their all, for our pleasure or conveniency.

The reasons alleged in vindication of this practice, are the following: that the several species of brutes being created to prey upon one another, affords a kind of analogy to prove that the human species were intended to feed upon them; that, if let alone, they would overrun the earth, and exclude mankind from the occupation of it; that they are requited for what they suffer at our hands, by our care and protection.

Upon which reasons I would observe, that *the analogy* contended for is extremely lame; since brutes have no power to support life by any other means, and since we have; for the whole human species might subsist entirely upon fruit, pulse, herbs, and roots, as many tribes of Hindoos actually do. The two other reasons may be valid reasons, as far as they go; for, no doubt, if man had been supported entirely by vegetable food, a great part of those animals which die to furnish his table, would never have lived: but they by no means justify our right over the lives of brutes to the extent in which we exercise it. What danger is there, for instance, of fish interfering with us, in the use of their element? Or what do *we* contribute to their support or preservation?

It seems to me, that it would be difficult to defend this right by any arguments which the light and order of nature afford; and that we are beholden for it to the permission recorded in Scripture, Gen. ix. 1,2,3: "And God blessed Noah and his sons, and said unto them, Be fruitful and multiply, and replenish the earth: and the fear of you, and the dread of you, shall be upon every beast of the earth, and upon every fowl of the air, and upon all that moveth upon the earth, and upon all the fishes of the sea; into your hand are they delivered: Every moving think shall be meat for you; even as the green herb, have I given you all things." To Adam and his posterity had been granted, at the creation, "every green herb for meat," and nothing more. In the last clause of the passage now produced, the old grant is recited, and extended to the flesh of animals: "even as the green herb, have I give you all things." But this was not till after the flood; the inhabitants of the antediluvian world had therefore no such permission, that we know of. Whether they actually refrained from the flesh of animals, is another question. Abel, we read, was a keeper of sheep; and for what purpose he kept them, but for food, is difficult to say (unless it were for sacrifices). Might not, however, some of the stricter sects among the antediluvians be scrupulous as to this point? And might not Noah and his family be of this description? For it is not probable that God would publish a permission, to authorize a practice which had never been disputed.

Wanton, and, what is worse, studied cruelty to brutes, is certainly wrong, as coming within none of these reasons.

A Vindication of Natural Diet

Percy Bysshe Shelley

Besides being one of Britain's finest poets, Shelley (1792–1822) was also something of an enfant terrible *of his day, championing before his untimely death such heterodox causes as atheism, free love, and vegetarianism. The latter is defended in his 1813* A Vindication of Natural Diet, *selections from which are reprinted here. In them, Shelley advocates abstinence from alcohol as well as meat on the grounds that such a "natural diet" enhances physical and mental fitness. But his vegetarianism is not based exclusively on considerations of health. Shelley was a convinced materialist and traced "all vice and misery" to physical "morbidity" and "disease." It followed for him that a dietary regimen which prevented destabilizing bodily malaise also struck at "the root of evil" by eliminating its cause. Consequently, Shelley regarded vegetarianism not merely as a prudential hygienic strategy. He also saw it as a necessary step in the moral perfection of humanity.*

Shelley's Vindication *was influenced by Plutarch's essay on abstinence; he even worked on a translation of it, although the manuscript has not survived. Like Plutarch, Shelley argues that humans are not designed by nature for flesh consumption; and, in book 8 of his "Queen Mab," published in the same year as the* Vindication, *he imagines a future in which humans, returned to a natural diet,*

enjoy "kindly passions," "pure desires," and are free from
the moral handicaps of "Hatred, despair and loathing."

> *Here now the human being stands adorning*
> *This loveliest earth with taintless body and mind;*
> *Blessed from his birth with all bland impulses,*
> *Which gently in his noble bosom wake*
> *All kindly passions and all pure desires.*
> *Him, still from hope to hope the bliss pursuing*
> *Which from the exhaustless lore of human weal*
> *Dawns on the virtuous mind, the thoughts that rise*
> *In time-destroying infiniteness, gift*
> *With self-enshrined eternity, that mocks*
> *The unprevailing hoariness of age,*
> *And man, once fleeting o'er the transient scene*
> *Swift as an unremembered vision, stands*
> *Immortal upon earth: no longer now*
> *He slays the lamb that looks him in the face,*
> *And horribly devours his mangled flesh,*
> *Which, still avenging nature's broken law,*
> *Kindled all putrid humours in his frame,*
> *All evil passions, and all vain belief,*
> *Hatred, despair, and loathing in his mind,*
> *The germs of misery, death, disease, and crime.*

Comparative anatomy teaches us that man resembles frugivorous animals in every thing, and carnivorous in nothing; he has neither claws wherewith to seize his prey, nor distinct and pointed teeth to tear the living fibre. A Mandarin of the first class, with nails two inches long, would probably find them alone inefficient to hold even a hare. After every subterfuge of gluttony, the bull must be degraded into the ox, and the ram into the wether, by an unnatural and inhuman operation, that the flaccid fibre may offer a fainter resistance to rebellious nature. It is only by softening and disguising dead flesh by culinary preparation, that it is rendered susceptible of mastication or digestion; and that the sight of its bloody juices and raw horror, does not excite intolerable loathing and disgust. Let the advocate of animal food, force himself to a decisive experiment on its fitness, and as Plutarch recommends, tear a living lamb with his teeth, and plunging his head into its vitals, slake his thirst with the steaming blood; when fresh from the deed of horror let him revert to the irresistible instincts of nature that would arise in judgment against it, and say, Nature formed me for such work as this. Then, and only, would he be consistent. . . .

What is the cause of morbid action in the animal system? Not the air we breathe, for our fellow denizens of nature, breathe the same uninjured; not the water we drink (if remote from the pollutions of man and his inventions), for the animals drink it too; not the earth we tread upon; not the unobscured sight of glorious nature, in the wood, the field, or the expanse of sky and ocean; nothing that we are or do in common, with the undiseased inhabitants of the forest. Something then wherein we differ from them: our habit of altering our food by fire, so that our appetite is no longer a just criterion for the fitness of its gratification. Except in children there remains no traces of that instinct, which determines in all other animals what aliment is natural or otherwise. . . .

Crime is madness. Madness is disease. Whenever the cause of disease shall be discovered, the root from which all vice and misery have so long overshadowed the globe, will lay bare to the axe. All the exertions of man, from that moment, may be considered as tending to the clear profit of his species. No sane mind in a sane body resolves upon a real crime. It is a man of violent passions, bloodshot eyes, and swollen veins, that alone can grasp the knife of murder. The system of a simple diet promises no utopian advantages. It is no mere reform of legislation, whilst the furious passions and evil propensities of the human heart, in which it had its origin, are still unassuaged. It strikes at the root of all evil, and is an experiment which may be tried with success, not alone by nations, but by small societies, families, and even individuals. In no cases has a return to vegetable diet produced the slightest injury; in most it has been attended with changes undeniably beneficial. Should ever a physician be born with the genius of Locke, I am persuaded that he might trace all bodily and mental derangements to our unnatural habits, as clearly as that philosopher has traced all knowledge to sensation. What prolific sources of disease are not those mineral and vegetable poisons that have been introduced for its extirpation! How many thousands have become murderers and robbers, bigots and domestic tyrants, dissolute and abandoned adventurers, from the use of fermented liquors, who, had they slacked their thirst only at the mountain stream, would have lived but to diffuse the happiness of their own unperverted feelings. How many groundless opinions and absurd institutions have not received a general sanction, from the sottishness and intemperance of individuals! Who will assert, that had the populace of Paris drank at the pure source of the Seine, and satisfied their hunger at the ever-furnished table of vegetable nature, that they would have lent their brutal suffrage to the proscription list of Robespierre? Could a set of men, whose passions were not perverted by unnatural stimuli, look with coolness on an auto da fé? Is it to be believed that a being of gentle feelings, rising from his meal of roots, would take delight in sports of blood? Was Nero a man of temperate life? Could you read calm health in his cheek, flushed with governable propensities of hatred for the human race? Did Muley Ismael's pulse beat evenly, was his skin transparent, did his eyes beam with healthfulness, and its invariable concomitants cheerfulness and benignity? Though history has decided none of these questions, a child could not hesitate to answer in the negative. Surely the bile-suffused cheek of Buonaparte, his wrinkled brow, and yellow eye, the ceaseless inquietude of his nervous system, speak no less plainly the character of his unresting ambition than his murders and his victories. It is impossible, that had Buonaparte descended from a race of vegetable feeders, that he could have had, either the inclination or the power to ascend the throne of the Bourbons. The desire of tyranny could scarcely be excited in the individual, the power to tyrannize would certainly not be delegated by a society, neither frenzied by inebriation nor rendered impotent and irrational by disease. Pregnant indeed with inexhaustible calamity, is the renunciation of instinct, as it concerns our physical matter. . . .

There is no disease, bodily or mental, which adoption of vegetable diet and pure water has not infallibly mitigated, wherever the experiment has been fairly tried. Debility is gradually converted into strength, disease into healthfulness, madness in all its hideous variety, from the ravings of the fettered maniac, to the unaccountable irrationalities of ill temper, that make a hell of domestic life, into a calm and considerate evenness of temper, that alone might offer a certain pledge of the future moral reformation of society. On a natural system of diet, old age would be our last and our only malady; the term of our existence would be protracted; we should enjoy life, and no longer preclude others from the enjoyment of it. All sensational delights would be infinitely more exquisite and perfect. The very sense of being would then be a continued pleasure, such as we now feel it in some few and favored moments of our youth. By all that is sacred in our hopes for the human race, I conjure those who love happiness and truth, to give a fair trial to the vegetable system. Reasoning is surely superfluous on a subject, whose merits an experience of six months would set for ever at rest. But is it only among the enlightened and benevolent, that so great a sacrifice of appetite and prejudice can be expected, even though its ultimate excellence should not admit of dispute? It is found easier, by the short-sighted victims of disease, to palliate their torments by medicine, than to prevent them by regimen. . . .

In proportion to the number of proselytes, so will be the weight of evidence, and when a thousand persons can be produced living on vegetables and distilled water, who have to dread no disease but old age, the world will be compelled to regard animal flesh and fermented liquors, as slow, but certain, poisons. The change which would be produced by simpler habits on political economy is sufficiently remarkable. The monopolizing eater of animal flesh would no longer destroy his constitution by devouring an acre at a meal, and many loaves of bread would cease to contribute to gout, madness and apoplexy, in the shape of a pint of porter, or a dram of gin, when appeasing the long-protracted famine of the hard-working peasant's hungry babes. The quantity of nutritious vegetable matter, consumed in fattening the carcass of an ox, would afford ten times the sustenance, undepraving indeed, and incapable of generating disease, if gathered immediately from the bosom of the earth. The most fertile districts of the habitable globe are now actually cultivated by men for animals, at a delay and waste of aliment absolutely incapable of calculation. It is only the wealthy that can, to any great degree, even now, indulge the unnatural craving for dead flesh, and they pay for the greater licence of the privilege by subjection to supernumerary diseases. Again, the spirit of the nation, that should take the lead in this great reform, would insensibly become agricultural; commerce, with all its vices, selfishness, and corruption, would gradually decline; more natural habits would produce gentler manners. . . .

The advantage of a reform in diet, is obviously greater than that of any other. It strikes at the root of the evil. To remedy the abuses of legislation, before we annihilate the propensities by which they are produced, is to suppose, that by taking away the effect, the cause will cease to operate. But the efficacy of this system depends entirely on the proselytism of individuals, and grounds its merits, as a benefit to the community, upon the total change of the dietetic habits in its members. It proceeds securely from a number of particular cases, to one that is universal, and has this advantage over the contrary mode, that one error does not invalidate all that has gone before.

Nineteenth-century defenses of ethical vegetarianism continued the theme which predominated in the preceding century: namely, that the slaughter of food animals tended to encourage morally undesirable habits in humans. But the focus of attention also shifted in the nineteenth century away from human-centered arguments about what flesh eating does to human character toward animal-centered ones that focus on the suffering carnivorism inflicts on food animals. Concerns about the brutalizing effects of carnivorism on humans is not neglected, but a greater sensitivity to animal welfare is now evidenced. Vegetarian societies sprang up in both Britain and America and were frequently accused of "sentimentalism" by their critics. But nineteenth-century advocates of ethical vegetarianism described the horrors of the slaughterhouse in such detail and with such passion that even their most ardent detractors couldn't help but take notice.

The French poet Alphonse de Lamartine tells us that he never forgot his childhood visit to a slaughterhouse and that the animal suffering he witnessed there convinced him that flesh eating is an evil. Richard Wagner, anticipating Albert Schweitzer's twentieth-century "reverence for life" ethic, argues that animals display "human-like traits" which ought to call forth from us "fellow-feeling." Leo Tolstoy provides a horrifying description of a visit to an abattoir, and Anna Kingsford insists that the slaughter of food animals ignores the fundamental ethical principle that the stronger ought to protect the weaker.

William A. Alcott deserves separate mention here. Although in many of his writings on ethical vegetarianism he repeats the nineteenth century's characteristic emphasis on animal suffering, he also offers in the selection here an argument that remarkably anticipates the global perspective typical of contemporary defenses of vegetarianism. He argues that flesh eating not only inflicts cruelty upon hapless animals, but also constitutes genocide of humans because it wastes food grains, thereby reducing the ability of present generations to feed and sustain future ones. This ethical concern for the welfare of future generations is a common theme in twentieth century moral discussions, but was relatively unknown in nineteenth ones.

A Shameful Human Infirmity

Alphonse De Lamartine

In this excerpt from his autobiographical Confidences, *the French poet Lamartine (1790–1869) denounces the slaughter of animals for food as a "shameful human infirmity." Raised by a progressive mother influenced by Pythagorean dietetics and Rousseau's* Emile, *Lamartine's boyhood was vegetarian. Although, like Seneca, he eventually "complied" with the culinary "rules of society," he never forgot nor renounced his mother's belief that carnivorism is "one of those curses cast upon man either by his fall or . . . his own perversity." The cruelty of animal slaughter is a constant theme in Lamartine's subsequent poetry, as is his insistence, as he says in his 1838 poem "La Chute d'un Ange," that "Le plus beau don de l'homme, c'est la Misericorde."*

My mother troubled herself but little about what is called instruction; she did not aspire to make me a "forward child for his age." She did not provoke me to that emulation which is but the jealousy of childish pride. She never had me compared to any one; she never exalted or humiliated me by such dangerous comparisons. She rightly thought that after my intellectual strength had been developed by time and health of body and mind, I would learn as easily as any other, that modicum of Greek, Latin, and figures, which constitutes that learned commonplace which is

77

called an education. Her wish was to make me a happy child, a sound mind, a loving soul; a creature of God and not one of man's dolls. . . .

My education was a secondhand philosophical education, a philosophical education corrected and softened down by motherly feelings. Physically, this education flowed in a great measure from Pythagoras and *Emile*. Consequently, the greatest simplicity in dress and the most rigorous frugality in food formed its basis. My mother was convinced, and on this head I have retained her firm belief, that to kill animals for the purpose of feeding on their flesh is one of the most deplorable and shameful infirmities of the human state; that it is one of those curses cast upon man either by his fall, or by the obduracy of his own perversity. She believed, and I am of the same belief, that these habits of hard-heartedness towards the gentlest animals, our companions, our auxiliaries, our brethren in toil and even in affection here below; that these immolations, these sanguinary appetites, this sight of palpitating flesh, are calculated to brutalize the instincts of the heart and make them ferocious. She believed, and I am of the same belief, that this nurture, which is seemingly much more succulent and much more energetic, contains in itself active causes of irritation and putridity, which sour the blood and shorten the days of mankind. In support of these ideas of abstinence, she quoted the innumerable gentle and pious tribes of India who deny themselves all that has had life; and the strong and healthy races of the shepherds and even of the laboring classes of our fields, who work harder than any, who live more innocently than any, and who do not eat meat ten times in the course of their lives. She never allowed me to eat any until I attained the age at which I was thrown into the helter-skelter life of colleges. To kill the desire for it, even if it had existed within me, she used no arguments, but appealed to instinct, which reasons much more powerfully in our breasts than logic.

I had a lamb which had been given to me by a peasant of Milly, and which I had taught to follow me all over like the most affectionate and faithful of dogs. We loved one another with that first fondness which little children and young animals naturally have for one another. One day the cook said to my mother before me:

"Madam, the lamb is fat, and the butcher has come for it; must I give it to him?"

I cried out upon it, threw myself before the lamb, and asked what the butcher wanted to do with it and what a butcher was. The cook answered that he was a man who killed lambs, sheep, little calves, and beautiful cows for money. I could hardly believe her. I prayed to my mother. I easily obtained that my little friend should be spared. A few days afterwards, my mother took me to town with her, and made me pass, as if by accident, through the yard of a slaughter house. I saw some men, their arms naked and besmeared with blood, knocking a bull in the head; others cutting the throats of calves and sheep, and separating their still heaving limbs. Streams of smoking gore ran along the pavement. An intense feeling of pity, mingled with horror, seized upon me. I asked to be led away quickly. The thought of these scenes, the necessary preliminaries of one of those dishes of meat which I had so often seen on the table, made me take a disgust to animal food and inspired me with a horror for butchers. Although the necessity of complying with the rules of the society in which we live has made me eat, since then, all that other people eat, I have retained a repugnance, based on reason, to cooked flesh, and it has always been difficult for me not to see in the butcher's trade something of the executioner's occupation.

Until the age of twelve, then, I only lived on bread, milk-food, vegetables, and fruit. My health was not less robust on this account, nor my growth less rapid, and it was to this diet, perhaps, that I was indebted for that purity of feature, that exquisite sensibility of feeling, and that quiet gentleness of humor and character which I had preserved up to that period.

The World is a
Mighty Slaughterhouse
and
Flesh-Eating and
Human Decimation

William A. Alcott

*A cousin of the Concord transcendentalist Bronson Alcott,
William (1798–1859) was a pioneer in both educational
and medical reform. Although he started out as a school-
master, his interests soon moved to the area of health and
hygiene. After earning a degree from Yale Medical School,
Alcott entered into a period of intensive lecturing and
writing on the subjects of education and health. He eventually published over one hundred volumes, including*
Vegetable Diet, *which appeared ten years before his
death. In this book, Alcott outlines several arguments in
favor of vegetarianism drawn from diverse areas such as
anatomy, physiology, medicine, politics, economics and
ethics. He thought the last the most persuasive, and it is
reproduced here in the first selection. In it, Alcott concludes that the slaughter of animals is contrary to moral
growth because of the callousness to cruelty it breeds. In
the second selection from* Vegetable Diet, *Alcott anticipates an argument popular among twentieth-century
advocates of ethical vegetarianism: that flesh consump-*

tion exacerbates the problem of world hunger by wasting food grains. His argument, however, has a unique twist. It claims that continued carnivorism deprives potential future humans of life by reducing the ability of present generations to feed and sustain them. For Alcott, this is a subtle form of murder. As he says, "We do not destroy [future generations] in the full sense of the term, it is true, for they never had an existence. But we prevent their coming into the possession of a joyous and happy existence; and though we have no name for it, is it not a crime?"

The World Is a Mighty Slaughterhouse

In one point of view, nearly every argument which can be brought to show the superiority of a vegetable diet over one that includes flesh or fish, is a moral argument.

Thus, if man is so constituted by his structure, and by the laws of his animal economy, that all the functions of the body, and of course all the faculties of the mind, and the affections of the soul, are in better condition—better subserve our own purposes, and the purposes of the great Creator—as well as hold out longer, on the vegetable system—then it is desirable, in a moral point of view, to adopt it. If mankind lose, upon the average, two years of their lives by sickness, as some have estimated it, saying nothing of the pain and suffering undergone, or of the mental anguish and soul torment which grow out of it, and often render life a burden; and if the simple primitive custom of living on vegetables and fruits, along with other good physical and mental habits, which seem naturally connected with it, will, in time, nearly if not wholly remove or prevent this amazing loss, then is the argument deduced therefrom . . . a moral argument.

If, as I have endeavored to show [in earlier sections], the adoption of the vegetable system by nations and individuals, would greatly advance the happiness of all, in every known respect, and if, on this account, such a change in our flesh-eating countries would be sound policy, and good economy—then we have another moral argument in its favor.

But, again: if it be true that all nations have been the most virtuous and flourishing, other things being equal, in the days of their simplicity in regard to food, drink, etc.; and if we can, in every instance, connect the decline of a nation with the period of their departure, as a nation, into the maze of luxurious and enervating habits; and if this doctrine is, as a general rule, obviously applicable to smaller classes of men, down to single families, then is the argument we derive from it in its nature a moral one. Whatever really tends, without the possibility of mistake, to the promotion of human happiness, here and hereafter, is, without doubt, moral.

But this, though much, is not all. The destruction of animals for food, in its details and tendencies, involves so much of cruelty as to cause every reflecting individual—not destitute of the ordinary sensibilities of our nature—to shudder. I recall: daily observation shows that such is not the fact; nor should it, upon second thought, be expected. Where all are dark, the color is not perceived; and so universally are the moral sensibilities which really belong to human nature deadened by the customs which prevail among us, that few, if any, know how to estimate, rightly, the evil of which I speak. They have no more a correct idea of a true sensibility—not a *morbid* one—on this subject, than a blind man has of colors; and for nearly the same reasons. And on this account it is, that I seem to shrink from presenting, at this time, those considerations which, I know, cannot, from the very nature of the case, be properly understood or appreciated, except by a very few.

Still, there are some things which, I trust, may be made plain. It must be obvious that the custom of rendering children familiar with the taking away of life, even when it is done with a good degree of tenderness, cannot have a very happy effect. But, when this is done, not only without tenderness or sympathy, but often with manifestations of great pleasure, and when children, as in some cases, are almost constant witnesses of such scenes, how dreadful must be the results!

In this view, the world, I mean our own portion of it, sometimes seems to me like one mighty slaughterhouse—one grand school for the suppression of every kind, and tender, and brotherly feeling—one grand process of education to the entire destitution of all moral principle—one vast scene of destruction to all moral sensibility, and all sympathy with the woes of those around us. Is it not so?

I have seen many boys who shuddered, at first, at the thought of taking the life, even of a snake, until compelled to it by what they conceived to be duty; and who shuddered still more at taking the life of a lamb, a calf, a pig, or a fowl. And yet I have seen these same boys, in subsequent life, become so changed, that they could look on such scenes not merely with indifference, but with gratification. Is this change of feeling desirable? How long is it after we begin to look with indifference on pain and suffering in brutes, before we begin to be less affected than before by human suffering?

I am not ignorant that sentiments like these are either regarded as morbid, and therefore pitiable, or as affected, and therefore ridiculous. . . .

I am not prepared to maintain, strongly, the old-fashioned doctrine, that a butcher who commences his employment at adult age, is necessarily rendered hard-hearted or unfeeling; or, that they who eat flesh have their sensibilities deadened, and their passions inflamed by it—though I am not sure that there is not some truth in it. I only maintain, that to render children familiar with the taking away of animal life—especially the lives of our own domestic animals, often endeared to us by many interesting circumstances of their history, or of our own, in relation to them—cannot be otherwise than unhappy in its tendency.

How shocking it must be to the inhabitants of Jupiter, or some other planet, who had never before witnessed these sad effects of the ingress of sin among us, to see the carcasses of animals, either whole or by piecemeal, hoisted upon our very tables before the faces of children of all ages, from the infant at the breast, to the child of ten or twelve, or fourteen, and carved, and swallowed; and this not merely once, but from day to day, through life! What could they—what would they—expect from such an education of the young mind and heart? What, indeed, but mourning, desolation, and woe!

On this subject the First Annual Report of the American Physiological Society thus remarks—and I wish the remark might have its due weight on the mind of the reader:

"How can it be right to be instrumental in so much unnecessary slaughter? How can it be right, especially for a country of vegetable abundance like ours, to give daily employment to twenty thousand or thirty thousand butchers? How can it be right to train our children to behold such slaughter? How can it be right to blunt the edge of their moral sensibilities, by placing before them, at almost every meal, the mangled corpses of the slain; and not only placing them there, but rejoicing while we feast upon them?"

One striking evidence of the tendency which an habitual shedding of blood has on the mind and heart, is found in the fact that females are generally so reluctant to take away life, that notwithstanding they are trained to a fondness for all sorts of animal food, very few are willing to gratify their desires for a stimulating diet, by becoming their own butchers. I have indeed seen females who would kill a fowl or a lamb rather than go without it; but they are exceedingly rare. And who would not regard female character as tarnished by a familiarity with such scenes as those to which I have referred? But if the keen edge of female delicacy and sensibility would be blunted by scenes of bloodshed, are not the moral sensibilities of our own sex affected in a similar way? And must it not, then, have a deteriorating tendency?

It cannot be otherwise than that the circumstances of which I have spoken, which so universally surround infancy and childhood, should take off, gradually, the keen edge of moral sensibility, and lessen every virtuous or holy sympathy. I have watched—I believe impartially—the effect on certain sensitive young persons in the circle of my acquaintance. I have watched myself. The result has confirmed the opinion I have just expressed. No child, I think, can walk through a common market or slaughterhouse without receiving a moral injury; nor am I quite sure that any virtuous adult can.

How have I been struck with the change produced in the young mind by that merriment which often accompanies the slaughter of an innocent fowl, or lamb, or pig! How can the Christian, with the Bible in hand, and the merciful doctrines of its pages for his text, "Teach me to feel another's woe,"—the beast's not excepted—and yet, having laid down that Bible, go at once from the domestic altar to make light of the convulsions and exit of a poor domestic animal?

Is it said that these remarks apply only to the *abuse* of a thing which, in its place, is proper? Is it said, that there is no necessity of levity on these occasions? Grant that there is none; still the result is almost inevitable. But there is, in any event, one way of avoiding, or rather preventing both the abuse and the occasion for abuse, by ceasing to kill animals for food; and I venture to predict that the evil never will be prevented otherwise.

The usual apology for hunting and fishing, in all their various and often cruel forms—whereby so many of our youth, from the setters of snares for birds, and the anglers for trout, to the whalemen, are educated to cruelty, and steeled to every virtuous and holy sympathy—is, the necessity of the animals whom we pursue for food. I know, indeed, that this is not, in most cases, the true reason, but it is the reason given—it is the substance of the reason. It serves as an apology. They who make it may often be ignorant of the true reason, or they or others may wish to conceal it; and, true to human nature, they are ready to give every reason for their conduct, but the real and most efficient one.

It must not, indeed, be concealed that there is one more apology usually made for these cruel sports; and made too, in some instances, by good men; I mean, by men whose intentions are in the main pure and excellent. These sports are healthy, they tell us. They are a relief to mind and body. Perhaps no good man, in our own country, had defended them with more ingenuity, or with more show of reason and good sense, than Dr. Comstack, in his recent popular work on human physiology. And yet, there is scarcely a single advantage which he has pointed out, as being derived from the "pleasures of the chase," that may not be gained in a way which savors less of blood. The doctor himself is too much in love with botany, geology, mineralogy, and the various branches of natural history, not to know what I mean when I say this. He knows full well the excitement, and, on his own principles, the consequent relief of body and mind from their accustomed and often painful round, which grows out of clambering over mountains and hills, and fording streams, and climbing trees and rocks, to need any very broad hints on the subject; to say nothing of the delights of agriculture and horticulture. How could he, then, give currency to practices which, to say the least—and by his own concessions, too—are doubtful in regard to their moral tendencies, by inserting his opinions in favor of sports, for which he himself happens to be partial, in a schoolbook? Is this worthy of those who would educate the youth of our land on the principles of the Bible?

Flesh-Eating and Human Decimation

Political economists tell us that the produce of an acre of land in wheat, corn, potatoes, and other vegetables, and in fruits, will sustain animal life sixteen times as long as when the produce of the same acre is converted into flesh, by feeding and fattening animals upon it.

But, if we admit that this estimate is too high, and if the real difference is only eight to one, instead of sixteen to one, the results may perhaps surprise us; and if we have not done it before, may lead us to reflection. Let us see what some of them are.

The people of the United States are believed to eat, upon the average, an amount of animal food equal to one whole meal once a day, and those of Great Britain one in two days. But taking this estimate to be correct, Great Britain, by substituting vegetable for animal food, might sustain forty-nine instead of twenty-one millions of inhabitants, and the United States sixty-six millions instead of twenty; and this, too, in their present comfort, and without clearing up any more new land. Here, then, we are consuming that unnecessarily—if animal food is unnecessary—which would sustain seventy-nine millions of human beings in life, health, and happiness.

Now, if life is a blessing at all—if it is a blessing to twenty-two millions in Great Britain, and twenty millions in the United States—then to add to this population an increase of seventy-nine millions, would be to increase, in the same proportion, the aggregate of human happiness. And if, in addition to this, we admit the very generally received principle, that there is a tendency, from the nature of things, in the population of any country, to keep up with the means of support, we, of Great Britain and America, keep down, at the present moment, by flesh-eating, sixty-three millions of inhabitants.

We do not destroy them, in the full sense of the term, it is true, for they never had an existence. But we prevent their coming into the possession of a joyous and happy existence; and though we have no name for it, is it not a crime? What! No crime for thirty-five millions of people to prevent and preclude the existence of sixty-three millions?

I see no way of avoiding the force of this argument, except by denying the premises on which I have founded my conclusions. But they are far more easily denied than disproved. The probability, after all, is that my estimates are too low, and that the advantages of an exclusively vegetable diet, in a national or political point of view, are even greater than is here represented. I do not deny, that some deduction ought to be made on account of the consumption of fish, which does not prevent the growth or use of vegetable products; but my belief is, that, including them, the animal food we use amounts to a great deal more than one meal a day, or one third of our whole living.

Suppose there was no *crime* in shutting human beings out of existence by flesh-eating, at the amazing rate I have mentioned— still, is it not, I repeat it, a great national or political loss? Or, will it be said, in its defence, as has been said in defence of war, if not of intemperance and some of the forms of licentiousness, that as the world is, it is a blessing to keep down its population, otherwise it would soon be overstocked? The argument would be as good in one case as in the other; that is, it is not valid in either. The world might be made to sustain, in comfort, even in the present comparatively infant state of the arts and sciences, at least forty or fifty times its present number of inhabitants. It will be time enough a thousand or two thousand years to come, to begin to talk about the danger of the world's being over-peopled; and, above all, to talk about justifying what we know is, in the abstract, very wrong, to prevent a distanced imagined evil; one, in fact, which may not, and probably will not ever exist.

Human Beasts of Prey
and
Fellow-Suffering

Richard Wagner

The great German composer Richard Wagner (1813–1883) was a longtime advocate of animal rights and vegetarianism, as well as an intensely outspoken critic of vivisection. The two selections here eloquently express the basis of his convictions. In the first, Wagner argues that humans have become "beasts of prey" by denying any kinship with the animals they slaughter for food, even though the latter are both sentient and display "human-like" traits such as loyalty and compassion. In the second, an excerpt from an 1858 letter to Mathilde Wesendonck, Wagner discusses his philosophy of "fellow-suffering," which he defines as a compassionate empathy "for even the commonest and least of beings." The concept of fellow-suffering, although in many respects characteristic of Wagner's nineteenth-century romanticism, has certain affinities to Albert Schweitzer's twentieth-century ethic of reverence for life. It certainly served as the basis for Wagner's own ethical vegetarianism.

Human Beasts of Prey

[W]hen first it dawned on human wisdom that the same thing breathed in animals as in mankind, it appeared too late to avert the

89

curse which, ranging ourselves with the beasts of prey, we seemed to have called down upon us through the taste of animal food: disease and misery of every kind, to which we did not see mere vegetable-eating men exposed. The insight thus obtained led further to the consciousness of a deep-seated guilt in our earthly being: it moved those fully seized therewith to turn aside from all that stirs the passions, through free-willed poverty and total abstinence from animal food. To these wise men the mystery of the world unveiled itself as a restless tearing into pieces, to be restored to restful unity by nothing save compassion. His pity for each breathing creature, determining his every action, redeemed the sage from all the ceaseless change of suffering existences, which he himself must pass until his last emancipation. Thus the pitiless was mourned by him for reason of his suffering, but most of all the beast, whose pain he saw without knowing it capable of redemption through pity. This wise man could but recognise that the reasonable being gains its highest happiness through free-willed suffering, which he therefore seeks with eagerness, and ardently embraces; whereas the beast but looks on pain, so absolute and useless to it, with dread and agonised rebellion. But still more to be deplored that wise man deemed the human being who consciously could torture animals and turn a deaf ear to their pain, for he knew that such a one was infinitely farther from redemption than the wild beast itself, which should rank in comparison as sinless as a saint.

Races driven to rawer climates, and hence compelled to guard their life by animal food, preserved till quite late times a feeling that the beasts did not belong to them, but to a deity; they knew themselves guilty of a crime with every beast they slew or slaughtered, and had to expatiate it to the god: they offered up the beast, and thanked the god by giving him the fairest portions of the spoil. What here was a religious sentiment survived in later philosophers, born after the ruin of religions, an axiom of humanity: one has only to read Plutarch's splendid treatise "On Reason in the Beasts of Land and Sea," to return with a tingle of shame to the precepts of our men of science.

Up to here, but alas! no further, can we trace the religious basis of our human forbears' sympathy with animals, and it seems that the march of civilization, by making him indifferent to "the God," turned man himself into a raging beast of prey. . . . [Now] our creed is: "Animals are useful; particularly if, trusting in our sanctuary, they yield

themselves into our hands. Come let us therefore make of them what
we deem good for human use; we have the right to martyr a thousand
faithful dogs the whole day long, if we can thereby help one human
creature to the cannibal well-being of five hundred swine."

―――――――

[T]he emergence of huge deserts, like the African Sahara, must
certainly have cast the dwellers on the once luxuriant coasts of
inland seas into such straits of hunger as we can only form an idea
of by recalling stories of the awful sufferings of the shipwrecked,
whereby completely civilized citizens of our modern states have
been reduced to cannibalism. On the swampy margins of Canadian
lakes animal species allied to the panther and tiger still live as
fruit-eaters, whereas upon those desert fringes the historic tiger
and lion have become the most bloodthirsty of all the beasts of
prey. That it must have been hunger alone, which first drove man
to slay the animals and feed upon their flesh and blood; and that
this compulsion was no mere consequence of his removal into
colder climes, as those assert who deem the consumption of ani-
mal-food in northern parts a duty of self-preservation, is proved by
the patent fact that great nations with ample supplies of grain suffer nothing in strength or endurance even in colder regions
through an almost exclusively vegetable diet, as is shewn by the
eminent length of life of Russian peasants; while the Japanese,
who know no other food than vegetables, are further renowned for
their warlike valor and keenness of intellect. We may therefore call
it quite an abnormality when hunger bred the thirst for blood, as
in the branches of the Malayan stock transplanted to the northern
steppes of Asia; that thirst which history teaches us can never
more be slaked, and fills its victims with a raging madness, not
with courage. One can only account for it all by the human beast
of prey having made itself monarch of the peaceful world, just as
the ravening wild beast usurped dominion of the woods: a result of
those preceding cataclysms which overtook primeval man while
yet all unprepared for either. And little as the savage animals have
prospered, we see the sovereign human beast of prey decaying too.
Owing to a nutriment against his nature, he falls sick with mal-
adies that claim but him, attains no more his natural span of life
or gentle death, but, plagued by pains and cares of body and soul

unknown to any other species, he shuffles through an empty life to its ever fearful cutting short.

[To] the beasts, who have been our schoolmasters in all the arts by which we trapped and made them subject to us, man was superior in nothing save deceit and cunning, by no means in courage or bravery; for the animal will fight to its last breath, indifferent to wounds and death: "It knows nor plea nor prayer for mercy, no avowal of defeat." To base man's dignity upon his pride, compared with that of animals, would be mistaken; and our victory over them, their subjugation, we can only attribute to our greater art of dissembling. That art we highly boast of; we call it "reason" and proudly think it marks us from the animals: for look you! it can make us like to God himself—as to which, however, Mephistopheles has his private opinion, concluding that the only use man made of reason was "to be more bestial than any beast." In its great veracity and naiveness the animal is unable to estimate the moral meanness of the arts through which we cowed it; in any case it finds something daemonic in them, which it obeys in timid awe: but if its master exercises kindness toward the daunted beast, we may assume that it recognises something divine in him, which it reveres and loves so strongly that it devotes its natural gifts of bravery entirely to the service of fidelity, to the point of agonising death. Just as the saint is driven irresistibly to attest his loyalty to God by martyrdom and death, so the animal with its love to a master as god. One only tie, which the saint has been able to break, still binds the animal to Nature, since it cannot be aught but sincere: compassion for its young. In resulting dilemmas, however, it knows how to choose for the best. A traveller once left his brach behind him in the stable of an inn, as she had just brought forth young, and pursued alone the three leagues journey to his house; next morning he finds on the straw in his yard the four sucklings, and beside them their dead mother: four times had she run the distance to and fro in haste and anguish, carrying home her litter one by one; only when she had brought the last pup safely to her master, whom she now had no more need to leave, did she yield to the lingering pains of death. This the "free" burgher of our Civilization calls "houndish fidelity," with a contemptuous accent on the "hound." Yet in a world from which all *reverence* has vanished, or tarries but as hypocritical pretence, is there no example for us to take from the affecting lesson of the animals we govern? Where devotion true till death is met between man and man, we need not be ashamed to regard it as already a noble bond of kinship with the animal kingdom, since there is good reason for believing that this virtue is purer, ah! diviner in its exercise by animals than by man: for, quite apart from their value in the eyes of the world, in his sufferings and death man is able to recognise a blessed expiation; whereas the beast, without one ulterior thought of moral advantage, sacrifices itself wholly and purely to love and loyalty—though this also is explained by our physiologists as a simple chemical reaction of certain elementary substances. . . .

Fellow-Suffering

Recently, while I was in the street, my eye was caught by a poulterer's shop; I stared unthinkingly at his piled-up wares, neatly and appetizingly laid out, when I became aware of a man at the side busily plucking a hen, while another man was just putting his hand in a cage, where he seized a live hen and tore its head off. The hideous scream of the animal, and the pitiful, weaker sounds of complaint that it made while being overpowered transfixed my soul with horror. Ever since then I have been unable to rid myself of this impression, although I had experienced it often before. It is dreadful to see how our lives—which, on the whole, remain addicted to pleasure—rest upon such a bottomless pit of the cruellest misery! This has been so self-evident to me from the very beginning, and has become even more central to my thinking as my sensibility has increased . . . I have observed the way in which I am drawn in the [direction of empathy for misery] with a force that inspires me with sympathy, and that everything touches me deeply only insofar as it arouses fellow-feeling in me, i.e. fellow-suffering. I see in this fellow-suffering the most salient feature of my moral being, and presumably it is this that is the well-spring of my art.

But what characterizes fellow-suffering is that it is by no means conditioned in its affections by the individual qualities of the suffering object but rather by the perception of suffering itself. In love it is otherwise: here we advance to a feeling of fellow-joy, and we can share the joy of an individual only if we find the latter's particular characteristics acceptable in the highest degree, and homogeneous. This is more likely in the case of common types, since here it is purely sexual relations which are almost exclusively at work. The more noble the nature, the more difficult it is to achieve fellow-joy through reintegration: but, if we succeed, there is nothing to equal it! Fellow-suffering, by contrast, is something we can feel for even the commonest and least of beings, a being which, apart from its suffering, is totally unsympathetic towards us, indeed, may even be antipathetic in what it is capable of enjoying. The reason for this, at all events, is infinitely profound and, if we recognize it, we shall thereby see ourselves raised above the very real barriers of our personality. For what we encounter when we exercise fellow-suffering in this way is suffering as such, divorced from all personality.

In order to steel themselves against the power of fellow-suffering, people commonly assert that it is demonstrably the case that lower natures feel suffering far less keenly than a higher organism: they argue that, as the sensibility that first makes fellow-suffering possible increases, so, proportionately, does suffering gain in reality: in other words, the fellow-suffering that we expend on lower natures is a waste of emotional effort, being an exaggeration, and even a pampering of feeling. This opinion, however, rests upon a fundamental error which is at the basis of every realistic philosophy, for it is precisely here that we see idealism in its truly moral stature inasmuch as it reveals the former as an example of egotistical narrow-mindedness. The question here is not what the other person suffers but what *I* suffer when I know him to be suffering. After all, we know what exists around us only inasmuch as we picture it in our imagination, and how *I* imagine it is how it is for *me*. If I ennoble it, it is because I myself feel deeply when I imagine his suffering, and whoever, by contrast, imagines it to be insignificant reveals in doing so that he himself is insignificant. Thus my fellow-suffering makes the other person's suffering an actual reality, and the more insignificant the being with which I can suffer, the wider and more embracing is the circle which suggests itself to my feelings. But here lies an aspect of my nature which others may see as a weakness. I admit that unilateral actions are much impeded by it; but I am certain that when I act, I then act in accordance with my essential nature, and certainly never cause pain to anyone intentionally. This consideration alone can influence me in all my actions: to cause others as little suffering as possible. On this point I am totally at one with myself, for only in this way can I hope to give others my joy, as well: for the only true, genuine joy is to be found in the conformity of fellow-suffering. But I cannot obtain this by force: it must be granted me by the other person's friendly nature, which is why I have only ever encountered a single perfect example of this phenomenon!

But I am also clear in my own mind why I can even feel greater fellow-suffering for lower natures than for higher ones. A higher nature is what it is precisely because it has been raised by its own suffering to the heights of resignation, or else has within it—and cultivates—the capacity for such a development. Such a nature is extremely close to mine, is indeed similar to it, and with it I attain to fellow-joy. That is why, basically, I feel less fellow-suffering for people than for animals. For I can see that the latter are totally denied the capacity to rise above suffering, and to achieve a state of resignation and deep, divine calm. And so, in the event of their suffering, as happens when they are tormented, all I see— with a sense of my own tormented despair—is their absolute, redemptionless suffering without any higher purpose, their only release being death, which confirms my belief that it would have been better for them never to have entered upon life. And so, if this suffering can have a purpose, it is simply to awaken a sense of fellow-suffering in man, who thereby absorbs the animal's defective existence, and becomes the redeemer of the world by recognizing the error of all existence. . . . But to see the individual's capacity for redeeming the world through fellow-suffering atrophy, undeveloped and most assiduously neglected, makes me regard people with utter loathing, and weakens my sense of fellow-suffering to the point where I feel only total insensitivity towards their distress. It is in his distress that the individual's road to salvation is to be found, a road which is not open to animals; if he does not recognize this to be so but insists upon considering it to be locked and barred to him, I feel an instinctive urge to throw this door wide open for him, and am capable of going to lengths of great cruelty in order to make him conscious of the need to suffer. Nothing leaves me colder than the philistine's complaint that he has been disturbed in his contentment: any compassion here would be pure complicity. Just as my entire nature involves shaking people out of their common condition, here, too, I feel an urge simply to spur them on in order to make them feel life's great anguish!

The Immorality of Carnivorism

Leo Tolstoy

This selection is excerpted from a longer piece entitled "The First Step," which Tolstoy (1828–1910) wrote as a preface for the 1892 Russian edition of The Ethics of Diet, *a still useful but long out-of-print history of vegetarianism written by Howard Williams. Tolstoy converted to vegetarianism in 1885, as did two of his daughters. His primary reason for doing so, as he says in this selection, was the conviction that flesh eating is "simply immoral, as it involves the performance of an act which is contrary to moral feeling—killing." Tolstoy makes clear that he was especially horrified by the inhumane and callous ways in which food animals are butchered, and his novelist's eye captures in stark detail the events he witnessed while visiting slaughter houses. His experiences convinced him that such practices diminished "spiritual capacity" because they suppressed "sympathy and pity toward living creatures," and that vegetarianism was a "first step" towards that self-restraint which should be the moral aspiration of humans.*

Fasting is an indispensable condition of a good life; but in fasting, as in self-control in general, the question arises, with what shall we begin—how to fast, how often to eat, what to eat, what to avoid eating? And as we can do no work seriously without regard-

97

ing the necessary order of sequence, so also we cannot fast without knowing where to begin—with what to commence self-control in food.

Fasting! And even an analysis of how to fast, and where to begin! The notion seems ridiculous and wild to the majority of men.

I remember how, with pride at his originality, an Evangelical preacher, who was attacking monastic asceticism, once said to me, "Ours is not a Christianity of fasting and privations, but of beef-steaks." Christianity, or virtue in general—and beefsteaks!

During a long period of darkness and lack of all guidance, Pagan or Christian, so many wild, immoral ideas have made their way into our life (especially into that lower region of the first steps toward a good life—our relation to food, to which no one paid any attention), that it is difficult for us even to understand the audacity and senselessness of upholding, in our days, Christianity or virtue with beefsteaks.

We are not horrified by this association, solely because a strange thing has befallen us. We look and see not: listen and hear not. There is no bad odor, no sound, no monstrosity, to which man cannot become so accustomed that he ceases to remark what would strike a man unaccustomed to it. Precisely so it is in the moral region. Christianity and morality with beefsteaks!

A few days ago I visited the slaughter house in our town of Toula. It is built on the new and improved system practised in large towns, with a view to causing the animals as little suffering as possible. It was on a Friday, two days before Trinity Sunday. There were many cattle there. . . .

Long before this . . . , I had wished to visit a slaughter house, in order to see with my own eyes the reality of the question raised when vegetarianism is discussed. But at first I felt ashamed to do so, as one is always ashamed of going to look at suffering which one knows is about to take place, but which one cannot avert; and so I kept putting off my visit.

But a little while ago I met on the road a butcher returning to Toula after a visit to his home. He is not yet an experienced butcher, and his duty is to stab with a knife. I asked him whether he did not feel sorry for the animals that he killed. He gave me the usual answer: "Why should I feel sorry? It is necessary." But when I told him that eating flesh is not necessary, but is only a luxury, he agreed; and then he admitted that he was sorry for the animals.

"But what can I do? I must earn my bread," he said. "At first I was *afraid* to kill. My father, he never even killed a chicken in all his life." The majority of Russians cannot kill; they feel pity, and express the feeling by the word "fear." This man had also been "afraid," but he was so no longer. He told me that most of the work was done on Fridays, when it continues until the evening.

Not long ago I also had a talk with a retired soldier, a butcher, and he, too, was surprised at my assertion that it was a pity to kill, and said the usual things about its being ordained; but afterwards he agreed with me: "Especially when they are quiet, tame cattle. They come, poor things! trusting you. It is very pitiful."

This is dreadful! Not the suffering and death of the animals, but that man suppresses in himself, unnecessarily, the highest spiritual capacity—that of sympathy and pity toward living creatures like himself—and by violating his own feelings becomes cruel. And how deeply seated in the human heart is the injunction not to take life!

Once, when walking from Moscow, I was offered a lift by some carters who were going from Serpouhof to a neighboring forest to fetch wood. It was the Thursday before Easter. I was seated in the first cart, with a strong, red, coarse carman, who evidently drank. On entering a village we saw a well-fed, naked, pink pig being dragged out of the first yard to be slaughtered. It squealed in a dreadful voice, resembling the shriek of a man. Just as we were passing they began to kill it. A man gashed its throat with a knife. The pig squealed still more loudly and piercingly, broke away from the men, and ran off covered with blood. Being near-sighted I did not see all the details. I saw only the human-looking pink body of the pig and heard its desperate squeal; but the carter saw all the details and watched closely. They caught the pig, knocked it down, and finished cutting its throat. When its squeals ceased the carter sighed heavily. "Do men really not have to answer for such things?" he said.

So strong is man's aversion to all killing. But by example, by encouraging greediness, by the assertion that God has allowed it, and, above all, by habit, people entirely lose this natural feeling.

On Friday I decided to go to Toula, and, meeting a meek, kind acquaintance of mine, I invited him to accompany me.

"Yes, I have heard that the arrangements are good, and have been wishing to go and see it; but if they are slaughtering I will not go in."

"Why not? That's just what I want to see! If we eat flesh it must be killed."

"No, no, I cannot!"

It is worth remarking that this man is a sportsman and himself kills animals and birds.

So we went to the slaughter house. Even at the entrance one noticed the heavy, disgusting, fetid smell, as of carpenter's glue, or paint on glue. The nearer we approached, the stronger became the smell. The building is of red brick, very large, with vaults and high chimneys. We entered the gates. To the right was a spacious enclosed yard, three-quarters of an acre in extent—twice a week cattle are driven in here for sale—and adjoining this enclosure was the porter's lodge. To the left were the chambers, as they are called—i.e., rooms with arched entrances, sloping asphalt floors, and contrivances for moving and hanging up the carcasses. On a bench against the wall of the porter's lodge were seated half a dozen butchers, in aprons covered with blood, their tucked-up sleeves disclosing their muscular arms also besmeared with blood. They had finished their work half an hour before, so that day we could only see the empty chambers. Though these chambers were open on both sides, there was an oppressive smell of warm blood; the floor was brown and shining, with congealed black blood in the cavities.

One of the butchers described the process of slaughtering, and showed us the place where it was done. I did not quite understand him, and formed a wrong, but very horrible, idea of the way the animals are slaughtered; and I fancied that, as is often the case, the reality would very likely produce upon me a weaker impression than the imagination. But in this I was mistaken.

The next time I visited the slaughter house I went in good time. It was the Friday before Trinity—a warm day in June. The smell of glue and blood was even stronger and more penetrating than on my first visit. The work was at its height. The duty yard was full of cattle, and animals had been driven into all the enclosures beside the chambers.

In the street, before the entrance, stood carts to which oxen, calves, and cows were tied. Other carts drawn by good horses and filled with live calves, whose heads hung down and swayed about, drew up and were unloaded; and similar carts containing the carcasses of oxen, with trembling legs sticking out, with heads and bright red lungs and brown livers, drove away from the slaughter house. The dealers themselves, in their long coats, with their whips and knouts in their hands, were walking about the yard, either marking with tar cattle belonging to the same owner, or bargaining, or else guiding oxen and bulls from the great yard into the enclosures which lead into the chambers. These men were evidently all preoccupied with money matters and calculations, and any thought as to whether it was right or wrong to kill these animals was as far from their minds as were questions about the chemical composition of the blood that covered the floor of the chambers.

No butchers were to be seen in the yard; they were all in the chambers at work. That day about a hundred head of cattle were slaughtered. I was on the point of entering one of the chambers, but stopped short at the door. I stopped both because the chamber was crowded with carcasses which were being moved about, and also because blood was flowing on the floor and dripping from above. All the butchers present were besmeared with blood, and had I entered I, too, should certainly have been covered with it. One suspended carcass was being taken down, another was being moved toward the door, a third, a slaughtered ox, was lying with its white legs raised, while a butcher with strong hand was ripping up its tight-stretched hide.

Through the door opposite the one at which I was standing, a big, red, well-fed ox was led in. Two men were dragging it, and hardly had it entered when I saw a butcher raise a knife above its neck and stab it. The ox, as if all four legs had suddenly given way, fell heavily upon its belly, immediately turned over on one side, and began to work its legs and all its hind-quarters. Another butcher at once threw himself upon the ox from the side opposite to the twitching legs, caught its horns and twisted its head down to the ground, while another butcher cut its throat with a knife. From beneath the head there flowed a stream of blackish-red blood, which a besmeared boy caught in a tin basin. All the time this was going on the ox kept incessantly twitching its head as if trying to get up, and waved its four legs in the air. The basin was quickly filling, but the ox still lived, and, its stomach heaving heavily, both hind and fore legs worked so violently that the butchers held aloof. When one basin was full, the boy carried it away on his head to the albumen factory, while another boy placed a fresh basin, which also soon began to fill up. But still the ox heaved its body and worked its hind legs.

When the blood ceased to flow the butcher raised the animal's head and began to skin it. The ox continued to writhe. The head, stripped of its skin, showed red with white veins, and kept the position given it by the butcher; on both sides hung the skin. Still the animal did not cease to writhe. Than another butcher caught hold of one of the legs, broke it, and cut it off. In the remaining legs and the stomach the convulsions still continued. The other legs were cut off and thrown aside, together with those of other oxen belonging to the same owner. Then the carcass was dragged to the hoist and hung up, and the convulsions were over.

Thus I looked on from the door at the second, third, fourth ox. It was the same with each: the same cutting off of the head with bitten tongue, and the same convulsed members. The only difference was that the butcher did not always strike at once so as to cause the animal's fall. Sometimes he missed his aim, whereupon the ox leaped up, bellowed, and, covered with blood, tried to escape. But then his head was pulled under a bar, struck a second time, and he fell.

I afterwards entered by the door at which the oxen were led in. Here I saw the same thing, only nearer, and therefore more plainly. But chiefly I saw here, what I had not seen before, how the oxen were forced to enter this door. Each time an ox was seized in the enclosure and pulled forward by a rope tied to its horns, the animal, smelling blood, refused to advance, and sometimes bellowed and drew back. It would have been beyond the strength of two men to drag it in by force, so one of the butchers went round each time, grasped the animal's tail and twisted it so violently that the gristle crackled, and the ox advanced.

When they had finished with the cattle of one owner, they brought in those of another. The first animal of his next lot was not an ox, but a bull—a fine, well-bred creature, black, with white spots on its legs, young, muscular, full of energy. He was dragged forward, but he lowered his head and resisted sturdily. Then the butcher who followed behind seized the tail, like an engine-driver grasping the handle of a whistle, twisted it, the gristle crackled, and the bull rushed forward, upsetting the men who held the rope. Then it stopped, looking sideways with its black eyes, the whites of which had filled with blood. But again the tail crackled, and the bull sprang forward and reached the required spot. The striker approached, took aim, and struck. But the blow missed the mark. The bull leaped up, shook his head, bellowed, and, covered with blood, broke free and rushed back. The men at the doorway all sprang aside: but the experienced butchers, with the dash of men inured to danger, quickly caught the rope; again the tail operation was repeated, and again the bull was in the chamber, where he was dragged under the bar, from which he did not again escape. The striker quickly took aim at the spot where the hair divides like a star, and, notwithstanding the blood, found it, struck, and the fine animal, full of life, collapsed, its head and legs writhing while it was bled and the head skinned.

"There, the cursed devil hasn't even fallen the right way!" grumbled the butcher as he cut the skin from the head.

Five minutes later the head was stuck up, red instead of black, without skin; the eyes, that had shone with such splendid color five minutes before, fixed and glassy.

Afterwards I went into the compartment where small animals are slaughtered—a very large chamber with asphalt floor, and tables with backs, on which sheep and calves are killed. Here the work was already finished; in the long room, impregnated with the smell of blood, were only two butchers. One was blowing into the leg of a dead lamb and patting the swollen stomach with his hand; the other, a young fellow in an apron besmeared with blood, was smoking a bent cigarette. There was no one else in the long, dark chamber, filled with a heavy smell. After me there entered a man, apparently an ex-soldier, bringing in a young yearling ram, black with a white mark on its neck, and its legs tied. This animal he placed upon one of the tables, as if upon a bed. The old soldier greeted the butchers, with whom he was evidently acquainted, and began to ask when their master allowed them leave. The fellow with the cigarette approached with a knife, sharpened it on the edge of the table, and answered that they were free on holidays. The live ram was lying as quietly as the dead inflated one, except that it was briskly wagging its short little tail and its sides were heaving more quickly than usual. The soldier pressed down its uplifted head gently, without effort; the butcher, still continuing the conversation, grasped with his left hand the head of the ram and cut its throat. The ram quivered, and the little tail stiffened and ceased to wave. The fellow, while waiting for the blood to flow, began to relight his cigarette, which had gone out. The blood flowed and the ram began to writhe. The conversation continued without the slightest interruption. It was horribly revolting.

———————

[A]nd how about those hens and chickens which daily, in thousands of kitchens, with heads cut off and streaming with blood, comically, dreadfully, flop about, jerking their wings?

And see, a kind, refined lady will devour the carcasses of these animals with full assurance that she is doing right, at the same time asserting two contradictory propositions:

First, that she is, as her doctor assures her, so delicate that she cannot be sustained by vegetable food alone, and that for her feeble organism flesh is indispensable; and, secondly, that she is so sensitive that she is unable, not only herself to inflict suffering on animals, but even to bear the sight of suffering.

Whereas the poor lady is weak precisely because she has been taught to live upon food unnatural to man; and she cannot avoid causing suffering to animals—for she eats them.

———————

[W]e cannot pretend that we do not know this. We are not ostriches, and cannot believe that if we refuse to look at what we do not wish to see, it will not exist. This is especially the case when what we do not wish to see is what we wish to eat. If it were really indispensable, or, if not indispensable, at least in some way useful! But it is quite unnecessary, and only serves to develop animal feelings, to excite desire, and to promote fornication and drunkenness. And this is continually being confirmed by the fact that young, kind, undepraved people—especially women and girls—without knowing how it logically follows, feel that virtue is incompatible with beef-steaks, and, as soon as they wish to be good, give up eating flesh.

What, then, do I wish to say? That in order to be moral people must cease to eat meat? Not at all.

I only wish to say that for a good life a certain order of good actions is indispensable; that if a man's aspirations toward right living be serious they will inevitably follow one definite sequence; and that in this sequence the first virtue a man will strive after will be self-control, self-restraint. And in seeking for self-control a man will inevitably follow one definite sequence, and in this sequence the first thing will be self-control in food—fasting. And in fasting, if he be really and seriously seeking to live a good life, the first thing from which he will abstain will always be the use of animal food, because, to say nothing of the excitation of the passions caused by such food, its use is simply immoral, as it involves the performance of an act which is contrary to the moral feeling—killing; and is called forth only by greediness and the desire for tasty food.

The Essence of True Justice

Anna Kingsford

Anna Kingsford (1846–1888) was one of the most remarkable women of the nineteenth century. An activist for animal and women's rights, a prolific author and speaker, and a medical doctor (University of Paris, 1880), Kingsford devoted most of her energy to championing a vegetarian lifestyle. Many of her books, particularly her bestselling The Perfect Way in Diet, *emphasize the health benefits of vegetarianism. But Kingsford was also interested in moral arguments for a vegetable diet.*

The selections here are excerpted from two "Addresses to Vegetarians" given by Kingsford to the British Vegetarian Society. Both stress that the essence of social justice is individual reformation and that the latter is closely connected with the ability on the part of humans to empathize with and show moral compassion for animals. The individual who acquiesces in the slaughter of animals for food ignores the moral dictum that the stronger have an obligation to protect the weaker.

I always speak with the greatest delight and satisfaction in the presence of my friends the members of the Vegetarian Society. With them I am quite at my ease, I have no reservation, I have no dissatisfaction. This is not the case when I speak for my friends the Anti-Vivisectionists, the Anti-Vaccinationists, the Spiritualists, or the advocates of freedom for women. I always feel that such of these as are not abstainers from flesh-food have unstable ground under their feet, and it is my great regret that, when helping them in their good works, I cannot openly and publicly maintain what I so ardently believe—that the Vegetarian movement is the bottom and basis of all other movements towards Purity, Freedom, Justice, and Happiness.

I think it was Benjamin D'Israeli who said that we had stopped short at Comfort, and had mistaken it for Civilisation, content to increase the former at the expense of the latter. Not a day passes without the perspicacity of this remark coming forcibly before me. Comfort, luxury, indulgence, and ease abound in this age, and in this part of the world; but, alas! Of Civilisation we have as yet acquired but the veriest rudiments. Civilisation means not mere physical ease, but moral and spiritual Freedom—Sweetness and Light—with which the customs of the age are in most respects at dire enmity. I named just now freedom for women. One of the greatest hindrances to the advancement and enfranchisement of the sex is due to the luxury of the age, which demands so much time, study, money, and thought to be devoted to what is called the "pleasures of the table." A large class of men seems to believe that women were created chiefly to be "housekeepers," a term which they apply almost exclusively to ordering dinners and superintending their preparation. Were this office connected only with the garden, the field, and the orchard, the occupation might be truly said to be refined, refining, and worthy of the best and most gentle lady in the land. But, connected as it is actually with slaughter-houses, butchers' shops, and dead carcases, it is an occupation at once unwomanly, inhuman, and barbarous in the extreme. Mr. Ruskin has said that the criterion of a beautiful action or of a noble thought is to be found in song, and that an action about which we cannot make a poem is not fit for humanity. Did he ever apply this test to flesh-eating? Many a lovely poem, many a beautiful picture, may be made about gardens and fruit-gathering, and the bringing home of the golden produce of harvest, or the burden of the vineyards, with groups of happy boys and girls, and placid, mild-eyed oxen bending their necks under their fragrant load. But I defy anyone to make beautiful verse or to paint beautiful pictures about slaughter-houses, running with streams of steaming blood, and terrified, struggling animals felled to the ground with pole-axes; or of a butcher's stall hung round with rows of gory corpses, and folks in the midst of them bargaining with the ogre who keeps the place for legs and shoulders and thighs and heads of the murdered creatures! What horrible surroundings are these for gentle and beautiful ladies! The word "wife" means, in the old Saxon tongue, a "weaver," and that of "husband" means, of course, a "husbandman." "Lady," too, is a word originally signifying "loaf-giver." In these old words have come down to us a glimpse of a fair picture of past times. The wife, or weaver, is the spinner, the maker, whose function it is to create forms of beauty and decorative art, to brighten, adorn, and make life lovely. Or if, as "lady" of the house, we look on her in the light of the provider and dispenser of good things, it is not loathsome flesh of beasts that she gives, but bread—sweet and pure, and innocent type of all human food. As for the man, he is the cultivator of the ground, a sower of grain, a tiller of the field. I would like to see these old times back, with all their sweet and tender Arcadian homeliness, in the place of the ugly lives which most folks lead in our modern towns, whose streets are hideous, above all at night with their crowded gin-palaces, blood-smeared butchers' stalls, reeling drunkards, and fighting women. People talk to me sometimes about peace conventions, and ask me to join societies for putting down war. I always say: "You are beginning at the wrong end, and putting the cart before the horse." If you want people to leave off fighting like beasts of prey, you must first get them to leave off living like beasts of prey. You cannot reform institutions without first reforming men. Teach men to live as human beings ought to live, to think wisely, purely, and beautifully, and to have noble ideas of the purpose and meaning of Humanity, and they will themselves reform their institutions. Any other mode of proceeding will result only in a patchwork on a worthless fabric, a whitening of a sepulchre full of dead men's bones and all uncleanness. Fleshmeats and intoxicating drinks—the pabulum of Luxury—are the baneful coil of hydra-headed Vice, whose ever-renewing heads we vainly strike, while leaving the body of the dragon still untouched. Strike there—at the heart—at the vitals of the destructive monster, and the work of Heracles, the Redeemer, is accomplished.

I have stood so often on this and on other platforms throughout England, as well as in Scotland and Switzerland, to speak to my

friends about the physiological, chemical, anatomical, and economical aspects of the non-flesh diet, that tonight, for a change, I am
going to take another and a higher line. We will, therefore, if you
please, take "as read" all the vindications of our mode of living fur-
nished by various scientific arguments: that we have the organisa-
tion of the fruit-eater; that the constituent elements of vegetable
food furnish all the necessary force and material of bodily vigour;
that it is cheaper to buy beans and meal than to buy pork and suet;
that land goes further and supports more people under a vegetable
cultivation than when laid out for pasture, and so forth. All these
arguments, more or less eloquently and clearly formulated, most of
you have by heart, and those who have not may buy them all for
sixpence of the Vegetarian Society. So I am going to talk to you
tonight about quite another branch of our subject, the loftiest and
fruitfulest branch of the whole tree. I am going to tell you that I see
in the doctrine we are here to preach the very culmination and
crown of the Gentle Life, that Life which, in some way, we all of us
in our best moments long to live, but which it is only given now and
again to some great and noble soul, almost divine, fully to realise
and glorify in the eyes of the world. I said just now that "in our best
moments" we all long to lead the Ideal Life. Some of us have many
"best moments," and long ones too: moments that dominate and top
our work-a-day efforts always, like a light of stars overhead,
through which the Heaven looks down on us. Some of us, again,
have very few "best moments," short and feeble, like lights over a
marsh, never steadfast, always flickering in and out, and paling
and flitting when we get abreast of them. With this class of persons
the Ideal is very faint and unstable, while with the former it is
strong and masterful. Societies like ours are made to encourage the
"best moments" of the weakly, and to glorify those of the strong.
Societies like ours are made to train soldiers and provide them with
leaders to fight for the Ideal. Beginners and feeble folk cannot
stand without encouragement in the teeth of a hot fire, nor rush
upon the enemy unless some hero heads them and shows the way.
The Ideal Life, the Gentle Life, has many enemies, and the
weapons used by these are various. They are pseudo-scientific,
pseudo-religious, pseudo-philanthropic, pseudo-aesthetic, and
pseudo-utilitarian. And the enemies are of all ranks, professions,
and interests. But of all the weapons used, the most deadly, the
most terrific, is—Ridicule. Yes, Ridicule slays its tens of thousands!

To be laughed at is far more awful to average mortals than to be preached at, groaned at, cursed at. It is the weapon which the journalists almost always handle with the greatest facility. These are the men who laugh for their living. They have replaced, in modern days, the paid domestic jesters of olden times. Every town keeps its paid jester now in the office of its local paper, just as, a few centuries back, great nobles kept their man in cap and motley to crack jokes on the guests at table. We have not changed in manners, but in manner only. And the very first thing that Reformers have to do is to get over minding the man in motley. Let him laugh. He cannot argue. Laughing is his stock-in-trade. If he laugh not too coarsely, and avoid blaspheming, he is, after all, very harmless. It is his privilege to laugh at all that is new and unwonted. All children do that, and the man in motley is but a clever child. Why let him knock you down with his fool's truncheon? Wince, and shrink, and expostulate: he sees his advantage then, and belabours you pitilessly. But heed him not, and go on doing your work with a great heart as though it were a royal thing to do, and he will soon be off to some other quarry. Only be sure in your own mind that you are *right;* only be set in dead earnest on keeping that royal thing in clear view and working up to it, and the Ideal will reward you by becoming the Real and Actual. It is not necessary to go very far afield to find this royal work. It does not lie—for most of us—in setting out to accomplish some vast task. Most of us will find it in just simply and calmly shaping out and lifting up our own lives so as to beautify and perfect and unify them, being just and merciful to all men and all creatures. We Vegetarians carry the Ideal a stage lower, and therefore a stage higher than do other folk. We find the duty to the lowliest the duty completest in blessing. Let me tell you a story. Once, in the far-away old days of romance, there was a Christian Knight of peerless repute, whose greatest longing and dearest hope it was to have the Vision of the Holy Grail. The Holy Grail is the name given in chivalry to the Chalice of the Altar containing the Sacred Blood of Christ, and this was said to be shown in a Vision by God to those whom He judged worthy of the sight of this supreme symbol of His Grace, in the moment when they pleased Him most. Well, the Knight of whom I speak, in pursuance of the Object of his desire, joined the Crusaders, and performed prodigies of valour and wonderful feats of arms in battle against the Infidels, but all in vain; he had no Vision and remained unblessed. Then he left Palestine and went and laid aside his sword in a monastery, and lived a life of long penance and meditation, desiring always a sight of the Holy Grail. But that, too, was in vain. At last, sorrowful and almost despairing, he returned homeward to his domain. As he drew near his castle, he saw gathered about its gates a crowd of beggars, sick, maimed, aged and infirm, old men, women, babes, and children— all who were left behind on the land while the hale and hearty went to fight the Saracens. Then he said to his squire: "What are these?" "They are beggars," the squire answered, "who can neither work nor fight. They clamour for bread; but why heed such a herd of useless, despicable wretches? Let me drive them away." "Nay," said the Knight, touched to the heart, "I have slain many abroad, let me save some at home. Call these poor folk together, give them bread and drink; let them be warmed and clothed." And lo! As the words passed his lips, a light from heaven fell upon him, and looking up, he saw, at last, the longed-for vision of the Holy Grail! Yes, that humble, simple, homely duty of charity was more precious in the Eyes Divine than all his deeds of prowess in the field of arms, or his long devotions in the cloister!

And so with us. Who so poor, so oppressed, so helpless, so mute and uncared for, as the dumb creatures who serve us—they who, but for us, must starve, and who have no friend on earth if man be their enemy? Even these are not too low for pity, nor too base for justice. And, without fear of irreverence or slight on the holy name that Christians love, we may truly say of them, as of the captive, the sick, and the hungry: "Inasmuch as ye do it unto the least of these, my brethren, ye do it unto me."

For, as St. Francis of Assisi has told us, all the creatures of God's hand are brethren. "My sisters the birds," he was wont to say, "My brothers the kine in the meadows." The essential of true justice is the sense of solidarity. All creatures, from highest to lowest, stand hand in hand before God. Nor shall we ever begin to spiritualise our lives and thoughts, to lighten and lift ourselves higher, until we recognise this solidarity, until we learn to look upon the creatures of God's hand, not as mere subjects for hunting and butchery, for dissecting and experimentation, but as *living souls* with whom, as well as with the sons of men, God's covenant is made.

Part IV

The Twentieth Century

Diet, Rights, and the Global Perspective

*Contemporary defenses of ethical vegetarianism are especially char-
acterized by their pluralistic approaches and by their broad range of
concerns. Twentieth-century critics of flesh consumption rest their
cases on a number of considerations. Some stress the ancient theme
of kinship between humans and animals; others focus on the eighteenth-century concern that carnivorism brutalizes humans; still
others are sympathetic to the nineteenth century's focus on the cruelties inflicted on food animals. But in addition to these more traditional apologies for ethical vegetarianism, twentieth-century
spokepersons also tend to focus on formal philosophical defenses of
the claim that animals possess ethical rights not to be treated cruelly or slaughtered as food sources. Moreover, there is a greater
appreciation of the widespread economic consequences of flesh consumption — consequences which, because they entail the needless
wastage of grain protein and hence contribute to the world problem
of hunger, have obvious moral overtones. Closely tied to global concerns about the availability of foodstuffs is the worry many ethical
vegetarians voice that the factory farming of flesh animals is detrimental to the planet's ecological integrity. Finally, there is a growing sensitivity to the possibility that carnivorism is a reflection of
patriarchal power structures that are inherently exploitative. Con-*

temporary discussions of ethical vegetarianism, then, are rich and complex.

In the selections that follow, J. Howard Moore and Albert Schweitzer tend to continue the defense of ethical vegetarianism based on the kinship between humans and animals. Romain Rolland, Henry Salt, Mohandas Gandhi, and Stephen Clark are concerned with the needless suffering imposed on animals by carnivorism, and Gandhi and Salt in particular worry about the brutalizing effects carnivorism has on human ethical sensitivity. The claim that animals possess rights, analogous to those enjoyed by humans, not to be eaten or gratuitously pained is defended here by Tom Regan, Peter Singer, and Thomas Auxter. Peter Wenz, Harriet Schleifer, Frances Moore Lappé, and Jon Wynne-Tyson approach the issue by arguing that vegetarianism encourages a scandalous misuse of both food staples and natural resources such as land and water. Moreover, Schleifer and Wynne-Tyson also condemn the twentieth-century agribusiness practice of factory farming. Finally, Carol Adams argues that the high premium western society puts on meat as a dietary necessity is intimately connected with patterns of racial and sexual oppression.

The Humanities of Diet

Henry S. Salt

Although little remembered today, Henry Salt (1851–1939) was probably the most astute and certainly the most tireless British spokesperson for ethical vegetarianism and animal rights in the late nineteenth and early twentieth centuries. A friend of other reformers such as Bernard Shaw and Gandhi, Salt was also an active participant in the movement to reform prisons and abolish the death penalty.

Salt wrote many books about animal rights and vegetarianism, the major ones including Animal Rights, The Logic of Vegetarianism, *and* The Humanities of Diet. *The selection here is taken from this last work. In it, Salt carefully spells out the vegetarian position and answers conventional objections to it. Although he writes briefly in response to those critics who argue that a meatless diet is unhealthy, Salt is primarily concerned with pointing out that vegetarianism is first and foremost an ethical, not a hygienic, position. Salt sees it as an aspect of a larger "humanitarian" movement that aims to eliminate all forms of brutality. His plea to humanize diet, then, is reflective of a larger concern to eliminate power structures at all levels that promote cruelty and needless suffering.*

S ome years ago, in an article entitled "Wanted, a New Meat," the *Spectator* complained that dietetic provision is made nowadays "not for man as humanised by schools of cookery, but for a race of fruit-eating apes." We introduce bananas, pines, Italian figs, pomegranates, and a variety of new fruits, but what is really wanted is "some new and large animal, something which shall combine the game flavour with the substantial solidity of a leg of mutton."[1] Surmising that there must exist "some neglected quadruped, which will furnish what we see," the *Spectator* proceeded to take anxious stock of the world's resources, subjecting in turn the rodents, the pachyderms, and the ruminants to a careful survey, in which the claims even of the wart-hog were conscientiously debated. In the end the ruminants won the day, and the choice fell upon the Eland, which was called to the high function of supplying a new flesh-food for "humanised" man.

This is not the sense in which I am about to speak of the "humanities" of diet. I have not been fired by the *Spectator's* enthusiasm for the rescue of some "neglected quadruped," nor have I any wish to see eviscerated Elands hanging a-row in our butchers' shops. On the contrary, I suggest that in proportion as man is truly "humanised," not by schools of cookery but by schools of thought, he will abandon the barbarous habit of his flesh-eating ancestors, and will make gradual progress towards a purer, simpler, more humane, and therefore more civilised diet-system.

There are many signs that the public is awaking to the fact that there is such a thing as food-reform. The reception of a new idea of this sort is always a strange process, and has to pass through several successive phases. First, there is tacit contempt; secondly, open ridicule; then a more or less respectful opposition; and lastly, a partial acceptance. During the third period, the one at which the Vegetarian question has now arrived, discussion is often complicated by the way in which the opponents of the new idea fail to grasp the *real* object of the reformers, and pleasantly substitute some exaggerated, distorted, or wholly imaginary concept of their own; after which they proceed to argue from a wrong basis, crediting their antagonists with mistaken aims and purposes, and then triumphantly impugning their consistency or logic. It is therefore of importance that, in debating the problem of food-reform, we should know exactly what the reformers themselves are aiming at.

Let me first make plain what I mean by calling Vegetarianism a *new* idea. Historically, of course, it is not new at all, either as a precept or a practice. A great portion of the world's inhabitants have always been practically Vegetarians, and some whole races and sects have been so upon principle. The Buddhist canon in the east, and the Pythagorean in the west, enjoined abstinence from flesh-flood on humane, as on other grounds; and in the writings of such "pagan" philosophers as Plutarch and Porphyry we find a humanitarian ethic of the most exalted kind, which, after undergoing a long repression during medieval churchdom, reappeared, albeit but weakly and fitfully at first, in the literature of the Renaissance, to be traced more definitely in the eighteenth century school of "sensibility." But it was not until after the age of Rousseau, from which must be dated the great humanitarian movement of the past century, that Vegetarianism began to assert itself as a system, a reasoned plea for the disuse of flesh-food. In this sense it is a new ethical principle, and its import as such is only now beginning to be generally understood.

I say *ethical* principle, because it is beyond doubt that the chief motive of Vegetarianism is the humane one. Questions of hygiene and of economy both play their part, and an important part, in a full discussion of food reform; but the feeling which underlies and animates the whole movement is the instinctive horror of butchery, especially the butchery of the more highly organized animals, so human, so near akin to man. Let me quote a short passage from the preface to Mr. Howard William's *Ethics of Diet,* an acknowledged textbook of Vegetarianism. "It has been well said," remarks Mr. Williams, "that there are steps on the way to the summit of dietetic reform, and if only one step be taken, yet that single step will not be without importance and without influence in the world. The step which leaves for ever behind it the barbarism of slaughtering our fellow beings, the mammals and birds, is, it is superfluous to add, the most important and influential of all."

Let us therefore be clearly understood that this step—the "first step," as Tolstoy has called it, in a scheme of humane living— has been the main object of all Vegetarian propaganda since the establishment of the Vegetarian Society in 1847. To secure the discontinuance of the shocking and inhuman practices that are inseparable from the slaughter-house—this, and no abstract theory of abstinence from all "animal" substances, no fastidious abhorrence of contact with the "evil thing," has been the purpose of modern food-reformers. They are, moreover, well aware that a change of this sort, which involves a reconsideration of our whole attitude towards the "lower animals," can only be gradually realised; nor do they invite the world, as their opponents seem to imagine, to an immediate hard-and-fast decision, a revolution in national habits which is to be discussed, voted, and carried into effect the day after tomorrow, to the grievous jeopardy and dislocation of certain time-honoured interests. They simply point to the need of progression towards humaner diet, believing, with Thoreau, that "it is part of the destiny of the human race, in its gradual improvement, to leave off eating animals, as surely as the savage tribes have left off eating each other, when they came in contact with the more civilised."

There are, however, many critics of Vegetarianism who have not grasped this ethical principle, and whose contentions are, therefore, quite irrelevant. It has been said, for example, that "the most enthusiastic Vegetarians scarcely venture to deny that the destruction of many animals is requisite for human existence. What Vegetarian would allow his premises to be swarming with mice, rats, and similar pests? Does he permit caterpillars, snails, and slugs to devour the produce of his vegetable garden? Perhaps he satisfies his conscience with the reflection that the destruction of vermin is a necessary act."

Perhaps the Vegetarian draws a distinction between the avowedly necessary destruction of garden and household pests, and the quite unnecessary (from the Vegetarian standpoint) butchery of oxen and sheep, who are bred for no other purpose than that of the slaughter-house, where they are killed in a most barbarous manner! *Perhaps* the Vegetarian "satisfies his conscience" with this distinction! I should rather think he did.

No wonder that food-reformers seem a strange and unreasonable folk to those who have thus failed to apprehend the very *raison d'être* of food-reform, and who persist in arguing as if the choice between the old diet and the new were a mere matter of personal caprice or professional adjustment, into which the moral question scarcely enters at all.

To this same misunderstanding is due the futile outcry that is raised every now and then against the term "Vegetarian," when some zealous opponent undertakes to "expose the delusions of those who boast that they live on vegetables, and yet take eggs, butter, and milk as regular articles of diet." Of course the simple fact is that Vegetarians are neither boastful of their diet, nor enamoured of their name; it was invented, wisely or unwisely, a full half-century ago, and, whether we like it or not, has evidently "come to stay" until we find something better. It is worth observing that the objection is seldom or never made in actual everyday life, where the word "Vegetarian" carries with it a quite definite meaning, viz., one who abstains from flesh-food but not necessarily from animal products; the verbal pother is always made by somebody who is sitting down to write an article against food-reform, and has nothing better to say. It all comes from the notion that Vegetarians are bent on some barren, logical "consistency," rather than on practical progress towards a more humane method of living—the only sort of "consistency" which in this, or any other branch of reform, is either possible in itself, or worth a moment's attention from a sensible man.

To show, however, that this question of the temporary use of animal products has not been shirked by food-reformers, I quote the following from my "Plea for Vegetarianism," published nearly thirty years ago.

> The immediate object which food-reformers aim at is not so much the disuse of animal substances in general, as the abolition of flesh-meat in particular; and if they can drive their opponents to make the important admission that actual flesh-food is unnecessary, they can afford to smile at the trivial retort that animal substance is still used in eggs and milk. . . . They are well aware that even dairy produce is quite unnecessary, and will doubtless be dispensed with altogether under a more natural system of diet. In the meantime, however, one step is sufficient. Let us first recognize the fact that the slaughter-house, with all its attendant horrors, might easily be abolished; that point gained, the question of the total disuse of all animal products is one that will be decided hereafter. What I wish to insist on is that it is not 'animal' food which we primarily abjure, but nasty food, expensive food, and unwholesome food.

If medical men, instead of quibbling about the word "Vegetarian," would recommend to their clients the use of animal products, as a substitute for "butchers' meat," there would be a great gain to the humanities of diet. Incidentally, it must be remarked, the doctors quite admit the efficiency of such substitutes; for in their eagerness to convict Vegetarians of inconsistency in using animal products, they guilelessly give away their own case by arguing that, of course, on *this* diet the Vegetarians do well enough! As for those ultra-consistent persons who sometimes write as if it were not worth while to discontinue the practice of cow-killing, unless we also immediately discontinue the practice of using milk—that is to say, who think the greater reform is worthless without the lesser and subsequent one—I can only express my respectful astonishment at such reasoning. It is as though a traveler were too "consistent" to start on a journey because he might be required to "change carriages" on the way.

But it is said, why not introduce "humane" methods of slaughtering, and so remedy the chief evil in the present system of diet? Well, in the first place, "humane slaughtering," if it be once admitted that there is no necessity to slaughter at all, is a contradiction in terms. But letting that pass, and recognising, as Vegetarians gladly do, that there would be a great reduction of suffering, if all flesh-eaters would combine for the abolition of *private* slaughter-houses and the substitution of well-ordered municipal abattoirs, we are still faced by the difficulty that these changes will take a long time to carry out, opposed as they are by powerful private interests, and that, even under the best possible conditions, the butchering of the larger animals must always be a horrible and inhuman business. Vegetarianism, as a movement, has nothing whatever to fear from the introduction of improved slaughtering; indeed, Vegetarians may take the credit for of having worked quite as zealously as flesh-eaters in that direction, feeling, as they do, that in our complex society no individuals can exempt themselves from a share in the general responsibility—the brand of the slaughterer is on the brow of every one of us. But there is no half-way resting-place in humane progress; and we may be quite sure that when the public conscience is once aroused on this dreadful subject of the slaughter-house, it will maintain its interest to a much more thorough solution of the difficulty than a mere improvement of methods.

One thing is quite certain. It is impossible for flesh-eaters to find any justification of their diet in the plea that animals *might* be slaughtered humanely; it is an obvious duty to carry out the improvements first, and to make the excuses afterwards. Those who admit that the Vegetarian, in his indictment of the slaughterhouse, hits a grievous blot in our civilisation, often try to escape from the inevitable conclusion on the ground that such allegations tell not against the use of animal food, but against the ignorance, carelessness, and brutality too often displayed in the slaughter-houses. This, however, is a libel on the working men who have to earn a livelihood by the disgusting occupation of butchering. The ignorance, carelessness, and brutality are not only in the rough-handed slaughtermen, but in the polite ladies and gentlemen whose dietetic habits render the slaughtermen necessary. The real responsibility rests not on the wage slave, but on the employer. "I'm only doing your dirty work," was the reply of a Whitechapel butcher to a gentleman who expressed the same sentiments as those I have quoted. "It's such as *you* makes such as *us*."

At this point it would presumably be the right thing to give some detailed description of the horrors enacted in our shambles, of which I might quote numerous instances from perfectly trust-worthy witnesses. If I do not do so, I can assure my readers that it is not from any desire to spare their feelings, for I think it might fairly be demanded of those who eat beef and mutton that they should not shrink from an acquaintance with facts of their own making; also we have often been told that it is the Vegetarians, not the flesh-eaters, who are the "sentimentalists" in this matter. I refrain for the simple reason that I fear, if I narrated the facts, this chapter would go unread. So, before passing on, I will merely add this, that in some ways the evils attendant on slaughtering grow worse, and not better, as civilisation advances, because of the more complex conditions of town life, and the increasingly long journeys to which animals are subjected in their transit from the grazier to the slaughter-man. The cattle-ships of the present day reproduce, in an aggravated form, some of the worst horrors of the slave-ship of fifty years back. I take it for granted, then, as not denied by our opponents, that the present system of killing animals for food is a very cruel and barbarous one, and a direct outrage on what I have termed the "humanities of diet."

It is also an outrage on every sense of refinement and good taste, for in this question the aesthetics are not to be dissociated from the humanities. Has the artist ever considered the history of the "chop" which is brought so elegantly to his studio? Not he. He would not be able to eat it if he thought about it. He has first employed a slaughterman ("It's such as you makes such as us") to convert a beautiful living creature into a hideous carcase, to be displayed with other carcases in that ugliest product of civilisation, a butcher's shop, and then he has employed a cook to conceal, as far as may be, the work of the slaughterman. This is what the *Spectator* calls being "humanised" by schools of cookery; I should call it being de-humanised. In passing a butcher's I have seen a concert-programme pinned prominently on the corpse of a pig, and I have mused on that suggestive though unintended allegory of the Basis of Art. I deny that it is the right basis, and I maintain that there will necessarily be something porcine in the art that is so upheld and exhibited. Nine-tenths of our literary and artistic gatherings, our social functions, and most sumptuous entertainments, are tainted from the same source. You take a beautiful girl down to supper, and you offer her—a ham sandwich! It is proverbial folly to cast pearls before swine. What are we to say of the politeness which casts swine before pearls?

It is no part of my purpose to argue in detail the *possibility* of a Vegetarian diet; nor is there any need to do so. The proofs of it are everywhere—in the history of races, in the rules of monastic orders, in the habits of large numbers of working populations, in biographies of well-known men, in the facts and instances of every-day life. The medical view of Vegetarianism, which at first (as in the similar case of teetotalism) was expressed by a severe negative and ominous head-shake, has very largely changed during the past ten or twenty years, and, in so far as it is still hostile, dwells rather on the superiority of the "mixed" diet than on the insufficiency of the other, while the solemn warnings which used to be addressed to the venturesome individual who had the hardihood to leave off eating his fellow-beings, have now lapsed into more general statements as to the probable failure of Vegetarianism in the long run, and on a more extended trial. Well, we know what that means. It is what has been said of every vital movement that the world has seen. It means that ordinary people, and dull people, and learned people, and specialists, need time to envisage new truths; but they *do* envisage them, some day. Already the medical preference for a flesh diet may be summed up under two heads—that flesh is more digestible, more easily assimilated, than vegetables, and that it is unwise to limit the sources of food which (to quote Sir Henry Thompson) "Nature has abundantly provided."

The first argument, as to the superior digestibility of flesh, is flatly denied by food-reformers on the plain grounds of experience, the notion that Vegetarians are in the habit of eating a greater bulk of food, in order to obtain an equal amount of nutriment, being one of those amazing superstitions which could not survive a day's comparative study of the parties in question. My own conviction is that the average flesh-eater eats at least twice as much bulk as the average Vegetarian; and I know that the experience of Vegetarians bears witness to a great reduction, instead of a great increase, in the amount of their diet. As for the second medical argument, the unwisdom of rejecting any of nature's bounties, it ignores the very existence of the ethical question, which is the Vegetarian's chief contention; nor does this appeal to "Nature" strike one as being very "scientific," inasmuch as (ethics apart) it might just as well justify cannibalism as flesh-eating. We can imagine how the medicine-men of some old anthropophagous tribe might deprecate the new-fangled civilised notion of abstinence from human flesh, on the ground that it is foolish to refuse the benefits which "Nature" has abundantly provided.

But what of the failures of those who have attempted the Vegetarian diet? Is not the movement hopelessly blocked by Mr. So-and-So 'six weeks' experiment? He became so very weak, you know, until his friends were quite alarmed about him, and he was really *obliged* to take something more nourishing. All of which symptoms, I would remark, could be matched by thousands of similar instances from the records of the temperance movement, and prove clearly enough, not that abstinence from flesh food or alcohol is impossible, but that (as any thoughtful person might have foreseen) a great change in the habits of a people cannot be effected suddenly, or without its inevitable percentage of failures. Every propagandist movement, religious, social, or dietetic, is sure to attract to itself a motley crowd of adherents, many of whom, after a trial of the new principles—some after a genuine trial, others after a very superficial one—revert to their former position. Let it be freely granted that a habit so ingrained as that of flesh-eating is likely, and, indeed certain, in some particular cases to be very hard to eradicate. What then? Is not that exactly what might have been expected in a change of this kind? And, on the other side, it is equally certain that a large number of the reported failures—nine-tenths of them, I should say—are caused by the half-hearted or ill-advised manner in which the attempt is made. It is just as possible to commit suicide on a Vegetarian diet as on any other, if you are bent on that conclusion; and really one might almost imagine, from the extraordinary folly sometimes shown in the selection of a diet, that certain experimentalists were "riding for a fall" in their dealings with Vegetarianism—taking up the thing in order to be able to say, "I tried it, and see the result!" I knew a man, a master at a great public school, who "tried Vegetarianism," and he tried it by making cabbage and potato the substitute for flesh, and after a month's trial he felt "very flabby," and then he gave it up.

An important factor in the success of a change of diet is the spirit in which such change is undertaken. As far as the mere chemistry of food is concerned, the majority of people may doubtless, with ordinary wisdom in the conduct of the change, substitute a Vegetarian for a "mixed" diet without inconvenience. But in some cases, owing perhaps to the temperament of the individual, or the nature of his surroundings, the change is much more difficult; and here it will make all the difference whether he have really at heart a sincere wish to take the first step towards a humaner diet, or whether he be simply experimenting out of curiosity or some other trivial motive. It is one more proof that the *moral* basis of Vegetarianism is the one that sustains the rest.

But are there not other reasons alleged against the practice of Vegetarianism? Ah, those dear old Fallacies, so immemorial yet ever new, how can I speak disrespectfully of what has so often refreshed and entertained me! Every food-reformer is familiar with them—the "law of nature" arguments, which would approximate human ethics to the standard of the tiger-cat or rattle-snake; the "necessity-of-taking-life" argument, which conscientiously ignores the practice of *un*necessary killing; the blubber argument, or, to put it more exactly, the "what-would-become-of-the-Esquimaux?" to which the only adequate answer is, a system of State-aided emigration; the "for-my-sake" argument, which may be called the family fallacy; the "what-should-we-do-without-leather?," that lurid picture of a shoeless world instantaneously converted to Vegetarianism; and the disinterested "what-would-become-of-the-animals?" which foresees the grievous wanderings of homeless herds who can find no kind protector to eat them. Best of all, I think, is what may be termed the logic of the larder, beloved of learned men, which urges that the animals would prefer to live and be eaten than not to live at all—an imaginary ante-natal choice in an imaginary antenatal condition!

I have now shown what I mean by those "humanities of diet," without which, as it seems to me, it is idle to dispute over the question of the "rights" of animals. A lively argument was lately raging between zoophilists and Jesuits, as to whether animals are "persons;" I would put it to both parties, is not the battle an unreal one, so long as the "persons" in question are by common agreement handed over to the tender mercies of the butcher, who will make exceeding short work of their "personality"?

I advance no exaggerated or fanciful claim for Vegetarianism. It is not, as some have asserted, a "panacea" for human ills; it is something much more rational—an essential part of the modern humanitarian movement, which can make no true progress without it. Vegetarianism is the diet of the future, as flesh-food is the diet of the past. In that striking and common contrast, a fruit shop side by side with a butcher's, we have a most significant object lesson. There, on the one hand, are the barbarities of a savage custom—the headless carcases, stiffened into a ghastly semblance of life, the joints and steaks and gobbets with their sickening odour, the harsh grating of the bone-saw, and the dull thud of the chopper—a perpetual crying protest against the horrors of flesh-eating. And, as if this were not witness sufficient, here, close alongside, is a wealth of golden fruit, a sight to make a poet happy, the only food that is entirely congenial to the physical structure and the natural instincts of mankind, that can entirely satisfy the highest human aspirations. Can we doubt, as we gaze at this contrast, that whatever intermediate steps may need to be gradually taken, whatever difficulties to be overcome, the path of progression from the barbarities to the humanities of diet lies clear and unmistakable before us?

Note

1. Cf. Richard Jefferies's complaint of "the ceaseless round of mutton and beef to which the dead level of civilisation reduces us." Yet Vegetarians are supposed to lack "variety"!

Universal Kinship

J. Howard Moore

An American zoologist, teacher, and author of several books advocating the humane treatment of animals as well as vegetarianism, J. Howard Moore (1862–1916) is a sadly neglected but fascinating turn-of-the-century champion of ethical vegetarianism. His approach is global, reminiscent of that of Schweitzer's, and in many respects anticipates Peter Singer's analysis of "speciesism." In the selections which follow, taken from Moore's The New Ethics *(1907) and* Universal Kinship *(1906), he argues that it is only arrogant "provincialism" that prevents humans from recognizing their kinship with animals, and he likens such an attitude to racism and national chauvinism. Animals, he argues, are sentient, and consequently have the same right as humans to be treated in such a way as to minimize their suffering and maximize their well-being. As Moore puts it, animals, like humans, should be regarded as ends, not means to dietary or sartorial indulgence, precisely because of their capacity for suffering. The "Great Law" of ethics, "act towards others as you would act toward a part of yourself," is consequently applicable to them. This is the fundamental principle of the ethics of universal kinship.*

The inhabitants of the earth are bound to each other by the ties and obligations of a common kinship. Man is simply *one* of a *series* of sentients, differing in degree, but not in kind, from the beings below, above, and around him. *The Great Law*—ACT TOWARD OTHERS AS YOU WOULD ACT TOWARD A PART OF YOUR OWN SELF—is a law not applicable to Aryans only, but to *all* men; and not to men only, but to *all beings*. There is the same obligation to act toward a German, a Japanese, or a Filipino, as one acts toward a part of his own organism, as there is to act in this way toward Americans or Englishmen; and, furthermore, there is the same reason for acting in this manner toward horses, cats, dogs, birds, fishes, and insects, as there is in acting so toward men. Restricting the application of this all-inclusive injunction to the human species, is a practice dictated solely by human selfishness and provincialism. The restriction is made, not because we are logical, but because we are diminutive.

How would it be for ants or elephants, or some other distinct group of the inhabitants of a world, to cut themselves off ethically from the rest, observing in their conduct toward each other THE GREAT LAW of social propriety, but ignoring this law in their conduct toward others, and acting toward all others, although these others were like them in every essential respect, as if they were without any of the ordinary rights and sensibilities of a common consciousness? Is it probable that men would have any difficulty in seeing clearly the untenableness of such an attitude? And yet it would be just as logical for any other group of animals to do this as it is for men to do it. The philosophies of this world have all been framed by, and from the standpoint of, a single species, and they are still managed and maintained in the interests of this species. What insects! The breadth of human sympathy and understanding is the catholicity of katydids who never see beyond the hedgerows that bound the little meadow in which they sing their lives away.

Moral practice and understanding are everywhere tribal and antagonistic. They have been *inherited, not reasoned out*. They have been handed along to us, not generated by us. They have come about as a result of the militant condition of things in the midst of which and in conformity with which life has been developed on the earth.

The ideal conception of social obligation is bigger than family and friends, bigger than the city and state in which one happens to

be born and raised, bigger than species, bigger even than the particular world of which one is a tenant. *There are no aliens anywhere,*
not even in hell, to the being who is as big morally as he ought to
be—only brothers. The universal heart goes out in tenderness
beyond all boundaries of form and color and architecture and accident of birth—into every place where quivers a living soul. *The*
Great Law is for the healing and consolation of all. Moral obligation
is as extensive as the power to feel. . . .

Man has defined himself as the "paragon of creation."

This is an overestimate. Man is no more a model animal than
the universe is a model universe. They are both of them very
immodel, as every one must know who has powers of understanding exceeding those of the infant.

Man is a bigot, and in his conception of himself and in his estimate of the relative importance of himself and others, he is true to
the weaknesses of his kind. But, omitting altogether the question of
whether man is the masterpiece of the universe or not, we may
affirm with perfect confidence, and without fear of contradiction,
that if man *is* the paragon of the universe, the universe has no
cause for dry eyes.

Man's treatment of his fellow-men, and especially his conduct
toward the forms of life differing anatomically from him, are such
as to stamp him as being anything but an ideal animal—anywhere
outside the psychologies of brigands, at any rate.

Human beings have been sufficiently enterprising and sufficiently devoted to each other to evolve into the master of the earth;
but instead of recognizing their responsibilities and converting
themselves into preceptors for the vanquished races, as an ideal
race would have done, they have become the butchers of the universe. Instead of becoming the models and schoolmasters of the
world in which they have outstripped, and striving to improve the
faulty natures, and guide the wayward feet of those by means of
whom they have been hoisted into distinction, they have become
colossal pedants, proclaiming themselves the pets and specials of
creation, and teaching each other that other races are mere things
to furnish pasture and pastime for them. They preach that it is the
ideal relation of associated beings for each to act toward the others
in the way in which he himself would like to have others act toward
him. This ideal of social rectitude was discovered two or three thousand years ago, and has been taught by the sages of the species ever

since. But in the application of this rule human beings restrict it hypocritically to the members of their own species. No nonhuman is innocent enough, or is sufficiently sensitive, intelligent, or beautiful, to be exempt from the most frightful wrongs, if by these wrongs human comfort, curiosity, or pastime are in any way whatever catered to. Our own happiness, and that of our species, are assumed to be so pre-eminent that we sacrifice without hesitancy the most sacred interests of others, in order that our own may be carefully provided for. Even for a tooth or a feather to wear on human vanity, forests are silenced and communities littered with the dead and dying. Beautiful beings that fill the groves with song and juvenility are compelled to sprawl lifeless and dishevelled on the heads of unconscionable sillies. . . .

Look at the scenes to be met with in our great cities! They are sufficient to horrify any being susceptible enough to the sufferings of others to be rated as one-fifth civilized. An army of butchers standing in blood ankle-deep and plunging great knives into writhing, shrieking living beings; helpless swine swinging by their hinders with their blood gushing from their slashed jugulars; unsuspecting oxen with trustful eyes looking up at the deadly pole-ax, and a moment later lying aquiver under its relentless thud; an atmosphere in perpetual churn with the groans and screams of the dying; streets thronged with unprocessioned funerals; dead bodies dangling from sale hooks or sprawling on chopping blocks; men and women going about praying and preaching, and sitting down two or three times a day and pouncing on the uncoffined remains of some poor creature cut down for them by the callous hands of hired cutthroats—such are the sights in all our streets and stockyards, and such are the crimes inflicted day after day by Christian cannibals on the defenseless dumb ones of this world.

Oh this killing, killing, killing—this awful, never-stopping, never-ending, worldwide butchery! What a world! "Ideal"?—and "perfect"?—and "all-wise"? Certainly—to tigers, and highwaymen, and people who are sound asleep; but to everybody else it is simply *monstrous*.

We are nothing but a lot of ferocious humbugs—that is the long and the short of it—leading lives all the way from a tenth to two-thirds decent in our conduct towards our fellow men, but almost absolutely savage in our treatment of not-men. A being who can look without weeping on the heart-rending facts that fill the cities of our so-called civilization has a psychology granitic enough to gaze unmoved on a hellful of roasting souls.

The Chicago stockyards alone grind up annually 4,500,000 sheep, 5,500,000 cattle, 450,000 calves, and 10,000,000 hogs— 20,500,000 *living beings a year,* or an average of *over 100 a minute* during every ten-hour working day!

What a mill! Just think of it! You who find it hard to realize vividly, and who stand blank and unconcerned in the presence of horrors that ought to make your very viscera crawl, and the very stones at your feet rise up, just remember, as you go about your daily duties, wherever you are and whatever you may be doing, that *every time the clock strikes,* 6,500 *innocent, intelligent, and highly sensitive beings have had their heads smashed with an axe, and their throats lunged through, and have struggled, and shuddered, and seen the world vanish from their eyes, here in these godless charnels.* And remember, too, that this appalling carnage goes on, and on, and on, day after day, month after month, year after year.

"What for"? Why, bless your life! In order that men and women may pray for mercy, and preach the Golden Rule, and deplore injustice, *with their bellies full of blood!*

I would like to retain respect for the religion of my boyhood, but when I see that religion look with indifference, and even levity, upon a hemorrhage wide as the continents, and horrible even to "heathens"—not only wink at it, but apologize for it, and even belittle those few emancipated souls who are trying to stop it—I can but feel that such a faith has no just claims on the allegiance of thinking men. "Does it not shame you," cried "pagan" Plutarch away in the dawning, "to mingle blood and murder with Nature's beneficent fruits? Other carnivora you call savage and ferocious—lions, tigers, and serpents—yet you yourselves come behind them in no species of barbarity." Men and women who hold shares in the responsibility for the common crimes of our civilization would do better to stop giving money for missionaries and begin on themselves; for they commit every day of their lives greater crimes and more of them than the so-called heathens they are trying to "convert" ever dream of. The gods pity this world if we have got to go on for ever as we have in the past—a globeful of lip-virtuous felons!

It has been claimed that man cannot be a consistent humanitarian, because it is necessary for him to exploit others in various ways in order to provide for his own needs and desires.

This is the most common objection. . . . It is the most common because it is the most selfish. So prominent is egoism in human psychology, and in the philosophies that have sprung from that psychology, that the most natural and convincing objections to any proposition are those prompted by and appealing to the selfish instincts. The question that arises in the mind of the ordinary man when a change in the arrangements of the world is suggested to him is not what will be the effect of the change on the universe, but what will be its effect on *him*—on that remarkable atom of the universe so zealously partitioned off from the rest of his own skin. Man has been so long accustomed to the undisputed privilege of spoliation, and has so long and so brilliantly imagined himself to be all there is in the world, that a proposition denying this privilege, however fair the proposition may be from an impartial point of view, is promptly classified as the allegation of a zany, and is supposed to be conclusively disposed of when it is shown to be capable of interfering with human convenience or pleasure.

[T]he complete denial by human animals of ethical relations to the rest of the animal world is a phenomenon not differing either in character of cause from the denial of ethical relations by a tribe, people, or race of human beings to the rest of the human world. The provincialism of Jews toward non-Jews, of Greeks toward non-Greeks, of Romans toward non-Romans, of Moslems toward non-Moslems, and of Caucasians toward non-Caucasians, is not one thing, and the provincialism of human beings toward non-human beings another. They are all manifestations of the same thing. The fact that these various actions are performed by different individuals and upon different individuals, and are performed at different times and places, does not invalidate the essential sameness of their natures. Crimes are not classified (except by savages or their immediate derivatives) according to the similarity of those who do them or those who suffer from them, but by grouping them according to the similarity of their intrinsic qualities. All acts of provincialism consist essentially in the disinclination or inability to be universal, and they belong in reality, all of them, to the same species of conduct. There is, in fact, but one great crime in the universe, and most of the instances of terrestrial wrong-doing are instances of this crime. It is the crime of exploitation—the considering by some beings of themselves as *ends*, and of others as their *means*—the refusal to recognize the equal, or the approximately equal, rights of all to life and its legitimate rewards—the crime of acting toward others as one would that others would *not* act toward him. For millions of years, almost ever since life began, this crime has been committed, in every nook and quarter of the inhabited globe.

Every being is an end. In other words, every being is to be taken into account in determining the ends of conduct. This is the only consistent outcome of the ethical process which is in course of evolution on the earth. This world was not made and presented to any particular clique for its exclusive use or enjoyment. The earth belongs, if it belongs to anybody, to the beings who inhabit it—to all of them. And when one being or set of beings sets itself up as the sole end for which the universe exists, and looks upon and acts toward others as mere means to this end, it is usurpation, nothing else and never can be anything else, it matters not by whom or upon whom the usurpation is practiced. A tyrant who puts his own welfare and aggrandizement in the place of the welfare of a people, and compels the whole people to act as a means to his own personal ends, is not more certainly a usurper than is a species or variety which puts its welfare in the place of the welfare of all the inhabitants of a world. The refusal to put one self in the place of others and to act toward them as one would that they would act toward him does not depend for its wrongfulness upon who makes the refusal or upon whether the refusal falls upon this or that individual or set. Deeds are right and wrong in themselves; and whether they are right or wrong, good or evil, proper or improper, whether they should be done or should not be done, *depends upon their effects upon the welfare of the inhabitants of the universe.* The basic mistake that has ever been made in this egoistic world in the judging and classifying of acts has been the mistake of judging and classifying them with reference to their effects upon some particular fraction of the inhabitants of the universe. In pure egoism conduct is judged as good or bad solely with reference to the results, immediate or remote, which that conduct produces, or is calculated to produce, on the self. To the savage, that is right or wrong which affects favorably or unfavorably himself or his tribe. And this sectional spirit of the savage has, as has been shown, characterized the moral conceptions of the peoples of all times. The practice human beings have today—the practice of those (relatively) broad and emancipated minds who are large enough to rise above the petty prejudices and "patriotisms" of the races and corporations of men, and are able to view "the world as their country" (the world of human beings, of course)—the practice such minds have of estimating conduct solely with reference to its effects upon the human species of animals is a practice which, while infinitely broader and more nearly ultimate than that of the savage, belongs logically in the same category with it. The partially emancipated human being who extends his moral sentiments to all the members of his own species, but denies to all other species the justice and humanity he accords to his own, is making on a larger scale the same ethical mess of it as the savage. The only consistent attitude, since Darwin established the unity of life (and the attitude we shall assume, if we ever become really civilized), is the attitude of universal gentleness and humanity.

The Unpardonable Crime

Romain Rolland

Winner of the 1915 Nobel Prize for Literature, French-born Romain Rolland (1866–1944) was a noted art historian as well as a novelist. Additionally, he was one of the early twentieth century's most eloquent champions of pacifism and worked with both Tolstoy and Gandhi in pursuit of world peace. His major novel, Jean-Christophe *(1904–1912), is a ten-volume exploration of the life and career of a composer and musician who, in his search for absolute beauty, discovers depths of compassion and sensitivity within himself that reflect Rolland's own humane world view. In the selection from this novel excerpted here, the hero Jean-Christophe, overwhelmed by what he sees as the unthinking cruelty of existence, has retreated to a small mountain village where he lives as a recluse. He reflects on the "field of battle in which man triumphed in the bloody slaughter of all other creatures" and is horrified by its extent. Even more repugnant to him is the realization that most people are indifferent to the suffering and death imposed by humans on food animals. This indifference to such cruelty, Rolland concludes, is the "unpardonable crime" whose enormity justifies "all that man may suffer." There are few more hauntingly beautiful meditations to be found in the literature of ethical vegetarianism.*

Only one living creature seemed to take any notice of his existence: this was an old St. Bernard, who used to come and lay his big head with its mournful eyes on Christophe's knees when Christophe was sitting on the seat in front of the house. They would look long at each other. Christophe would not drive him away. Unlike the sick Goethe, the dog's eyes had no uneasiness for him. Unlike him, he had no desire to cry: "Go away! . . . Thou goblin, thou shalt not catch me, whatever thou doest!"

He asked nothing better than to be engrossed by the dog's suppliant sleepy eyes and to help the beast: he felt that there must be behind them an imprisoned soul imploring his aid.

In those hours when he was weak with suffering, torn alive away from life, devoid of human egoism, he saw the victims of men, the field of battle in which man triumphed in the bloody slaughter of all other creatures: and his heart was filled with pity and horror. Even in the days when he had been happy he had always loved the beasts: he had never been able to bear cruelty towards them: he had always had a detestation of sport, which he had never dared to express for fear of ridicule: but his feeling of repulsion had been the secret cause of the apparently inexplicable feeling of dislike he had had for certain men: he had never been able to admit to his friendship a man who could kill an animal for pleasure. It was not sentimentality: no one knew better than he that life is based on suffering and infinite cruelty: no man can live without making others suffer. It is no use closing our eyes and fobbing ourselves off with words. It is no use either coming to the conclusion that we must renounce life and sniveling like children. No. We must kill to live, if, at the time, there is no other means of living. But the man who kills for the sake of killing is a miscreant. An unconscious miscreant, I know. But, all the same, a miscreant. The continual endeavor of man should be to lessen the sum of suffering and cruelty: that is the first duty of humanity.

In ordinary life those ideas remained buried in Christophe's inmost heart. He refused to think of them. What was the good? What could he do? He had to be Christophe, he had to accomplish his work, live at all costs, live at the cost of the weak. . . . It was not he who had made the universe. . . . Better not think of it, better not think of it. . . .

But when unhappiness had dragged him down, him, too, to the level of the vanquished, he had to think of these things. Only a

little while ago he had blamed Olivier for plunging into futile
remorse and vain compassion for all the wretchedness that men
suffer and inflict. Now he went even farther: with all the vehe-
mence of his mighty nature he probed to the depths of the tragedy
of the universe: he suffered all the sufferings of the world, and was
left raw and bleeding. He could not think of the animals without
shuddering in anguish. He looked into the eyes of the beasts and
saw there a soul like his own, a soul which could not speak: but the
eyes cried for it:

"What have I done to you? Why do you hurt me?"

He could not bear to see the most ordinary sights that he had
seen hundreds of times—a calf crying in a wicker pen, with its big,
protruding eyes, with their bluish whites and pink lids, and white
lashes, its curly white tufts on its forehead, its purple snout, its
knock-kneed legs:—a lamb being carried by a peasant with its four
legs tied together, hanging head down, trying to hold its head up,
moaning like a child, bleating and lolling its gray tongue:—fowls
huddled together in a basket:—the distant squeals of a pig being
bled to death:—a fish being cleaned on the kitchen-table. . . . The
nameless tortures which men inflict on such innocent creatures
made his heart ache. Grant animals a ray of reason, imagine what a
frightful nightmare the world is to them: a dream of cold-blooded
men, blind and deaf, cutting their throats, slitting them open, gut-
ting them, cutting them into pieces, cooking them alive, sometimes
laughing at them and their contortions as they writhe in agony. Is
there anything more atrocious among the cannibals of Africa? To a
man whose mind is free there is something even more intolerable in
the sufferings of animals than in the sufferings of men. For with the
latter it is at least admitted that suffering is evil and that the man
who causes it is a criminal. But thousands of animals are uselessly
butchered every day without a shadow of remorse. If any man were
to refer to it, he would be thought ridiculous.—And that is the
unpardonable crime. That alone is the justification of all that men
may suffer. It cries vengeance upon God. If there exists a good God,
then even the most humble of living things must be saved. If God is
good only to the strong, if there is no justice for the weak and lowly,
for the poor creatures who are offered up as a sacrifice to humanity,
then there is no such thing as goodness, no such thing as justice.

Diet and Morality

Mohandas Gandhi

M. K. Gandhi (1869–1948), the great Indian reformer and champion of satyagraha, *or peaceful civil disobedience, was also one of the contemporary era's great advocates of ethical vegetarianism. Raised as a vegetarian by his Vaishnavas Hindu parents, Gandhi secretly "experimented" as a young man with carnivorism. His hope was that emulating the diet of India's British occupiers would give him the strength and courage he associated with them. But the experiment was short-lived. As Gandhi tells us in his autobiography,* The Story of My Experiments with Truth, *he suffered guilt because of the deception toward his parents as well as the realization that his meat eating occasioned the death of innocent animals. So he returned to vegetarianism, but with a new appreciation of its moral foundation.*

As a university and law student in England, Gandhi was an active member of the Vegetarian Society and published several articles in various newspapers defending the vegetarian alternative. As a young lawyer in South Africa, he continued his journalistic advocacy, and the first selection here dates from that period. In "The Superiority of Vegetarianism," a letter to The Natal Mercury *(3 February 1896), Gandhi argues that abstention from animal flesh is conducive to both physical and spiritual health. In the second selection, portions of a speech*

139

Gandhi delivered before the London Vegetarian Society
some thirty-five years later, he argues that an authentic
commitment to vegetarianism should be based on ethical
rather than merely hygienic reasons. As he tells his audi-
ence, an adoption of a vegetarian lifestyle should be built
on the conviction that bodily needs ought not be satisfied
by killing "our fellow creatures." In saying this, Gandhi is
clearly suggesting that the vegetarian alternative is a cor-
relative of his doctrine of ahimsa, *or nonviolence.*

The Superiority of Vegetarianism

[B]ut for the unfortunate characteristic of this "self-indulgent" age, in which "nothing is more common than to hear men warmly supporting a theory in the abstract without any intention of submitting to it in practice," we should all be vegetarians. For, why should it be otherwise when Sir Henry Thompson calls it "a vulgar error" to suppose that flesh foods are indispensable for our sustenance, and the most eminent physiologists declare that fruit is the natural food of man, and when we have the example of Buddha, Pythagoras, Plato, Porphyry, Ray, Daniel, Wesley, Howard, Shelley, Sir Isaac Pitman, Edison, Sir W. B. Richardson, and a host of other eminent men as vegetarians. The Christian vegetarians claim that Jesus was also a vegetarian, and there does not seem to be anything to oppose that view, except the reference to His having eaten broiled fish after the Resurrection. The most successful missionaries in South Africa (the Trappists) are vegetarians. Looked at from every point of view, vegetarianism has been demonstrated to be far superior to flesh-eating. The Spiritualists hold, and the practice of the religious teachers of all the religions, except, perhaps, the generality of Protestant teachers, shows that nothing is more detrimental to the spiritual faculty of man than the gross feeding on flesh. The most ardent vegetarians attribute the agnosticism, the materialism, and the religious indifference of the present age to too much flesh-eating and wine-drinking, and the consequent disappearance, partial or total, of the spiritual faculty in man. Vegetarian admirers of the intellectual in man point to the whole host of the most intellectual men of the world, who were invariably abstemious in their habits, especially at the time of writing their best works, to demonstrate the sufficiency, if not the superiority, of the vegetarian diet from an intellectual standpoint. The columns of the vegetarian magazines and reviews afford a most decisive proof that where beef and its concoctions, with no end of physic thrown in, have lamentably failed, vegetarianism has triumphantly succeeded. Muscular vegetarians demonstrate the superiority of their diet by pointing out that the peasantry of the world are practically vegetarians, and that the strongest and most useful animal, the horse, is a vegetarian, while the most ferocious and practically useless animal, the lion, is a carnivore. Vegetarian moralists mourn over the fact that selfish men would—for the sake of gratifying their lustful and diseased appetite—force the butcher's trade on a portion of mankind, while they themselves would shrink with horror from such a calling. They moreover lovingly implore us to bear in mind that without the stimulants of flesh foods and wine it is difficult enough to restrain our passions and escape Satan's clutches, and not to add to those difficulties by resorting to meats and drinks which, as a rule, go hand in hand. For, it is claimed that vegetarianism, in which juicy fruits find the foremost place, is the safest and surest cure for drunkenness, while meat-eating induces or increases the habit. They also argue that since meat-eating is not only unnecessary but harmful to the system, indulgence in it is immoral and sinful, because it involves the infliction of unnecessary pain to and cruelty towards harmless animals. Lastly, vegetarian economists without fear of contradiction, assert that vegetarian foods are the cheapest diet, and their general adoption will go a long way towards mitigating, if not altogether suppressing, the rapidly growing pauperism side by side with the rapid march of the materialistic civilization and the accumulation of immense riches in the hands of a few.

Vegetarianism as Moral Choice

When I received the invitation to be present at this meeting [the London Vegetarian Society], I need not tell you how pleased I was, because it revived old memories and recollections of pleasant friendships formed with vegetarians. I feel especially honoured to find on my right Mr. Henry Salt. It was Mr. Salt's book, *A Plea for Vegetarianism*, which showed me why, apart from a hereditary habit, and apart from my adherence to a vow administered to me by my mother, it was right to be a vegetarian. He showed me why it was a moral duty incumbent on vegetarians not to live upon fellow-animals. It is, therefore, a matter of additional pleasure to me that I find Mr. Salt in our midst.

I do not propose to take up your time by giving you my various experiences of vegetarianism, nor do I want to tell you something of the great difficulty that faced me in London itself in remaining staunch to vegetarianism, but I would like to share with you some of the thoughts that have developed in me in connection with vegetarianism. Forty years ago I used to mix freely with vegetarians. There was at that time hardly a vegetarian restaurant in London that I had not visited. I made it a point, out of curiosity, and to study the possibilities of vegetarian restaurants in London, to visit every one of them. Naturally, therefore, I came into close contact with many vegetarians. I found at the tables that largely the conversation turned upon food and disease. I found also that the vegetarians who were struggling to stick to their vegetarianism were finding it difficult from [a] health point of view. I do not know whether, nowadays, you have those debates, but I used at that time to attend debates that were held between vegetarians and vegetarians, and between vegetarians and nonvegetarians. . . . Then vegetarians had a habit of talking of nothing but food and nothing but disease. I feel that is the worst way of going about the business. I notice also that it is those persons who become vegetarians because they are suffering from some disease or other—that is, from purely the health point of view—it is those persons who largely fall back. I discovered that for remaining staunch to vegetarianism a man requires a moral basis.

For me that was a great discovery in my search after truth. At an early age, in the course of my experiments, I found that a selfish basis would not serve the purpose of taking a man higher and higher along the paths of evolution. What was required was an altruistic purpose. I found also that health was by no means the monopoly of vegetarians. I found many people having no bias one way or the other, and that nonvegetarians were able to show, generally speaking, good health. I found also that several vegetarians found it impossible to remain vegetarians because they had made food a fetish and because they thought that by becoming vegetarians they could eat as much lentils, haricot beans, and cheese as they liked. Of course, those people could not possibly keep their health. Observing along these lines, I saw that a man should eat sparingly and now and then fast. No man or woman really ate sparingly or consumed just that quantity which the body requires and no more. We easily fall a prey to the temptations of the palate, and, therefore, when a thing tastes delicious, we do not mind taking a morsel or two more. But you cannot keep health under those circumstances. Therefore, I discovered that in order to keep health, no matter what you ate, it was necessary to cut down the quantity of the food and reduce the number of meals. Become moderate; err on the side of less, rather than on the side of more. When I invite friends to share their meals with me, I never press them to take anything except only what they require. On the contrary, I tell them not to take a thing if they do not want it.

What I want to bring to your notice is that vegetarians need to be tolerant if they want to convert others to vegetarianism. Adopt a little humility. We should appeal to the moral sense of the people who do not see eye to eye with us. If a vegetarian became ill, and a doctor prescribed beef-tea, then I would not call him a vegetarian. A vegetarian is made of sterner stuff. Why? Because it is for the building of the spirit and not of the body. Man is more than meat. It is the spirit in man for which we are concerned. Therefore, vegetarians should have that moral basis—that a man was not born a carnivorous animal, but born to live on the fruits and herbs that the earth grows. I know we must all err. I would give up milk if I could but I cannot. I have made that experiment times without number. I could not, after a serious illness, regain my strength unless I went back to milk. That has been the tragedy of my life. But the basis of my vegetarianism is not physical, but moral. If anybody said that I should die if I did not take beef-tea or mutton, even under medical advice, I would prefer death. That is the basis of my vegetarianism. I would love to think that all of us who called ourselves vegetarians should have that basis. There were thousands of meat-eaters who did not stay meat-eaters. There must be a definite reason for our making that change in our lives, for our adopting habits and customs different from society, even though sometimes that change may offend those nearest and dearest to us. Not for the world should you sacrifice a moral principle. Therefore the only basis for having a vegetarian society and proclaiming a vegetarian principle is, and must be, a moral one. I am not to tell you, as I see and wander about the world, that vegetarians, on the whole, enjoy much better health than meat-eaters. I belong to a country which is predominantly vegetarian by habit or necessity. Therefore, I cannot testify that that shows much greater endurance, much greater courage, or much greater exemption from disease. Because it is a peculiar, personal thing. It requires obedience, and scrupulous obedience, to all the laws of hygiene.

Therefore, I think that what vegetarians should do is not to emphasize the physical consequences of vegetarianism, but to explore the moral consequences. While we have not yet forgotten that we share many things in common with the beast, we do not sufficiently realize that there are certain things which differentiate us from the beast. Of course, we have vegetarians in the cow and the bull—which are better vegetarians than we are—but there is something much higher which calls us to vegetarianism. Therefore I thought that during the few minutes which I give myself the privilege of addressing you, I would just emphasize the moral basis of vegetarianism. And I would say that I have found from my own experience, and the experience of thousands of friends and companions, that they find satisfaction, so far as vegetarianism is concerned, from the moral basis they have chosen for sustaining vegetarianism.

The Ethic of Reverence for Life

Albert Schweitzer

There are few contemporary thinkers who have defended the virtue of nonviolence as eloquently and memorably as Albert Schweitzer (1875–1965). In his 1923 Civilization and Ethics, *he makes his case for an "ethic of reverence for life," excerpted here. Schweitzer argues that the "fundamental moral principle" is what might be described as empathic "fellow-feeling" (it is instructive to compare this notion with Richard Wagner's earlier principle of "fellow-suffering"). For Schweitzer, all organisms possess what he calls a "will-to-live." This drive ought to be respected in all animals, regardless of their position in the organic chain. Although Schweitzer's essay is not an explicit brief for vegetarianism, his insistence that the "fundamental principle" entails responsible compassion for nonhuman species surely points to the obligation to refrain from the butchery of animals for food whenever possible. As he says toward the end of his essay, the history of pain inflicted upon animals in both the abbatoir and the laboratory imposes an obligation upon humans to "do as much good as we possibly can to all creatures in all circumstances." Such actions in some measure atone for the "crimes against animals" perpetrated by humankind.*

J ust as in my own will-to-live there is a yearning for more life, and for that mysterious exaltation of the will-to-live which is called pleasure, and terror in face of annihilation and that injury to the will-to-live which is called pain; so the same obtains in all the will-to-live around me, equally whether it can express itself to my comprehension or whether it remains unvoiced.

Ethics thus consists in this, that I experience the necessity of practising the same reverence for life toward all will-to-live, as toward my own. Therein I have already the needed fundamental principle of morality. It is *good* to maintain and cherish life; it is *evil* to destroy and to check life.

As a matter of fact, everything which in the usual ethical valuation of inter-human relations is looked upon as good can be traced back to the material and spiritual maintenance or enhancement of human life and to the effort to raise it to its highest level of value. And contrariwise everything in human relations which is considered an evil, is in the final analysis found to be material or spiritual destruction or checking of human life and slackening of the effort to raise it to its highest value. Individual concepts of good and evil which are widely divergent and apparently unconnected fit into one another like pieces which belong together, the moment they are comprehended and their essential nature is grasped in this general notion.

The fundamental principle of morality which we seek as a necessity for thought is not, however, a matter only of arranging and deepening current views of good and evil, but also of expanding and extending these. A man is really ethical only when he obeys the constraint laid on him to help all life which he is able to succor, and when he goes out of his way to avoid injuring anything living. He does not ask how far this or that life deserves sympathy as valuable in itself, nor how far it is capable of feeling. To him life as such is sacred. He shatters no ice crystal that sparkles in the sun, tears no leaf from its tree, breaks off no flower, and is careful not to crush any insect as he walks. If he works by lamplight on a summer evening, he prefers to keep the window shut and to breathe stifling air, rather than to see insect after insect fall on his table with singed and sinking wings.

If he goes out into the street after a rainstorm and sees a worm which has strayed there, he reflects that it will certainly dry up in the sunshine, if it does not quickly regain the damp soil into which it can creep, and so he helps it get back from the deadly paving stones into the lush grass. Should he pass by an insect which has fallen into a pool, he spares the time to reach it a leaf or stalk on which it may clamber and save itself.

He is not afraid of being laughed at as sentimental. It is indeed the fate of every truth to be an object of ridicule when it is first acclaimed. It was once considered foolish to suppose that colored men were really human beings and ought to be treated as such. What was once foolishness has now become a recognized truth. Today it is considered as exaggeration to proclaim constant respect for every form of life as being the serious demand of a rational ethic. But the time is coming when people will be amazed that the human race was so long before it recognized that thoughtless injury to life is incompatible with real ethics. Ethics is in its unqualified form extended responsibility to everything that has life.

The general idea of ethics as a partaking of the mental atmosphere of reverence for life is not perhaps attractive. But it is the only complete notion possible. Mere sympathy is too narrow a concept to serve as the intellectual expression of the ethical element. It denotes, indeed, only a sharing of the suffering of the will-to-live. But to be ethical is to share the whole experience of all the circumstances and aspirations of the will-to-live, to live with it in its pleasures, in its yearnings, in its struggles toward perfection.

Love is a more inclusive term, since it signifies fellowship in suffering, in joy, and in effort. But it describes the ethical element only as it were by a simile, however natural and profound the simile may be. It places the solidarity created by ethics in analogy to that which nature has caused to come into being in a more or less superficial physical manner, and with a view to the fulfillment of their destiny, between two sexually attracted existences, or between these and their offspring.

Thought must strive to find a formula for the essential nature of the ethical. In so doing it is led to characterize ethics as self-devotion for the sake of life, motivated by reverence for life. Although the phrase "reverence for life" may perhaps sound a trifle unreal, yet that which it denotes is something which never lets go its hold of the man in whose thought it has once found a place. Sympathy, love, and, in general, all enthusiastic feeling of real value are summed up in it. It works with restless vitality on the mental nature in which it has found a footing and flings this into the rest-less activity of a responsibility which never ceases and stops nowhere. Reverence for life drives a man on as the whirling thrash-ing screw forces a ship through the water.

The ethic of reverence for life, arising as it does out of an inward necessity, is not dependent on the question as to how far or how little it is capable of development into a satisfactory view of life. It does not need to prove that the action of ethical man, as directed to maintaining, enhancing and exalting life, has any sig-nificance for the total course of the world-process. Nor is it dis-turbed by the consideration that the preservation and enhance-ment of life which it practises are of almost no account at all beside the mighty destruction of life which takes place every moment as the result of natural forces. Determined as it is to act, it is yet able to ignore all the problems raised as to the result of its action. The fact that in the man who has become ethical a will informed by rev-erence for life and self-sacrifice for the sake of life exists in the world, is itself significant for the world.

The universal will-to-live experiences itself in my personal will-to-live otherwise than it does in other phenomena. For here it enters on an individualization, which, so far as I am able to gather in trying to view it from the outside, struggles only to live itself out, and not at all to become one with will-to-live external to itself. The world is indeed the grisly drama of will-to-live at variance with itself. One existence survives at the expense of another of which it yet knows nothing. But in me the will-to-live has become cognizant of the existence of other will-to-live. There is in it a yearning for unity with itself, a longing to become universal.

Why is it that the will-to-live has this experience only in myself? Is it a result of my having become capable of reflection about the totality of my existence? Whither will the evolution lead which has thus begun in me?

There is no answer to these questions. It remains a painful enigma how I am to live by the rule of reverence for life in a world ruled by creative will which is at the same time destructive will, and by destructive will which is also creative.

I can do no other than hold on to the fact that the will-to-live appears in me as will-to-live which aims at becoming one with other will-to-live. This fact is the light which shines for me in the darkness. My ignorance regarding the real nature of the objective world no longer troubles me. I am set free from the world. I have been cast by my reverence for life into a state of unrest foreign to the world. By this, too, I am placed in a state of beatitude which the world cannot give. If in the happiness induced by our independence of the world I and another afford each other mutual help in understanding and in forgiveness, when otherwise will would harass other will, then the will-to-live is no longer at variance with itself. If I rescue an insect from a pool of water, then life has given itself for life, and again the self-contradiction of the will-to-live has been removed. Whenever my life has given itself out in any way for other life, my eternal will-to-live experiences union with the eternal, since all life is one. I possess a cordial which secures me from dying of thirst in the desert of life.

Therefore I recognize it as the destiny of my existence to be obedient to the higher revelation of the will-to-live which I find in myself. I choose as my activity the removal of the self-contradiction of the will-to-live, as far as the influence of my own existence extends. Knowing as I do the one thing needful, I am content to offer no opinion about the enigma of the objective world and my own being.

Thought becomes religious when it thinks itself out to the end. The ethic of reverence for life is the ethic of Jesus brought to philosophical expression, extended into cosmical form, and conceived as intellectually necessary.

The surmising and longing of all deeply religious personalities is comprehended and contained in the ethic of reverence for life. This, however, does not build up a worldview as a completed system, but resigns itself to leave the cathedral perforce incomplete. It is only able to finish the choir. Yet in this true piety celebrates a living and continuous divine service. . . .

[W]hat does the reverence for life teach us about the relations of man and the non-human animals?

Whenever I injure life of any kind I must be quite clear as to whether this is necessary or not. I ought never to pass the limits of the unavoidable, even in apparently insignificant cases. The countryman who has mowed down a thousand blossoms in his meadow as fodder for his cows should take care that on the way home he does not, in wanton pastime, switch off the head of a single flower growing on the edge of the road, for in so doing he injures life without being forced to do so by necessity.

Those who test operations or drugs on animals, or who inoculate them with diseases so that they may be able to help human beings by means of the results thus obtained, ought never to rest satisfied with the general idea that their dreadful doings are performed in pursuit of a worthy aim. It is their duty to ponder in every separate case whether it is really and truly necessary thus to sacrifice an animal for humanity. They ought to be filled with anxious care to alleviate as much as possible the pain which they cause. How many outrages are committed in this way in scientific institutions where narcotics are often omitted to save time and trouble! How many also when animals are made to suffer agonizing tortures, only in order to demonstrate to students scientific truths which are perfectly well known. The very fact that the animal, as a victim of research, has in his pain rendered such services to suffering men, has itself created a new and unique relation of solidarity between him and ourselves. The result is that a fresh obligation is laid on each of us to do as much good as we possibly can to all creatures in all sorts of circumstances. When I help an insect out of his troubles all that I do is to attempt to remove some of the guilt contracted through these crimes against animals.

Whenever any animal is forced into the service of man, the sufferings which it has to bear on that account are the concern of every one of us. No one ought to permit, in so far as he can prevent it, pain or suffering for which he will not take the responsibility. No one ought to rest at ease in the thought that in so doing he would mix himself up in affairs which are not his business. Let no one shirk the burden of his responsibility. When there is so much maltreatment of animals, when the cries of thirsting creatures go up unnoticed from the railway trucks, when there is so much roughness in our slaughter-houses, when in our kitchens so many animals suffer horrible deaths from unskillful hands, when animals endure unheard of agonies from heartless men, or are delivered to the dreadful play of children, then we are all guilty and must bear the blame.

We are afraid of shocking or offending by showing too plainly how deeply we are moved by the sufferings which man causes to the non-human creatures. We tend to reflect that others are more "rational" than we are, and would consider that which so disturbs us as customary and as a matter of course. And then, suddenly, they let fall some expression which shows us that they, too, are not really satisfied with the situation. Strangers to us hitherto, they are now quite near our own position. The masks, in which we had each concealed ourselves from the other, fall off. We now know that neither of us can cut ourselves free from the horrible necessity which plays ceaselessly around us. What a wonderful thing it is thus to get to know each other!

The ethic of reverence for life forbids any of us to deduce from the silence of our contemporaries that they, or in their case we, have ceased to feel what as thinking men we all cannot but feel. It prompts us to keep a mutual watch in this atmosphere of suffering and endurance, and to speak and act without panic according to the responsibility which we feel. It inspires us to join in a search for opportunities to afford help of some kind or other to the animals, to make up for the great amount of misery which they endure at our hands, and thus to escape for a moment from the inconceivable horrors of existence.

The Moral Basis of Vegetarianism

Tom Regan

Tom Regan (1938–   ), professor of philosophy at North Carolina State University, first published his classic "The Moral Basis of Vegetarianism" in 1975. In his subsequent book All That Dwell Therein *(University of California Press, 1982), he tells us that he deliberately wrote the piece in a "G. E. Moorish," analytical style because he was "determined not to let any extravagance, any emotion, any 'rhetorical device' find a place in the argument. This was to be hard core philosophy—clear, rigorous, dispassionate; written in an appropriate style, a style that might be fairly characterized as 'ponderously prodding.'" This is not, of course, to say that Regan is not passionate about his moral convictions, but only that he felt it necessary to establish their philosophical respectability.*

In this selection, which reproduces the second half of Regan's essay, he argues that it is the killing of food animals, and not merely the infliction of pain upon them, that is morally significant. This conclusion, which is based on the argument that if humans have a natural right to live so do animals, undercuts the claim of those who would insist that the slaughter of food animals is morally acceptable if done painlessly.

My argument in this section turns on considerations about the natural "right to life" that we humans are sometimes said uniquely to possess, and to possess to an equal degree. . . . What I will try to show is that arguments that might be used in defense of the claim that all human beings have this natural right, to an equal extent, would also show that animals are possessors of it, whereas arguments that might be used to show that animals do not have this right would also show that not all human beings do either. . . . I have not been able to consider all the arguments that might be advanced in this context; all that I have been able to do is consider what I think are the most important ones.

Let us begin, then, with the idea that all humans possess an equal natural right to life. And let us notice, once again, that it is an *equal natural* right that we are speaking of, one that we cannot acquire or have granted to us, and one that we all are supposed to have just because we are human beings. On what basis, then, might it be alleged that all and only human beings possess this right to an equal extent? Well, a number of familiar possibilities come immediately to mind. It might be argued that all and only human beings have an equal right to life because either (a) all and only human beings have the capacity to reason, or (b) all and only human beings have the capacity to make free choices, or (c) all and only human beings have a concept of "self," or (d) all and only human beings have all or some combination of the previously mentioned capacities. And it is easy to imagine how someone might argue that, since animals do not have any of these capacities, *they* do not possess a right to life, least of all one that is equal to the one possessed by humans.

I have already touched upon some of the difficulties such views must inevitably encounter. Briefly, it is not clear, first, that no nonhuman animals satisfy one (or all) of these conditions, and, second, it is reasonably clear that not all human beings satisfy them. The severely mentally feeble, for example, fail to satisfy them. Accordingly, *if* we want to insist that they have a right to life, then we cannot also maintain that they have it because they satisfy one or another of these conditions. Thus, *if* we want to insist that they have an equal right to life, despite their failure to satisfy these conditions, we cannot consistently maintain that animals, because they fail to satisfy these conditions, therefore lack this right.

Another possible ground is that of sentience, by which I understand the capacity to experience pleasure and pain. But this view, too, must encounter a familiar difficulty—namely, that it could not justify restricting the right *only* to human beings.

What clearly is needed, then, if we are to present any plausible argument for the view that all and only human beings have an equal natural right to life, is a basis for this right that is invariant and equal in the case of all human beings and only in their case. It is against this backdrop, I think, that the following view naturally arises.[1] This is the view that the life of every human being has "intrinsic worth"—that, in Kant's terms, each of us exists as "an end in himself"—*and* that this intrinsic worth which belongs *only* to human beings, is shared *equally* by all. "Thus," it might be alleged, "it is because of the equal intrinsic worth of all human beings that we all have an equal right to life."

This view, I think, has a degree of plausibility which those previously discussed lack. For by saying that the worth that is supposed to attach to a being just because he or she is human is intrinsic, and that it is because of this that we all have an equal natural right to life, this view rules out the possibility that one human being might give this right to or withhold it from another. It would appear, therefore, that this view could make sense of the alleged *naturalness* of the right in question. Moreover, by resting the equal right to life on the idea of the equal intrinsic worth of all human beings, this view may succeed, where the others have failed, in accounting for the alleged *equality* of this right.

Despite these apparent advantages, however, the view under consideration must face certain difficulties. One difficulty lies in specifying just what it is supposed to mean to say that the life of every human being is "intrinsically worthwhile."[2] Now, it cannot mean that "each and every human being has a natural right to life." For the idea that the life of each and every human being has intrinsic worth was introduced in the first place to provide a basis for saying that each and every human being has an equal right to life. Accordingly, if, say, "Jones' life is intrinsically worthwhile" ends up meaning "Jones has an equal right to life," then the claim that the life of each and every individual is equally worthwhile, judged intrinsically, cannot be construed as a *basis* for saying that each and every human being has an equal right to life. For the two claims would mean the same thing, and one claim can never be construed as being the basis for another, if they both mean the same.

But a second and, for our purposes, more important difficulty is this: on what grounds is it being alleged that each and every human being, and only human beings, are intrinsically worthwhile? Just what is there, in other words, about being human, and only about being human, that underlies this ascription of unique worth? Well, one possible answer here is that there isn't "anything" that underlies this worth. The worth in question, in short, just belongs to anyone who is human, and only to those who are. It is a worth that we simply recognize or intuit, whenever we carefully examine that complex of ideas we have before our minds when we think of the idea, "human being." I find this view unsatisfactory, both because it would seem to commit us to an ontology of value that is very difficult to defend, and because I, for one, even after the most scrupulous examination I can manage, fail to intuit the unique worth in question. I do not know how to prove that the view in question is mistaken in a few swift strokes, however. All I can do is point out the historic precedents of certain groups of human beings who have claimed to "intuit" a special worth belonging to their group and not to others within the human family, and say that it is good to remember that alluding to a special, intuitive way of "knowing" such things could only serve the purpose of giving an air of intellectual respectability to unreasoned prejudices. And, further, I can only register here my own suspicion that the same is true in this case, though to a much wider extent. For I think that falling into talk about the "intuition of the unique intrinsic worth of being human" would be the last recourse of men who, having found no good reason to believe that human beings have an unique intrinsic worth, would go on believing that they do anyhow.

Short of having recourse to intuition, then, we can expect those who believe that human beings uniquely possess intrinsic worth to tell us what there is about being human, in virtue of which this worth is possessed. The difficulty here, however, as can be anticipated, is that some familiar problems are going to raise their tiresome heads. For shall we say that it is the fact that humans can speak, or reason, or make free choices, or form a concept of their own identity that underlies this worth? These suggestions will not work here, anymore than they have before. For there are some beings who are human who cannot do these things, and there very well may some beings who are not human who can. None of these capacities, therefore, could do the job of providing the basis for a kind of worth that all humans and only humans are supposed to possess.

But suppose we try to unpack this notion of intrinsic worth in a slightly different way.[3] Suppose we say that the reasons we have for saying that all and only human beings exist as ends in themselves are, first, that every human being has various positive interests, such as desires, goals, hopes, preferences and the like, the satisfaction or realization of which brings intrinsic value to their lives, in the form of intrinsically valuable experiences; and, second, that the intrinsic value brought to the life of any one man, by the satisfaction of his desires or the realization of his goals, is just as good, judged in itself, as the intrinsic value brought to the life of any other man by the satisfaction or realization of those comparable desires and goals he happens to have. In this sense, then, all men are equal, and it is because of this equality among all men, it might be alleged, that each man has as much right as any other to seek to satisfy his desires and realize his goals, so long, at least, that, in doing so, he does not violate the rights of any other human being. "Now, since," this line of argument continues, "no one can seek to satisfy his desires or realize his goals if he is dead, and in view of the fact that every man has as much right as any other to seek to satisfy his desires and realize his goals, then to take the life of any human being will always be prima facie to violate a right which he shares equally with all other human beings—namely, his right to life."

What shall we make of this argument? I am uncertain whether it can withstand careful scrutiny. Whether it can or not, however, is not a matter I feel compelled to try to decide here. What I do want to point out is that, of the arguments considered here, this one has a degree of plausibility the others lack, not only because, as I have already remarked, it addresses itself both to the alleged naturalness and the alleged equality of the right in question, but also because it rests on what I take to be a necessary condition of being human—namely, that a being must have interests. For these reasons, then, I do not think I can be accused of "straw-man" tactics by choosing this as the most plausible among a cluster of possible arguments that might be urged in support of the contention that all human beings have an equal natural right to life. At the same time, however, as can be anticipated, I believe that, whatever plausibility this argument might have in this connection, it would also have in connection with the claim that animals, too, have an equal natural right to life.

For even if it is true that this argument provides us with adequate grounds for ascribing a natural right to life equally to all human beings, there is nothing in it that could tend to show that this is a right that belongs *only* to those beings who are human. On the contrary, the argument in question would equally well support the claim that any being who has positive interests which, when satisfied, bring about experiences that are just as intrinsically valuable as the satisfaction of the comparable interests of any other individual, would have an equal right to life. In particular, then, it would support the view that animals have an equal right to life, if they meet the conditions in question. And a case can be made for the view that they do. For, once again, it seems clear that animals have positive interests, the satisfaction or realization of which would appear to be just as intrinsically worthwhile, judged in themselves, as the satisfaction or realization of any comparable interest a human being might have. True, the interests animals have may be of a comparatively low-grade, when we compare them to, say, the contemplative interests of Aristotle's virtuous man. But the same is true of many human beings: their interests may be largely restricted to food and drink, with occasional bursts of sympathy for a few. Yet we would not say that such a man has less of a right to life than another, assuming that all men have an equal right to life. Neither, then, can we say that animals, because of their "base" interests, have any less of a right to life.

One way to avoid this conclusion . . . is to avoid that animals have interests.[4] But on what basis might this denial rest? A by now familiar basis is that animals cannot speak; they cannot use words to formulate or express anything; thus, they cannot have an interest in anything. But this objection obviously assumes that only those beings who are able to use words to formulate or express something can have interests, and this, even ignoring the possibility that at least some animals might be able to do this, seems implausible. For we do not suppose that infants, for example, have to learn to use a language before they can have any interests. Moreover, the behavior of animals certainly seems to attest to the fact that they not only can, but that they actually do have interests. Their behavior presents us with many cases of preferential choice and goal directed action, in the fact of which, and in the absence of any rationally compelling argument to the contrary, it seems both arbitrary and prejudicial to deny the presence of interests in them.

The most plausible argument for the view that humans have an equal natural right to life, therefore, seems to provide an equally plausible justification for the view that animals have this right also. But . . . we would not imply that the right in question can never be overridden. For there may arise circumstances in which an individual's right to life could be outweighed by other, more pressing moral demands, and where, therefore, we would be justified in taking the life of the individual in question. But even a moment's reflection will reveal that we would not condone a practice which involved the routine slaughter of human beings simply on the grounds that it brought about this or that amount of pleasure, or this or that amount of intrinsically good experiences for others, no matter how great the amount of good hypothesized. For to take the lives of individuals, for this reason, is manifestly not to recognize that their life is just as worthwhile as anybody else's or that they have just as much right to life as others do. Nor need any of this involve considerations about the amount of pain that is caused the persons whose lives are taken. Let us suppose that these persons are killed painlessly; that still would not alter the fact that they have been treated wrongly and that the practice in question is immoral.

If, then, the argument in the present section is sound; and assuming that no other basis is forthcoming which would support the view that humans do, but animals do not, have an equal right to life; then the same is true of any practice involving the slaughter of animals, and we have, therefore, grounds for responding to the two objections raised, but not answered, at the end of the first section [not printed here: editors]. These objections were, first, that since the only thing wrong with the way animals are treated in the course of being raised and slaughtered is that they are caused a lot of undeserved pain, the thing to do is to desensitize them so that they don't feel anything. What we can see now, however, is that the undeserved pain animals feel is not the only morally relevant consideration; it is also the fact that they are killed that must be taken into account.

Similarly, to attempt to avoid the force of my argument . . . by buying meat from farms that do not practice intensive rearing methods or by hunting and killing animals oneself . . . will not meet the total challenge vegetarians can place before their meat eating friends. For the animals slaughtered on even the most otherwise idyllic farms, as well as those shot in the wild, are just as much killed, and just as much dead, as the animals slaughtered under the most ruthless of conditions.

Unless or until, then, we are given a rationally compelling argument that shows that all and only human beings have an equal right to life; and so long as any plausible argument that might be advanced to support the view that all human beings have this right can be shown to support, to the same extent, the view that animals have this right also; and so long as we believe we are rationally justified in ascribing this right to humans and to make reference to it in the course of justifying our judgment that it is wrong to kill a given number of human beings simply for the sake of bringing about this or that amount of good for this or that number of people; given all these conditions, then I believe we are equally committed to the view that we cannot be justified in killing any one or any number of animals for the intrinsic good their deaths may bring to us. I do not say that there are no possible circumstances in which we would be justified in killing them. What I do say is that we cannot justify doing so in their case, anymore than we can in the case of the slaughter of human beings, by arguing that such a practice brings about intrinsically valuable experiences for others.

Once again, therefore, the onus of justification lies, not on the shoulders of those who are vegetarians, but on the shoulders of those who are not. If the argument [here] is sound, it is the non-vegetarian who must show us how he can be justified in eating meat, when he knows that, in order to do so, an animal has had to be killed. It is the non-vegetarian who must show us how his manner of life does not contribute to practices which systematically ignore the right to life which animals possess, if humans are supposed to possess it on the basis of the most plausible argument considered here. And it is the non-vegetarian who must do all this while being fully cognizant of the fact that he cannot defend his way of life merely by summing up the intrinsic goods—the delicious taste of meat, for example—that come into being as a result of the slaughter of animals.

This is not to say that practices that involve taking the lives of animals cannot possibly be justified. In some cases, perhaps, they can be, and the grounds on which we might rest such a justification would, I think, parallel those outlined in the preceding section in connection with the discussion of when we might be morally justified in approving a practice that caused animals non-trivial, undeserved pain. What we would have to show in the present case, I think, in order seriously to consider approving of such a practice, is (1) that such a practice would prevent, reduce or eliminate a much greater amount of evil, including the evil that attaches to the taking of the life of a being who has as much claim as any other to an equal natural right to life; (2) that, realistically speaking, there is no other way to bring about these consequences; and (3) that we have very good reason to believe that these consequences will, in fact, obtain. Now, perhaps there are some cases in which these conditions are satisfied. For example, perhaps they are satisfied in the case of the eskimo's killing of animals and in the case of having a restricted hunting season for such animals as deer. But to say that this is (or may be) true of *some* cases is not to say that it is true of all, and it will remain the task of the non-vegetarian to show that what is true in these cases, assuming that it is true, is also true of any practice that involves killing animals which, by his actions, he supports.

Two final objections deserve to be considered before ending. The first is that, even assuming that what I have said is true of *some* nonhuman animals, it does not follow that it is true of *all* of them. For the arguments given have turned on the thesis that it is only beings who have interests who can have rights, and it is quite possible that, though some animals have interests, not all of them do. I think this objection is both relevant and very difficult to answer adequately. The problem it raises is how we can know when a given being has interests. The assumption I have made throughout is that this is an empirical question, to be answered on the basis of reasoning by analogy—that, roughly speaking, beings who are very similar to us, both in terms of physiology and in terms of nonverbal behavior, are, like us, beings who have interests. The difficulty lies in knowing how far this analogy can be pushed. Certain animals, I think, present us with paradigms for the application of this reasoning—the primates, for example. In the case of others, however, the situation is less clear, and in the case of some, such as the protozoa, it is very grey indeed. There are, I think, at least two possible ways of responding to this difficulty. The first is to concede that there are some beings who are ordinarily classified as animals who do not have interests and who cannot, therefore, possess rights. The second is to insist that all those beings who are ordinarily classified as animals do have interests and can have rights. I am inclined to think that the former of these two alternatives is the correct one, though I cannot defend this judgment here. And thus I think that the arguments I have presented do not, by themselves, justify the thesis that *all* animals have interests and can, therefore, possess rights. But this exaggeration has been perpetrated in the interests of style, and does not, I think, detract from the force of my argument, when it is taken in context. For the cases where we would, with good reason, doubt whether an animal has interests—for example, whether protozoa do—are cases which are, I think, irrelevant to the moral status of vegetarianism. The question of the obligatoriness of vegetarianism, in other words, can arise only if and when the animals we eat are the kind of beings who have interests. Whatever reasonable doubts we may have about which animals do and which do not have interests do not apply, I think, to those animals that are raised according to intensive rearing methods or are routinely killed, painlessly or not, preparatory to our eating them. Thus, to have it pointed out that there are or may be some animals who do not have interests does not in any way modify the obligation not to support practices that cause death or non-trivial, undeserved pain to those animals that do.

Finally, a critic will object that there are no natural rights, not even natural rights possessed by humans. "Thus," he will conclude, "no animals have natural rights either and the backbone of your argument is broken." This objection raises problems too large for me to consider here, and I must content myself, in closing, with the following two remarks. First, I have not argued that either human beings or animals do have natural rights; what I have argued, rather, is that what seems to me to be the most plausible arguments for the view that all humans possess the natural rights I have discussed can be used to show that animals possess these rights also. Thus, if it should turn out that there is no good reason to believe that we humans have any natural rights, it certainly would follow that my argument would lose some of its force. Even so, however, this would not alter the principal logical points I have endeavored to make.

But, second, even if it should turn out that there are no natural rights, that would not put an end to many of the problems discussed here. For even if we do not possess natural rights, we would still object to practices that caused non-trivial, undeserved pain for some human beings if their "justification" was that they brought about this or that amount of pleasure or other forms of intrinsic good for this or that number of people; and we would still object to any practice that involved the killing of human beings, even if killed painlessly, if the practice was supposed to be justified in the same way. But this being so, what clearly would be needed, if we cease to invoke the idea of rights, is some explanation of why practices which are not right, when they involve the treatment of people, can be right (or at least permissible) when they involve the treatment of animals. What clearly would be needed, in short, is what we have found to be needed and wanting all along—namely, the specification of some morally relevant feature of being human which is possessed by *all* human beings and *only* by those beings who are human. Unless or until some such feature can be pointed out, I do not see how the differential treatment of humans and animals can be rationally defended.

Notes

1. For an example of this kind of argument, see Gregory Vlastos' "Justice and Equality" in *Social Justice*. Edited by Richard B. Brandt. Englewood Cliffs, New Jersey: Prentice-Hall, Incorporated, 1962.

2. This is a point that first became clear to me in discussion with Donald VanDeVeer.

3. Vlastos, *op. cit.*

4. See, for example, H. J. McCloskey's "Rights," *Philosophical Quarterly* (1965). McCloskey denies that animals have interests, but does not, so far as I can see, give any reason for believing that this is so.

All Animals Are Equal

Peter Singer

Although Peter Singer (1946–   ) claims not to have coined the term "speciesism," he's certainly done more than any other individual to ensure it a place in popular parlance. Speciesism, as Singer defines it, is the assumption that the interests of the human species always and everywhere take precedence over the interests of nonhuman species. This assumption of superiority is just as unwarranted and exploitative as, for example, racism or sexism.

According to Singer, the speciesist bias has traditionally provided a pseudojustification for the slaughter and (more recently) factory farming of food animals. But it ignores what Singer takes to be the important ethical principle that all creatures capable of suffering equally deserve moral consideration. Consequently, since carnivorism needlessly inflicts suffering upon sentient animals, it is prima facie suspect. In the following selection, taken from an early essay which anticipated the argument of his classic Animal Liberation, *Singer explains his position.*

A liberation movement demands an expansion of our moral horizons and an extension or reinterpretation of the basic moral principle of equality. Practices that were previously regarded as natural and inevitable come to be seen as the result of an unjusti-fiable prejudice. Who can say with confidence that all his or her attitudes and practices are beyond criticism? If we wish to avoid being numbered amongst the oppressors, we must be prepared to re-think even our most fundamental attitudes. We need to consider them from the point of view of those most disadvantaged by our attitudes, and the practices that follow from these attitudes. If we can make this unaccustomed mental switch we may discover a pat-tern in our attitudes and practices that consistently operates so as to benefit one group—usually the one to which we ourselves belong—at the expense of another. In this way we may come to see that there is a case for a new liberation movement. My aim is to advocate that we make this mental switch in respect of our atti-tudes and practices towards a very large group of beings: members of species other than our own—or, as we popularly though mis-leadingly call them, animals. In other words, I am urging that we extend to other species the basic principle of equality that most of us recognise should be extended to all members of our own species.

All this may sound a little far-fetched, more like a parody of other liberation movements than a serious objective. In fact, in the past the idea of "The Rights of Animals" really has been used to parody the case for women's rights. When Mary Wollstonecraft, a forerunner of later feminists, published her *Vindication of the Rights of Women* in 1792, her ideas were widely regarded as absurd, and they were satirized in an anonymous publication enti-tled *A Vindication of the Rights of Brutes*. The author of this satire (actually Thomas Taylor, a distinguished Cambridge philosopher) tried to refute Wollstonecraft's reasonings by showing that they could be carried one stage further. If sound when applied to women, why should the arguments not be applied to dogs, cats, and horses? They seemed to hold equally well for these "brutes"; yet to hold that brutes had rights was manifestly absurd; therefore the reasoning by which this conclusion had been reached must be unsound, and if unsound when applied to brutes, it must also be unsound when applied to women, since the very same arguments had been used in each case.

One way in which we might reply to this argument is by saying that the case for equality between men and women cannot validly be extended to nonhuman animals. Women have a right to vote, for instance, because they are just as capable of making rational decisions as men are; dogs, on the other hand, are incapable of understanding the significance of voting, so they cannot have the right to vote. There are many other obvious ways in which men and women resemble each other closely, while humans and other animals differ greatly. So, it might be said, men and women are similar beings, and should have equal rights, while humans and non-humans are different and should not have equal rights.

The thought behind this reply to Taylor's analogy is correct up to a point, but it does not go far enough. There *are* important differences between humans and other animals, and these differences must give rise to *some* differences in the rights that each have. Recognizing this obvious fact, however, is no barrier to the case for extending the basic principle of equality to non-human animals. The differences that exist between men and women are equally undeniable, and the supporters of Women's Liberation are aware that these differences may give rise to different rights. Many feminists hold that women have the right to an abortion on request. It does not follow that since these same people are campaigning for equality between men and women they must support the right of men to have abortions too. Since a man cannot have an abortion, it is meaningless to talk of his right to have one. Since a pig can't vote, it is meaningless to talk of its right to vote. There is no reason why either Women's Liberation or Animal Liberation would get involved in such nonsense. The extension of the basic principle of equality from one group to another does not imply that we must treat both groups in exactly the same way, or grant exactly the same rights to both groups. Whether we should do so will depend on the nature of the members of the two groups. The basic principle of equality, I shall argue, is equality of consideration; and equal consideration for different beings may lead to different treatment and different rights.

So there is a different way of replying to Taylor's attempt to parody Wollstonecraft's arguments, a way which does not deny the differences between humans and non-humans, but goes more deeply into the question of equality, and concludes by finding nothing absurd in the idea that the basic principle of equality applies to so-called "brutes." I believe that we reach this conclusion if we examine the basis on which our opposition to discrimination on grounds of race or sex ultimately rests. We will then see that we would be on shaky ground if we were to demand equality for blacks, women, and other groups of oppressed humans while denying equal consideration to non-humans.

When we say that all human beings, whatever their race, creed or sex, are equal, what is it that we are asserting? Those who wish to defend a hierarchical, inegalitarian society have often pointed out that by whatever test we choose, it simply is not true that all humans are equal. Like it or not, we must face the fact that humans come in different shapes and sizes; they come with differing moral capacities, differing intellectual abilities, differing amounts of benevolent feeling and sensitivity to the needs of others, differing abilities to communicate effectively, and differing capacities to experience pleasure and pain. In short, if the demand for equality were based on the actual equality of all human beings, we would have to stop demanding equality. It would be an unjustifiable demand.

Still, one might cling to the view that the demand for equality among human beings is based on the actual equality of the different races and sexes. Although humans differ as individuals in various ways, there are no differences between the races and sexes *as such*. From the mere fact that a person is black, or a woman, we cannot infer anything else about that person. This, it may be said, is what is wrong with racism and sexism. The white racist claims that whites are superior to blacks, but this is false—although there are differences between individuals, some blacks are superior to some whites in all of the capacities and abilities that could conceivably be relevant. The opponent of sexism would say the same: a person's sex is no guide to his or her abilities, and this is why it is unjustifiable to discriminate on the basis of sex.

This is a possible line of objection to racial and sexual discrimination. It is not, however, the way that someone really concerned about equality would choose, because taking this line could, in some circumstances, force one to accept a most inegalitarian society. The fact that humans differ as individuals rather than as races or sexes, is a valid reply to someone who defends a hierarchical society like, say, South Africa, in which all whites are superior in status to all blacks. The existence of individual variations that cut across the lines of race or sex, however, provides us with no defence at all against a more sophisticated opponent of equality, one who proposes that, say, the interests of those with ratings above 100. Would a hierarchical society of this sort really be so much better than one based on race or sex? I think not. But if we tie the moral principle of equality to the factual equality of the different races or sexes, taken as a whole, our opposition to racism and sexism does not provide us with any basis for objecting to this kind of inegalitarianism.

There is a second important reason why we ought not to base our opposition to racism and sexism on any kind of factual equality, even the limited kind that asserts that variations in capacities and abilities are spread evenly between the different races and sexes: we can have no absolute guarantee that these abilities and capacities really are distributed evenly, without regard to race or sex, among human beings. So far as actual abilities are concerned, there do seem to be certain measurable differences between both races and sexes. These differences do not, of course, appear in each case, but only when averages are taken. More important still, we do not yet know how much of these differences is really due to the different genetic endowments of the various races and sexes, and how much is due to environmental differences that are the result of past and continuing discrimination. Perhaps all of the important differences will eventually prove to be environmental rather than genetic. Anyone opposed to racism and sexism will certainly hope that this will be so, for it will make the task of ending discrimination a lot easier; nevertheless it would be dangerous to rest the case against racism and sexism on the belief that all significant differences are environmental in origin. The opponent of, say, racism who takes this line will be unable to avoid conceding that if differences in ability did after all prove to have some genetic connection with race, racism would in some way be defensible.

It would be folly for the opponent of racism to stake his whole case on a dogmatic commitment to one particular outcome of a difficult scientific issue which is still a long way from being settled. While attempts to prove that differences in certain selected abilities between races and sexes are primarily genetic in origin have certainly not been conclusive, the same must be said of attempts to prove that these differences are largely the result of environment. At this stage of the investigation we cannot be certain which view is correct, however much we may hope it is the latter.

Fortunately, there is no need to pin the case for equality to one particular outcome of this scientific investigation. The appropriate response to those who claim to have found evidence of genetically-based differences in ability between the races or sexes is not to stick to the belief that the genetic explanation must be wrong, whatever evidence to the contrary may turn up: instead we should make it quite clear that the claim to equality does not depend on intelligence, moral capacity, physical strength, or similar matters of fact. Equality is a moral ideal, not a simple assertion of fact. There is no logically compelling reason for assuming that a factual difference in ability between two people justifies any difference in the amount of consideration we give to satisfying their needs and interests. The principle of the equality of human beings is not a description of an alleged actual equality among humans: it is a prescription of how we should treat humans.

Jeremy Bentham incorporated the essential basis of moral equality into his utilitarian system of ethics in the formula: "Each to count for one and none for more than one." In other words, the interests of every being affected by an action are to be taken into account and given the same weight as the like interests of any other being. A later utilitarian, Henry Sidgwick, put the point in this way: "The good of any one individual is of no more importance, from the point of view (if I may say so) of the Universe, than the good of any other."[2] More recently, the leading figures in contemporary moral philosophy have shown a great deal of agreement in specifying as a fundamental presupposition of their moral theories some similar requirement which operates so as to give everyone's interests equal consideration—although they cannot agree on how this requirement is best formulated.[3]

It is an implication of this principle of equality that our concern for others ought not to depend on what they are like, or what abilities they possess—although precisely what this concern requires us to do may vary according to the characteristics of those affected by what we do. It is on this basis that the case against racism and the case against sexism must both ultimately rest; and it is in accordance with this principle that speciesism is also to be condemned. If possessing a higher degree of intelligence does not entitle one human to use another for his own ends, how can it entitle humans to exploit non-humans?

Many philosophers have proposed the principle of equal consideration of interests, in some form or other, as a basic moral principle; but . . . not many of them have recognised that this principle applies to members of other species as well as to our own. Bentham was one of the few who did realize this. In a forward-looking passage, written at a time when black slaves in the British dominions were still being treated much as we now treat non-human animals, Bentham wrote:

> The day *may* come when the rest of the animal creation may acquire those rights which never could have been withholden from them but by the hand of tyranny. The French have already discovered that the blackness of the skin is no reason why a human being should be abandoned without redress to the caprice of a tormentor. It may one day come to be recognised that the number of the legs, the villosity of the skin, or the termination of the *os sacrum*, are reasons equally insufficient for abandoning a sensitive being to the same fate. What else is it that should trace the insuperable line? Is it the faculty of reason, or perhaps the faculty of discourse? But a full-grown horse or dog is beyond comparison a more rational, as well as a more conversable animal, than an infant of a day, or a week, or even a month, old. But suppose they were otherwise, what would it avail? The question is not, Can they reason? Nor Can they *talk*?, But, *Can they suffer?*[4]

In this passage Bentham points to the capacity for suffering as the vital characteristic that gives a being the right to equal consideration. The capacity for suffering—or more strictly, for suffering and/or enjoyment or happiness—is not just another characteristic like the capacity for language, or for higher mathematics. Bentham is not saying that those who try to mark "the insuperable line" that determines whether the interests of a being should be considered happen to have selected the wrong characteristic. The capacity for suffering and enjoying things is a pre-requisite for having interests at all, a condition that must be satisfied before we can speak of interests in any meaningful way. It would be nonsense to say that it was not in the interests of a stone to be kicked along the road by a schoolboy. A stone does not have interests because it cannot suffer. A mouse, on the other hand, does have an interest in not being tormented, because it will suffer if it is.

If a being suffers, there can be no moral justification for refusing to take that suffering into consideration. No matter what the nature of the being, the principle of equality requires that its suffering be counted equally with the like suffering—in so far as rough comparisons can be made—of any other being. If a being is not capable of suffering, or of experiencing enjoyment or happiness, there is nothing to be taken into account. This is why the limit of sentience (using the term as a convenient, if not strictly accurate, shorthand for the capacity to suffer or experience enjoyment or happiness) is the only defensible boundary of concern for the interests of others. To mark this boundary by some characteristic like intelligence or rationality would be to mark it in an arbitrary way. Why not choose some other characteristic, like skin color?

The racist violates the principle of equality by giving greater weight to the interests of members of his own race, when there is a clash between their interests and the interests of those of another race. Similarly the speciesist allows the interests of his own species to override the greater interests of members of other species.[5] The pattern is the same in each case. Most human beings are speciesists. I shall now very briefly describe some of the practices that show this.

For the great majority of human beings, especially in urban, industrialized societies, the most direct form of contact with members of other species is at meal-times: we eat them. In doing so we treat them purely as means to our ends. We regard their life and well-being as subordinate to our taste for a particular kind of dish. I say "taste" deliberately—this is purely a matter of pleasing our palate. There can be no defence of eating flesh in terms of satisfying nutritional needs, since it has been established beyond doubt that we could satisfy our need for protein and other essential nutrients far more efficiently with a diet that replaced animal flesh by soy beans, or products derived from soy beans, and other high-protein vegetable products.[6]

It is not merely the act of killing that indicates what we are ready to do to other species in order to gratify our tastes. The suffering we inflict on the animals while they are alive is perhaps an even clearer indication of our speciesism than the fact that we are prepared to kill them.[7] In order to have meat on the table at a price that people can afford, our society tolerates methods of meat production that confine sentient animals in cramped, unsuitable conditions for the entire durations of their lives. Animals are treated like machines that convert fodder into flesh, and any innovation that results in a higher "conversion ratio" is liable to be adopted. As one authority on the subject has said, "cruelty is acknowledged only when profitability ceases."[8] So hens are crowded four or five to a cage with a floor area of twenty inches by eighteen inches, or around the size of a single page of the *New York Times*. The cages will have wire floors, since this reduces cleaning costs, though wire is unsuitable for the hens' feet; the floors slope, since this makes the eggs roll down for easy collection, although this make it difficult for the hens to rest comfortably. In these conditions all the birds' natural instincts are thwarted: they cannot stretch their wings fully, walk freely, dustbathe, scratch the ground, or build a nest. Although they have never known other conditions, observers have noticed that the birds vainly try to perform these actions. Frustrated at their inability to do so, they often develop what farmers call "vices," and peck each other to death. To prevent this, the beaks of young birds are often cut off.

This kind of treatment is not limited to poultry. Pigs now are also being reared in cages inside sheds. These animals are comparable to dogs in intelligence, and need a varied, stimulating environment if they are not to suffer from stress and boredom. Anyone who kept a dog in the way in which pigs are frequently kept would be liable to prosecution, in England at least, but because our interest in exploiting pigs is greater than our interests in exploiting dogs, we object to cruelty to dogs while consuming the produce of cruelty to pigs. Of the other animals, the condition of veal calves is perhaps worst of all, since these animals are so closely confined that they cannot even turn around or get up and lie down freely. In this way they do not develop unpalatable muscle. They are also made anaemic and kept short of roughage, to keep their flesh pale, since white veal fetches a higher price; as a result they develop a craving for iron and roughage, and have been observed to gnaw wood off the sides of their stalls, and lick greedily at any rusty hinge that is within reach.

Since, as I have said, none of these practices cater for anything more than our pleasures of taste, our practice of rearing and killing other animals in order to eat them is a clear instance of the sacrifice of the most important interests of other beings in order to satisfy trivial interests of our own. To avoid speciesism we must stop this practice, and each of us has a moral obligation to cease supporting the practice. Our custom is all the support that the meat-industry needs. The decision to cease giving it that support may be difficult, but it is no more difficult than it would have been for a white Southerner to go against the traditions of his society and free his slaves; if we do not change our dietary habits, how can we censure those slaveholders who would not change their own way of living?

Notes

1. Passages of this article appeared in a review of *Animals, Men and Morals*, edited by S. and R. Godlovitch and J. Harris (Gollancz and Taplinger, London 1972) in *The New York Review of Books*, April 5, 1973. The whole direction of my thinking on this subject I owe to talks with a number of friends in Oxford in 1970–71, especially Richard Keshen, Stanley Godlovitch, and, above all, Roslind Godlovitch.

2. *The Methods of Ethics* (7th Ed.), p. 382.

3. For example, R. M. Hare, *Freedom and Reason* (Oxford, 1963) and J. Rawls, *A Theory of Justice* (Harvard, 1972); for a brief account of the essential agreement on this issue between these and other positions, see R. M. Hare, "Rules of War and Moral Reasoning," *Philosophy and Public Affairs*, vol. I, no. 2 (1972).

4. *Introduction to the Principles of Morals and Legislation*, ch. XVII.

5. I owe the term "speciesism" to Dr. Richard Ryder.

6. In order to produce 1 pound of protein in the form of beef or veal, we must feed 21 pounds of protein to the animal. Other forms of livestock are slightly less inefficient, but the average ratio in the United States is still 1:8. It has been estimated that the amount of protein lost to humans in this way is equivalent to 90 percent of the annual world protein deficit. For a brief account, see Frances Moore Lappé, *Diet for a Small Planet* (Friends of the Earth/Ballantine, New York, 1971), pp. 4–11.

7. Although one might think that killing a being is obviously the ultimate wrong one can do to it, I think that the infliction of suffering is a clearer indication of speciesism because it might be argued that at least part of what is wrong with killing a human is that most humans are conscious of their existence over time, and have desires and purposes that extend into the future—see, for instance, M. Tooley, "Abortion and Infanticide," *Philosophy and Public Affairs*, vol. 2, no. 1 (1972). Of course, if one

took this view one would have to hold—as Tooley does—that killing a human infant or mental defective is not in itself wrong, and is less serious than killing certain higher mammals that probably do have a sense of their own existence over time.

8. Ruth Harrison, *Animal Machines* (Stuart, London, 1964). This book provides an eye-opening account of intensive farming methods for those unfamiliar with the subject.

The Right Not to Be Eaten

Thomas Auxter

Thomas Auxter (1945–   ), professor of philosophy at the University of Florida, argues in this essay that wild animals have the right not to be eaten and that the practice of stock farming for meat production ought to be discontinued. He does not base his case upon an abstract analysis of rights, however, or upon the attempt to show that animals possess certain attributes analogous to human ones that would guarantee their moral standing. Instead, he more broadly approaches the question from the perspective of teleological ethical theory, arguing that the latter provides a basis for moral vegetarianism by focusing on the issue of the maximum development of a species consistent with the diversification of nature. Using this standard of telic development, Auxter believes that an individual or species has a right to both existence and well-being if "such an existence figures into a system of beings which would be richer and more developed through the existence of that individual or species or . . . , the individual or species does not undermine such development." In light of these functional standards, Auxter concludes that we are justified in ascribing to animals a right not to be eaten, even if non-vegetarians refuse to grant them an intrinsic right not to be eaten.

The debate over the rights of animals has had some effects which are not satisfactory from a vegetarian point of view. Often, meat-eating philosophers who listen to the arguments that animals have rights respond by expressing reservations about whether animals can satisfy the conditions for the attribution of rights. Usually it is noted that animals do not have a developed language, cannot make contracts, cannot even agree to something, cannot complain when rights are violated, cannot exercise coercion in the absence of respect for rights, etc. In short, it is argued that animals cannot do everything that human beings can do and that the distinctly human capacities are precisely those features which qualify one for rights. Furthermore, since human beings typically think of rights in terms of the exercise of such powers, it is not altogether surprising that these philosophers should find it "odd" to think of other types of beings which have moral claims on human conduct and yet do not exercise human-life powers in articulating and defending these claims. The conclusion of the meat-eating philosopher who hears the vegetarian arguments is that the contention that animals have rights is "doubtful" in view of the "complications," and consequently there are not sufficient grounds for changing a practice which is otherwise quite agreeable. The vegetarian philosopher is—rightly, I believe—angry at this outcome. He/she observes that the line of reasoning is typical of those who commit moral outrages, proceeding from an "impartial" hearing to an endorsement of the status quo without ever seriously examining what is at issue. But such charges are not themselves arguments (although they may be of some use in discouraging attitudes of complacency), and a more systematic response is necessary if there is to be an advance in the debate.

It should be clear that the vegetarian's feeling of moral outrage will not be diminished by claims that the bearer of rights must have human capacities. It should also be clear that those who eat animals will not be persuaded that they have violated rights when this concept is—for them—so loaded with properties which apply only to human beings. Are we at an impasse? Is there nothing more to be said which will take the debate a step further? At this point one might be motivated to search for an alternative approach if one believes our philosophic concepts are not doing an adequate job of reflecting our moral sensibilities. Is it possible that moral outrage *is* a legitimate response to the practice of slaughtering animals but that the vocabulary (and logical geography) of the concept of rights is not *in itself* adequate to express these justifiable protests? Might it not be the case that our concept of rights needs to be amplified so that we are able to acknowledge both the rights which are claimed and defended in human conflicts and those "rights in effect" which we attribute to animals because we think they are something more than a material to be manipulated at will? Moreover, one might also be motivated to search for an alternative philosophical language and theory if one believes that "rights talk" begins to sound artificial when "rights" are added to "rights" without any consideration of what it would take to honor them. Fortunately, the philosophical tradition readily supplies a likely candidate in the kind of teleological ethic which follows the lines of investigation pursued by Plato and Aristotle. In this tradition, which is taken up by such thinkers as Leibniz and Whitehead, we are urged to seek the highest good, which is generally understood as the most perfect or complete state of affairs possible.[1] Here a right is not understood in the "rigorous" sense of an inviolable claim which ought to condition the conduct of everyone regardless of the circumstances. Instead, an individual or species has a right to existence and well-being if either (a) such an existence figures into a system of beings which would be richer and more developed through the existence of that individual or species or, (b) the individual or species does not undermine such development.[2] It is only when we take into account the effects a particular being has on the total system of beings that we will be able to decide whether that being has a right to exist— including the right not to be eaten. In other words, there can be no determination of the value of a creature, or of the rights which should or should not be ascribed to it as a consequence of the determination of its value, apart from an assessment of its impact on the organization of a life-system.

Thus, in the absence of indications that the issue of animal rights can be settled by an abstract discussion of the concept of rights, it seems advisable to ask what sort of guidance a teleological ethic might provide—especially since such an approach allows us to consider empirical evidence concerning effects on the natural environment, which otherwise does not find its way into discussions of the rights of animals. A further advantage of this approach is that it avoids the criticism that philosophers are arbitrarily expanding the list of rights without any regard to what kind of natural environment and social context would be required to support them. It is in this larger (teleological) context that I propose to discuss the conditions which determine which creatures *ought not* to be eaten.

There are some animals who are usually thought to have the right not to be eaten. Ordinarily, we say that "the rational animal" has this right, and our horror at the idea of a cannibal has more to it than merely sympathy for the one who is to be eaten. In fact, most people would probably say that chimpanzees have the right not to be eaten and would feel moral indignation at the thought of people eating them. But how far this right extends and why it extends no further are the issues which concern us here. In line with the teleological approach we will not begin with the question of the constitution of a rights-bearing creature. Instead, we will look for that type of conduct which serves to sustain the highest level of organization of life.

One reason why this approach to the question is promising is that the meat-eating philosophers usually concede it is morally relevant to consider the level of organization of life in decisions concerning how animals are to be treated and used. The recognition of this higher/lower division can be seen (at least indirectly) in two types of arguments which have been made by meat-eating philosophers. In the first place it is said we should treat animals kindly (although we are always, of course, free to eat them) because, in the words of Aquinas, "whoever is practiced in the affection of pity towards animals is thereby more disposed to the affection of pity toward men,"[3] or in the words of Kant, "Tender feelings toward dumb animals develop humane feelings toward mankind."[4] The persistence of this argument in the history of philosophy leads one to believe that there is considerable uneasiness over how to reconcile the total denial of animal rights at the moment an animal is slaughtered for the dinner table with the undeniable feeling that there is something wrong with torturing an animal. But if killing an animal is permissible *because* the creature has no rights against human beings, then obviously an animal can have no right not to be tortured either. The only way that the outrage against our moral sensibilities can be accounted for on the meat eater's scheme is to claim that we are undermining our moral responsiveness *to human beings* by this kind of behavior. The animal itself has already been denied any rights to be violated. This explains, I believe, why this argument has been so popular with meat-eating philosophers. But I am concerned at present with noticing something else: no one argues against cruelty to plants. This, I take it, is tacitly an admission that in comparison with plants animals are (a) more highly organized in that they share many features with human beings which make them capable of being tortured and (b) more valuable since their welfare is singled out for special attention (although in a somewhat backhanded fashion).[5] In the second place we can see a recognition of the division between higher and lower types of beings—and its importance for values—in the concession that "in experiments on living animals for scientific purposes, it is right to prefer the less highly organized animal to the more highly organized, whenever the lower type is clearly sufficient for the purposes of the experiment."[6] This and similar concessions which can be won from the meat eater in discussions of the issue of animal rights lead me to believe that even the meat eater would require a moral justification for how an animal was being treated and used if it were to appear that a member of a higher species were being sacrificed when a member of a lower species would do. But if this is true, then the meat eater needs to explain why his/her taste for animal flesh ought to be made an exception to the rule.

At this point an obvious objection needs to be considered. The meat eater may well reply that if we were always to favor the more highly organized being, we would soon find ourselves saddled with some unacceptable consequences. The consequences become apparent when we imagine the natural order which would result from the consistent application of the proposed moral standard. If the value of a creature is a function of the comparative degree of organization of its constitution, and if the human species is the highest species by this measure, then we would be required to protect, and even increase, the membership of this species at every available opportunity. Furthermore, because it happens to be true that grain yields the greatest amount of protein for human use[7] (while the domestication of animals for food uses up more protein than it generates), the policy of always preferring the survival (i.e., Nourishment and continued existence) of the more highly organized being would eventually result in the polarization of all life-forms into the human species on the one hand and grain yielding plants on the other. In order to observe the moral standard we would have to eliminate the non-human animal population because it competes with some human beings for food. Thus the very moral standard which was designed to protect animal life actually encourages the destruction of animal life. If the vegetarian wants to place a value on animal life, he/she can hardly advocate a consistent preference for the more highly organized being.

There are two answers to this type of objection. First, there are prudential considerations (and is should be noted that such considerations can only assume their proper pivotal role in a teleological ethic). We have learned from recent ecological disasters that it is perilous for even the highest species to assume omniscience about nature's complex patterns and that we should not effect major dislocations in natural balances because the consequences do not make themselves known until it is too late. It is also dangerous to reduce the world to a few mutually dependent species for if something (e.g., disease) were to happen to one of the species, the consequences for the other species would be devastating. Thus merely for human safety and preservation we should not accept this master plan for re-arranging nature.

But the second consideration is more concerned with the nature of the moral ideal itself. The question here is what we mean by the "most highly organized" as a moral ideal. Do we mean "the greatest quantity of the most developed species"? Or, do we mean "the natural order which encompasses the most developed and diverse types of beings in patterns of mutual adaptation and support?" In the former, organization is a standard which is only used to compare the various species, and we are asked to favor the highest species at the expense of all the others. In the latter, organization is a standard which is used to compare natural systems, and we are asked to favor that natural order which most successfully incorporates the characteristics of harmony, diversity, and subtlety of response. Among the classical teleological ethical theories there is not unanimity on this question of which organizational ideal would be the basis for our value judgments, but the latter view clearly predominates. Although it would be instructive to compare the classical philosophers who advance the latter kind of ideal and assess the coherence and plausibility of their various formulations, it is not necessary to do so for the purposes of this paper. While it is clear that we have many teleological theories to choose from, it does not especially matter whether the *telos* we choose is a "great chain of being," a religious conception of cosmological design, a naturalistic conception of evolution, etc. All we really need is an indication of the outlines of a non-anthropocentric teleological system so that we can decide how we ought to behave with respect to animals. Among those who adopt this type of view there is general agreement on three highly relevant theses: (1) that value is not to be placed solely in human projects and interests, (2) that there is special value in a situation in which a great variety of beings are adjusted to or are seeking adjustment to each other; i.e., when beings are subtle (more fully adapted) in their responses to each other, and (3) that the most perfect and complete state of affairs is one in which every species finds a place in the natural order and in which the existence and functioning of any one species is not a threat to the existence and functioning of any other species. In other words, there is agreement on the ideal of a rich and developed natural order.

If we now examine the effects of the human institution of meat production, we will see that this practice is inconsistent with holding to the teleological ideal of a diversified and highly-evolved environment for natural life. Indeed, it impoverishes the natural order in a way paralleled by few other practices. In order to fatten animals for slaughter, vast quantities of grain must be produced and fed to them.[8] This in turn requires that vast wilderness areas must be converted into farm lands, and this in turn means that the wild animals which flourished in those wilderness areas will die. The institution of meat production replaces these wild and high-spirited species with what may be an equal quantity of animal life, but the replacements are creatures which are remarkable only in their singularly dull countenance.[9] Their environment is purposely designed to avoid stimulation in any way except those that will put pounds of meat on their bones.

If this practice "de-animalizes" animals, it also de-humanizes human beings. The vast stores of grain which are processed through these lethargic beasts are withheld from large numbers of people who face starvation or a debilitating malnutrition. Consequently, the de-humanization is evident in two ways: it directly affects those who are losing their human capacities to deal with the world, and it indirectly affects those whose moral sensibilities are subverted by the daily duplicity of stuffing themselves with meat while complaining about the miserable state of the world.

None of this is necessary. It is not necessary to continue to convert wilderness into farm land, wild animals into domesticated animals, or real human beings into zombies. It is one and the same practice which has all of these effects, and its prompt discontinuation will mean that we can begin to place a proper value on both natural life *and* human life.

The right not to be eaten gains new significance when it is placed in this larger context. The conclusion of this line of reasoning is not that every animal which now exists has the right to exist. The conclusion is that the natural *telos* is a diversified environment in which organic beings are capable of symbiosis as well as spontaneity (localized autonomy) and that any practice which inhibits the development of this type of environment ought to be discontinued. Since meat-eating is a conspicuous example of a human practice which has this effect, it should be discontinued, and a right not to be eaten should be *ascribed* to animals. However, it does not follow that the right not to be eaten must be ascribed to every member of the current generation of *domesticated* animals. These animals are elements of the very process by which wilderness and spontaneous animal life are destroyed, and it is a complicated empirical question as to how this type of being can be phased out and how a richer natural life can be restored.

This way of analyzing the issue removes the artificial character of the debate over the rights of animals. It rejects the assumption that the issue can be resolved by an appeal to the nature of the concept of rights (*in abstracto*). By examining the total natural and social context in which values and rights are grounded, we are in a position to notice that appetites which occasion large-scale transformations in a life-supporting natural system deny the *rights* of all beings that could have prospered in this natural order.[10] This way of analyzing the issue also has the advantage of providing a basis for our moral intuition that it is wasteful to sacrifice a more highly organized being when a lesser being will do. Our intuition is that adaptation and subtlety of response are intrinsic to the environment of value which has been discussed above. Thus in normal circumstances we do not feel morally justified in destroying the most highly evolved creatures in this natural system.

Regardless of what is to be done with the domesticated animals now living, it should be clear that a teleological ethic—if it is consistently applied to our practices in the natural world—gives us a mandate for ascribing rights to animals (that is to say, to wild animals). The ideal of developed natural beings in developed natural relationships places an obligation on the human species. The obligation is to cease the destruction of wild (developed) animal life for the sake of satisfying an unnecessary and wasteful appetite. The vegetarian's moral intuition is correct even if the vegetarian's absolute and rigorous (deontological) way of formulating the problem is not. We are justified in *ascribing* a right not to be eaten to animals inasmuch as (a) they need not be sacrificed in order to maintain human life and health (i.e., a lower being will do),[11] and (b) the practice of meat production has the effect of decimating the population of wild animals. Moreover, the human institution of meat-eating has the further effects of both destroying the balanced natural environment which is necessary for sustaining a multitude of life-forms and undermining the abilities of human beings to function in human ways. While a teleological ethic does not forbid us from killing animals under any circumstances, it does place upon us the obligation to discontinue the production and consumption of meat and to take up those alternative styles of living which will allow natural life to be natural and human life to be human.

Notes

1. A teleological theory of obligation can be simply defined as a theory which "maintains the moral rightness or wrongness of an action is a function of the good that is produced in the world, and nothing else" (Richard T. Garner and Bernard Rosen, *Moral Philosophy*, Macmillan & Co., New York 1967, p. 24). A wide variety of ethical positions can find a place within the general designation "teleological ethic." As Robert Olson has observed, virtually every ethic up through the early modern (pre-Kantian) period can be classified as teleological. (Cf. "Teleological Ethics" in *Encyclopedia of Philosophy,* Collier Macmillan, New York 1967, Vol. 8, p. 88.) Among the classical teleological ethical theories are Plato's ethical idealism, Aristotle's natural teleology, and the various formulations of the "great chain of being" ethic (including Leibniz's process teleology). What all of these ethics have in common is the conviction that one must come to grips with the basic nature of the highest good before other questions concerning value can be satisfactorily answered. Furthermore, they all share the belief that harmony, diversity, and subtlety of response are essential constituent properties of the system which is guided by the *telos*. While

there are serious disagreements on how much emphasis should be placed on each of these factors, as well as on how the various factors are related to each other, often reflecting developments in the debate over the One and the Many, there is sufficient agreement on the nature and status of the highest good for the purposes of this paper, viz. to show that the values implicit in a teleological ethic of this kind should lead us to major changes in the ways we think of and treat animals. Although it is not always clear exactly what a teleological ethic includes, it is clear that such an ethic provides the basis for ruling out any practice (including meat production) which causes great losses in diversity and mutual adaptation.

2. This formulation of the concept of rights presupposes that the ideal which is put forward in classical teleological theories can be stated without an anthropocentric bias. The fact that many of these classical ethical theories were also "eudaemonistic," i.e. primarily concerned with human happiness, has obscured their more general thesis about a system of value achievement. . . .

3. Saint Thomas Aquinas, *Summa Theologica* (Benziger Brothers, 1918), Part II, Question 65, Article 3.

4. Immanuel Kant, *Lectures on Ethics,* trans. By Louis Infield (Harper and Row, 1965), p. 241.

5. The comparison of animals with plants does not prove either (a) that plant life is not valuable, or (b) that in a choice between the well-being of a particular grouping of animal life and a particular grouping of plant life the former should always be preserved at the expense of the latter. A teleological ethic does not force us into such dilemmas because it takes into consideration the total environment bearing on value achievement. Thus it is in principle possible to place a very high priority on the preservation of a particular species of plant life if such a species is implicated in the survival of a complex ecosystem. Nevertheless, what the comparison does show (in a teleological ethic) is that *ceteris paribus* the more highly developed individual is to be favored.

6. D. G. Ritchie, "Why Animals Do Not Have Rights," in Regan and Singer (eds.), *Animal Rights and Human Obligations* (Prentice-Hall, 1976), p. 184.

7. For an estimate of the relative amounts of protein provided by grain v. Beef, see Note 8 below.

8. Peter Singer has noted that 21 lbs. of grain protein must be fed to a steer for each pound of beef protein produced. Even if the ratio is lower than this (and it is for some other animals), the waste from and moral implications of this practice are still extraordinary.

9. It might be argued that if we dramatically reduced the human population, we could continue to eat meat while restoring the kind of natural life discussed here. However, this argument is not consistent with the endorsement of a teleological ethic which favors the maximum development of the more highly organized beings consistent with the diversification of nature. There would be reductions in human beings in order to have greater quantities of unresponsive, domesticated animals. There would be a loss of active, highly organized beings in both human and animal life.

10. Cf. Note 5 above. If it takes 21 pounds of grain protein to feed a steer enough to produce every 1 pound of beef protein, then the person who eats the beef protein is in effect depriving twenty other persons of an equivalent amount of protein—protein which cannot be available to them while meat production and consumption are in fashion.

11. In fact a lower being would be much better. Saturated fat is the principal cause of circulatory ailments and heart disease.

An Ecological Argument
for Vegetarianism

Peter S. Wenz

*In this essay, Peter Wenz (1942–   ), a philosophy profes-
sor at Sangamon State University, proceeds from the nor-
mative assumption that "healthy ecosystems are of value,
that the value of an ecosystem is positively related to its
degree of health, and that at least part of this value is independent of the interests of human and other sentient
beings." According to Wenz, if this assumption is granted,
one must also concede "the prescription to become a vegetarian." He does not argue that a* strict *vegetarianism is
implied: individuals requiring special diets or societies
whose well-being would be jeopardized by large-scale vegetarianism are morally exempt. But the focus of Wenz's
defense is squarely upon ecological integrity, not animal
rights or human welfare. Vegetarianism reduces needless
cruelty to animals and the waste of foodstuffs available to
humans, but it foremost protects the ability of ecosystems to
maintain and regenerate themselves. He concludes his discussion by responding to critics such as J. Baird Callicott
who argue that ecological stability is enhanced rather than
harmed by carnivorism, demonstrating that such a position does not hold up. It is important to keep in mind that
Wenz does not offer his position as an alternative to other
defenses of vegetarianism based on either utility theory or
animal rights. Instead, it is intended to complement them.*

189

I

To the prudential, humanitarian, utilitarian, and deontological arguments for vegetarianism, I would like to add an ecological argument.[1] I will suppose, for the sake of argument, that healthy ecosystems are of value, that the value of an ecosystem is positively related to its degree of health, and that at least part of this value is independent of the interests of human and other sentient beings. This is not to deny that human interests and sentient experiences have value, but to affirm that the value of a healthy ecosystem does not rest entirely upon these other values.

The following argument is thus hypothetical in form. If one accepts the independent value of healthy ecosystems, then one must accept the prescription to become a vegetarian. The antecedent is controversial. Kantians and hedonistic utilitarians will not accord the required value to ecosystems, whereas W. D. Ross's formalism and G. E. Moore's idealistic utilitarianism are compatible with this value. Rather than repeat the arguments here, I refer the reader to the appropriate literature and move on to the vegetarian implications of believing that healthy ecosystems are intrinsically good.[2]

The "vegetarian implication" that I endorse in the present paper is limited, but nonetheless of great practical significance. Except for those relatively few people whose health would be endangered by vegetarianism, members of industrial societies have an absolute duty, as opposed to a merely prima facie duty, to adopt a diet that does not include the meat of animals that have been deliberately raised for food, nor of animals acquired through the hunting methods employed almost universally in industrial societies. This would be a diet without MacDonald's hamburgers, without ground meat, or steak or chicken or port from the grocery store, without Kentucky Fried Chicken, and without pepperoni or sausage or ham on one's pizza, to mention but a few of the ways in which the prescribed diet differs from that of most Americans. The implications of the argument are thus considerable. But the argument falls short of prescribing anything at all for some people (traditional hunter-gatherers and those with special dietary problems), and does not prescribe strict vegetarianism for anyone (because strict vegetarianism excludes eating even the small quantities of fish that may be acquired through ecologically benign fishing). In these respects, the argument is like the utilitarian argument for vegetarianism. Yet, as in the case of the utilitarian argument, the argument presented here prescribes so many dietary changes in the direction of vegetarianism for so many of our society's omnivores, that it is not unreasonably labeled an argument for vegetarianism.

II

If healthy ecosystems are of value, and the value of an ecosystem is positively related to its health, then, according to both ethical theories that are compatible with this value, one has a moral reason to avoid needlessly impairing the health of any ecosystem. To do so is to diminish the good, which runs afoul of both the formalistic duty of nonmaleficence and the (ideal) utilitarian duty to maximize the good. The same theories endorse repairing the damage one has done to an ecosystem's health. Formalism includes a duty of reparation, and repairing damage would, all other things being equal, maximize the good. Further, one ought, when possible, to promote or improve the health of ecosystems. This accords with both the formalist duty of beneficence and the utilitarian duty to maximize the good.

However, the value of healthy ecosystems is just one among many values. So on either ethical theory, the duties to avoid harming, to repair damage and to improve the health of ecosystems are only prima facie. They apply when all other things are equal.

This may suggest to some people that these duties are overridden whenever they call for behavior that the agent finds inconvenient or irksome. But such a view ignores the distinction between moral and prudential obligations. A moral obligation is affected by and responsive to considerations relating not only to the agent, but to at least some other beings as well. A purely prudential obligation, by contrast, is affected by and responsive to considerations relating to the agent alone. The slightest inconvenience to the agent could override an obligation only if no weight is accorded to considerations relating to others, which is to say, only if the obligation in question is prudential rather than moral. Any prima facie moral obligation requires more, if it is to be overridden, than the slightest inconvenience to the agent. Since the obligations to refrain from harming, to repair harm done, and to promote the health of ecosystems are moral obligations, they cannot be overridden by the slightest inconvenience to the agent.

III

One way that people can reduce their negative impact upon, and promote the health of ecosystems is by becoming vegetarians (of the sort mentioned earlier). Less cultivation is needed to feed vegetarians than omnivores because the animals eaten by omnivores must themselves be fed by vegetation grown on the land. But most of the nutritional value of this vegetation is used by the animals for their own bodies' maintenance. So people who eat plants instead of feeding them to animals can feed themselves by growing fewer plants and cultivating less land.[3]

The cultivation of land is almost universally detrimental to an ecosystem's health. One ecosystem is healthier than another if it has a greater ability to regenerate itself. In the words of Aldo Leopold, "Health is the capacity of the land for self-renewal."[4] The surface of the Moon and Parmenides' One are paradigm cases of non-ecosystems. They include neither generation nor regeneration. Central Illinois is typical of land under cultivation. A few species, such as human beings, corn and soybeans are overrepresented, while the general diversity of species is very small (compared to a wilderness area). The soil is eroding faster than it is being built (hence the massive use of fertilizers) and insect populations tend toward inordinate growth (hence the massive use of pesticides). The capacity for self-regeneration is thus very limited. Take away the fertilizers, pesticides and herbicides, and the fields of corn and soybeans would change rapidly; they would not regenerate in their current form.

Healthy ecosystems may be compared to healthy organisms. A healthy plant or animal has the power to regenerate itself in the context of the environmental conditions to which it is adapted by evolution. By contrast, an animal that is seriously ill may require blood transfusions, a respirator, and other artificial life-support systems if it is to remain alive. If it dies, the matter of which it is composed will continue to exist, but will no longer participate in the same system of relationships that characterized the living organism.

The herbicides, pesticides and fertilizers used in Central Illinois are like the artificial life-support systems that may be used to keep an animal alive. Just as the necessity of artificial life support indicates ill health in an organism, the necessity of pesticides and the like indicates ill health in Central Illinois' agricultural ecosystems. In both cases, ill health is indicated by the inability of a system (or organism) to regenerate itself. Central Illinois would be ecologically healthier were it not farmed.

The ecologically disruptive impact of agriculture is not due entirely to the use of modern agricultural methods. In the ancient Near East the emergence of agriculture caused "the local extinction of large wild animals, deserts replacing forests, the degradation of grasslands and the disappearance of soil.[5] In the Far East, as well, agriculture accounts for eroded slopes surrounding ancient cities, their burial under successive layers of silt, and periodic floods and pestilence. Wilderness areas are almost universally healthier than areas that are farmed.

Some land is not suitable for growing plants that humans can eat, but can be used to grow vegetation that animals can eat. People can make nutritional use of this land only by eating the animals raised upon it. However, this method of deliberately raising animals for food also degrades the ecosystems involved. The herded species are overrepresented in the ecosystem just as is corn in Central Illinois. So are the plant species upon which the herds feed. The general variety of animal species is reduced because predators are eliminated to protect the flock, and other grazing animals are crowded out of the limited food supply. The man-made machines used in the process of controlling and moving the herd are ecologically disruptive, and range overuse often causes ecological difficulties. The result is a diminished capacity for self-regeneration. Just as a sick individual may need to have fluids drained from her body in an artificial manner, so members of the herded species must be eliminated by massive human intervention, because humans are the species' only predators. If human beings ignore the flock for a considerable period of time, overgrazing will denude the landscape. Rains will then wash away the topsoil, reducing floral regeneration. The herd will starve for lack of food. They will be unable to regenerate themselves. In short, the ecosystem will die, to be replaced by another.

A vegetarian population would allow such land to remain in the ecologically healthier wilderness state. Thus, whether animals are raised for human consumption through farming or herding, people could feed themselves in a less ecologically disruptive manner by being vegetarians. Their prima facie obligation to reduce their negative impact upon and promote the health of ecosystems thus gives them a prima facie obligation to be vegetarians.

IV

It is true that alfalfa cropping enriches soils by adding nitrogen to them. Nitrogen enrichment can enhance an area's generative and regenerative capacities. So one way of improving the ecological health of an area that has nitrogen depleted soil is to grow alfalfa there before allowing the area to return to a wilderness state. People can make nutritional use of the resulting alfalfa only by going through the animal cycle. From the purely ecological perspective meat should occasionally be raised this way and consumed by people. This would allow some of people's nutritional requirements to be met in a way that, unlike most agricultural production, is ecologically constructive, rather than destructive. The same reasoning supports raising animals for human consumption on garbage, the waste from vegetable processing, and the like.

But some human beings have special needs for the consumption of meat and are therefore exempt from the current argument for vegetarianism. It is assumed that their physical health is of greater value than is the ecological disvalue that is typically caused by eating meat. Occasional alfalfa cropping and the like makes it possible to feed (many of) these people without any ecological disvalue. But this does not justify anyone else eating meat grown deliberately for human consumption.

There are, of course, objections to eating meat that are distinct from the ecological considerations raised here. Peter Singer objects to meat consumption on utilitarian grounds,[6] and Tom Regan on the basis of animal rights.[7] Any concessions made in this paper to the practice of eating meat relate solely to ecological considerations, and are not meant to imply that the practice is acceptable from the perspectives of utilitarianism or animal rights. I am here considering the implications only of the ecological perspective.

Some meat is available from animals that have not been deliberately raised for human consumption. These are animals that have grown in the wild. They can be acquired through ecologically benign hunting, such as that undertaken by many hunter-gatherers, and by such hunting advocates as Aldo Leopold and Paul Shepard. Such hunting is ecologically benign because it does not detract from the ecosystem's ability to regenerate itself. However, ecologically benign hunting represents an insignificantly small percentage of the hunting conducted world-wide. The small quantities of meat acquired by it should, for humanitarian and ecological reasons, be reserved for those with special medical problems, since alfalfa cropping and the like are unlikely to be sufficient for their needs.

An exception should be made in this regard for some contemporary hunter-gatherers. Their entire way of life depends upon the (ecologically benign) hunt meeting some of their nutritional needs. The loss they would experience by becoming vegetarians, like that of people with special medical problems, is more than can be justified by the ecological good that their vegetarianism would do.

Some fishing could be ecologically benign and result in large catches, though at present little fishing is conducted in this manner. But if a great deal were, healthy people would be able to eat some fish, but probably much less than at present. (Again, this is the case when the issue is viewed solely from the ecological perspective).

V

Some people might be surprised to learn that vegetarianism is ecologically better than omnivorous eating, because they think that if everyone became a vegetarian, the world would be populated by increasing hordes of cows, hogs and chickens, who would plague humanity and cause ecological disaster. However, this fear is ill-founded. Farmers currently control the size of their flocks and so would be able to reduce them appropriately as the demand for meat diminished. But most species need not become extinct, either. Some of their members could probably be returned to suitable wilderness area (after sufficient research, so as to avoid such ecological disruption as that caused by burros in the Grand Canyon, mustangs in Wyoming and camels in the California desert).

The fact that omnivorous diets are ecologically destructive does not imply that all vegetarian diets are ecologically benign. It is, for example, ecologically damaging to raise tomatoes and pineapples monoculturally. But this does not diminish one's prima facie obligation to be a vegetarian. It means merely that being a vegetarian does not discharge completely one's prima facie obligation to reduce one's negative impact upon and promote the health of ecosystems. The obligation requires (prima facie) that we alter many aspects of our lives, in areas as diverse as transportation, recreation and family planning. But the point of the present paper is that we are required to become vegetarians.

If the arguments above are correct, I have so far shown that people have a prima facie obligation to be vegetarians, and that this obligation is not overridden by very slight inconveniences to the agent. I will now show that except for those with special health problems, people have an obligation true and simple, one that is not prima facie, to *become* vegetarians.

For healthy people, no loss in nutrition or health need accompany a change to a vegetarian diet. There will be some loss in gustatory pleasure, but this need be no more than temporary. Delicious vegetarian meals can be made as easily, and often more inexpensively, than the dishes they replace. Thus, the major obstacle to becoming a vegetarian is the trouble associated with abandoning old patterns of behavior and adopting new ones. This inconvenience is considerable, but temporary, lasting only a matter of months, at most. If one can remain a vegetarian for many years, then the burden of becoming one is smaller per unit of time during which one can be a vegetarian, than is the ecological benefit per unit of time of a vegetarian over an omnivorous diet. This is because each day a person is a vegetarian, the strain that his or her food consumption puts on the biosphere is cut by more than one-half.[8]

Because individuals differ, no one can be certain that his or her longterm experience of loss will not be very great. But the testimony of those who have already become vegetarians gives everyone very good evidence that in the long run being a vegetarian involves very little loss. So everyone has an obligation, which is not prima facie, to at least *become* a vegetarian, and remain so long enough for the formation of habits that have for other people made vegetarianism convenient and aesthetically pleasurable.

The value of healthy ecosystems does not diminish the value of human well-being, so the consequences for the general level of human well-being of a massive shift to vegetarianism must be

assessed. These consequences are mostly positive. It would be easier and less expensive to feed a vegetarian than an omnivorous population. Thus, we would all gain at the supermarket. More important, it would be easier to eliminate malnutrition and starvation
among human beings as nutritious food was produced more efficiently. (Of course, this does not by itself guarantee that the poor
would actually be fed.) The improved ecosystems resulting from
vegetarianism could be of recreational, esthetic and scientific benefit to people.

On the negative side, the meat industry would be ruined, cre-
ating hardships for those who depend upon it for income. There is
however, a general belief in our society that the commercial hardships created by changing consumption patterns are more than
compensated for by the benefits associated with such changes.
Thus, we do not censure those who are voluntarily buying small,
fuel-efficient cars, even though this creates difficulties in the auto
industry. We do not look back with moral disdain upon those who
chose eighty years ago to light their homes with electricity, rather
than gas. We have no more reason to question the moral propriety
of a change to vegetarianism. Indeed, we have less, due to the obviously great human benefits to be derived from the change, and to
the fact that the change is called for by the obligations to minimize
the harm one does to ecosystems and to promote their health.

VI

J. Baird Callicott, in his generally excellent article "Animal Liberation: A Triangular Affair,"[9] maintains that the earth's biosphere is
best protected by people remaining omnivores rather than becoming vegetarians. One's prima facie obligation to reduce one's negative impact upon and promote the health of ecosystems would thus
require that one continue eating meat. Callicott does not dissent
from the view urged here that, all other things being equal, vegetarian humans are lesser burdens on the biosphere than their
omnivorous counterparts. He notes, however, that vegetarianism
"increases available food resources for human beings. The human
population would probably, as past trends overwhelmingly suggest,
expand in accordance with the potential thus afforded. The new
result would be fewer nonhuman beings and more human beings

who, of course, have requirements of life far more elaborate than even those of domestic animals, requirements which would tax other 'natural resources' (trees for shelter, minerals mined at the expense of topsoil and its vegetation, etc.) more than under present circumstances. A vegetarian human population is therefore *probably* ecologically catastrophic."

The first thing to note is that the argument here is not that general vegetarianism would be ecologically catastrophic, but that an increased human population would be so, which is of course correct. So Callicott is not denying the ecological advantages of the prescriptions that people *both* stop eating meat *and* stabilize or decrease their population.

He maintains, however, on the basis of "past trends" (he might have invoked Malthus, as well) that the human population tends to expand in accordance with the food available to people. Following the first prescription, vegetarianism, thus makes it unlikely that people will follow the second, population stabilization or reduction. But the Malthusian prediction is surely ill-founded. Contemporary industrial and post-industrial societies (i.e. Western Europe, Japan and the United States) illustrate almost universally that an increased availability of food, whether created by altered agricultural practices or by agricultural imports paid for with manufactured goods, need not be accompanied by population increase. The populations in these countries are either levelling off, stable or declining slightly. Is there any reason to think that if food became increasingly available due not to increased agricultural or industrial output, but because people became vegetarians, that the effect on population would be any different? I see none. Quite to the contrary, if people were so moved by the ecological argument presented here as to change their eating habits, the last thing one would expect them to do is apply the money they save on food to the birth and rearing of a child they would not otherwise have had. So the connection between vegetarianism and population increase upon which Callicott's argument turns is factually ill-founded and psychologically implausible.

Reliance upon a Malthusian assumption about human behavior is inappropriate in an argument against vegetarianism for yet another reason. Suppose the assumption were correct, that people could be relied upon to increase their population so as to fully use their food production potential. Twentieth century technology has made that potential so great that the corresponding population increase would be great enough to lead to nothing short of world-wide ecological disaster. All roads would lead to perdition. Whether people were vegetarians or omnivores, whether industry were powered by solar energy or nuclear energy, whether there were disarmament or a continued arms race, population increase would destroy the biosphere. The danger of ecological disaster would, therefore, not serve to favor any one course of action over its opposite, and so would not favor either an omnivorous or a vegetarian diet over the other. Thus, even when his Malthusian assumption is granted, Callicott does not present a cogent argument against vegetarianism.

Finally, Callicott raises a consideration which does not so much argue against vegetarianism as denigrate its importance. He writes in relation to the horror that animal liberationists have of factory farming, "The land ethic takes as much exception to the transmogrification of plants by mechanicochemical means as to that of animals. The important thing, I would think, is not to eat vegetables as opposed to animal flesh, but to resist factory farming in all its manifestations, including especially its liberal application of pesticides, herbicides, and chemical fertilizers to maximize the production of vegetable crops."

The ecological perspective of the present paper supports this call to eat "organically as opposed to mechanicochemically produced food," because pesticides, herbicides and chemical fertilizers damage the biosphere greatly. But this in no way diminishes the moral importance, from the same ecological perspective, of avoiding the consumption of meat. Presently, most of the meat consumed in our society is produced by feeding animals mechanicochemically produced grains. Cutting these animals out of the human food chain would therefore drastically reduce the mechanicochemical production of vegetables. Second, current food production methods are used, as Callicott notes, because they "maximize the production of *vegetable* crops." Making the transition that he and I both advocate to organic vegetable production will result in a food shortage unless the relative "inefficiency" of organic farming is compensated for by some additional efficiency elsewhere. So long as the human population is over two or three billion, which means in the foreseeable future, vegetarianism will be needed to create additional efficiency in the human food chain in order to make the transition to organic agriculture feasible. So contrary to Callicott's view, the importance of eliminating the mechanicochemical production of vegetables strengthens rather than weakens the ecological argument for vegetarianism.

Notes

1. Peter Singer alludes to an ecological argument for vegetarianism in *Animal Liberation* (New York: Avon Books, 1975), pp. 177–178 and 257, but he does not develop the argument. More oblique reference to this theme is made by Michael W. Fox, "Philosophy, Ecology, Animal Welfare, and the 'Rights' Question," *Ethics and Animals*, Harlan B. Miller and William H. Williams, eds. (Clifton, NJ: The Humana Press, 1983), pp. 308–310. Frances Moore Lappé, *Diet for a Small Planet* (New York: Ballantine Books, 1975), Part 1, relates vegetarianism to decreased human land use, but does so in the context of a humanitarian rather than an ecological argument for vegetarianism.

W. D. Ross's formalist theory of "What Makes Right Acts Right" is compatible with the ecological argument presented here when it is combined with G. E. Moore's "ideal utilitarian" conception of the good. Ross's duty of beneficence then requires that, all other things being equal, people should preserve and promote healthy ecosystems. See *The Right and the Good* (Oxford, 1930), pp. 24–26. In sum, I am alluding to Ross's theory of the right, not his theory of the good. The others mentioned in this footnote supply appropriate theories of the good for the purposes of this paper.

2. G. E. Moore's *Principia Ethica* (Cambridge: Cambridge University Press, 1903), pp. 81–85. Christopher Stone, "Should Trees Have Standing? Toward Legal Rights for Natural Objects," *Southern California Law Review* 45 (1972), 450–501; Holmes Rolston III, "Is There An Ecological Ethics?", *Ethics* 85 (1975–1975), 93–101, and "Are Values in Nature Subjective or Objective?", *Environmental Ethics* 4 (1982), 125–151; John Rodman, "The Liberation of Nature?", *Inquiry* 20 (1977), 83–141; Tom Regan, "The Nature and Possibility of an Environmental Ethic," *Environmental Ethics* 3 (1981), 19–34; William Godfrey-Smith, "The Value of Wilderness," *Environmental Ethics* 1 (1979), 309–319.

3. John Harris, "Killing for Food" in *Animals, Men and Morals*, ed. Godlovitch and Harris (New York: Taplinger Publishing Co., 1972), p. 107.

4. Aldo Leopold, *A Sand County Almanac* (New York: Ballantine Books, 1970), p. 258.

5. Paul Shepard, *The Tender Carnivore and the Sacred Game* (New York: Charles Scribner's Sons, 1973), p. 20.

6. *Animal Liberation.*

7. *The Case for Animal Rights* (Berkeley: The University of California Press, 1983).

8. See footnote 3 and Lappé, pp. 9–12.

9. J. Baird Callicott, "Animal Liberation: A Triangular Affair," *Environmental Ethics* 2 (Winter, 1980), pp. 311–389. See especially pp. 335–336.

The Pretext of "Necessary Suffering"

⚜

Stephen R. L. Clark

In this selection from his 1977 The Moral Status of Animals, *Stephen R. L. Clark (1945–   ), lecturer in moral philosophy at the University of Glasgow, takes on those individuals who grant that it is wrong to cause unnecessary suffering to sentient creatures but then go on to argue that a certain degree of imposed suffering to animals is inevitable if conventional dietary customs are to continue. Clark accuses such individuals of bad faith. It is pointless if not dishonest to concede the immorality of inflicting needless suffering on animals "if anything at all will do as a context for calculating necessity." A carnivorous diet, although often appealed to as a justification for causing animals to suffer, is in fact a flimsy pretext. Humans do not need animal flesh to survive or prosper. Nor will the simple craving for flesh suffice as a legitimate excuse: it could be less cruelly assuaged by eating dead humans. It follows, then, that flesh eating poses no genuine exception to the minimal ethical precept that one ought not, directly or indirectly, to inflict unnecessary suffering on sentient creatures. Given the nonnecessity of carnivorism, Clark even more strongly concludes that "those who still eat flesh when they could do otherwise have no claim to be serious moralists."*

L et us admit, then, that animals in varying degrees feel pain and fear, and that we have no general reason to think them less subject to these ills than we: if they have fewer forebodings, if they do, then by the same token they are buoyed by fewer hopes. A burning cat is as agonized as any burning baby. Even where we do have reason to impute a lesser pain, yet pain is painful. It has been urged, in a last desperate throw, that animals, who lack any consciousness of themselves, must find each pang of agony a new thing without past or future, so that they do not seem to themselves to suffer any long pain. Even if we grant the premises—which I do not—yet even pangs of agony are ill to be borne.

To be distressed by something is to find it an evil. We are so constituted that we are inclined to make others' distress our own, the more sincerely the closer these others touch us. Our solidarity in suffering with other sentient life, so Ruland thought . . . , was enough to induce in us a respect for the life and dignity of non-human animals.[1] He was too sanguine. But at least it is very common now to pay lip-service to the thesis that it is wrong to cause unnecessary suffering to an animal. Necessity, of course, is often defined in terms of human activities that are simply unquestioned, so that (at most) such a rubric merely rules out technical incompetence. Such incompetency, being a symptom of inefficiency, might be left to the technicians' care were it not that a fundamental inattention to animals as beings to be taken seriously so often blinds men even to their own profit. . . .

The difficulty about this slogan (that animals be spared unnecessary pains), minimal as it is, is that it already proves too much for the orthodox to stomach. I emphasized that it *is* a minimal principle, that it makes no mention of rights to life, and indeed allows "rights" only in the sense that animals are not reckoned mere "stocks and stones." As a radical moralizer I would go much further . . . ; but here for a moment I will take my stand, on the claim that one should not cause unnecessary suffering to animals. Incompetence is to be ruled out, and so also are certain ends which are merely specious, or immoral in themselves. Wanton torture, or torture to impress a friend, or demonstrate man's superiority (to whom?), or to satisfy a particular minor whim for some food-stuff whose production involves enormous suffering, or to save oneself the trouble of taking due care must all, precisely, be counted wanton. The human ends within which we calculate necessity must be of some weight, otherwise the principle is *entirely* meaningless—for it licenses even incompetence: "if I am to conduct this experiment, run this farm with the minimum of care and attention and without troubling my head or heart about the problematic distress of the lower creatures, a certain amount of suffering in my stock will be *necessary*." "It is of little use to claim 'rights' for animals . . . if we show our determination to subordinate those rights to anything that can be construed into a human want."[2] It is of little use claiming that it is wrong to inflict unnecessary suffering if anything at all will do as a context for calculating necessity.

Consider then: it is not necessary to imprison, torture or kill animals if we are to eat. The laborious transformation of plant proteins into animal protein, indeed, is notoriously inefficient, and wastes a great deal of food that would greatly assist human beings in less carnivorous places. It is not necessary for us to do this: I say nothing of what may be necessary for the Eskimos, for whom the orthodox display a sudden, strange affection when confronted by zoophiles (though the health of Eskimos might be better served by supplying plant-food). It is not necessary for us, and our affection for other human beings would perhaps be better shown by ceasing to steal their plant protein in order to process it into a form that pleases our palates.

But perhaps flesh-eating, for some reason that escapes me, is held to be an end of sufficient weight. Consider then: it is not necessary to submit animals to their present distress if we are to eat meat. Indeed, it is not strictly necessary to submit them to any distress: now that liberal orthodoxy has apparently decreed that any concern over the integrity of the human corpse is a mere anti-social superstition (witness the demand for transplantable organs), it would seem a simple solution both to our flesh-craving and to the increasing storage problem to cook the victims of automobile accidents. But even if this economical solution is rejected, and our flesh-craving must be satisfied with the death of animals, it is still not necessary to submit them to the foul distresses involved in factory farming. The only case under which these distresses *are* necessary is if we are to go on eating flesh in our present quantities and without attention to their well-being—but that is a reason for changing our habits, not for defending them.

What follows for our obligations? Simply, that if we are to

mean what we say in outlawing the unnecessary suffering of animals, we must become, at the least, vegetarians. I repeat that I say nothing here about the Eskimos, nor have I any interest in the desert-island castaway. We are not on a desert-island. Nor have I yet seen an orthodox moralist defend rape or even fornication merely on the ground that most males trapped in solitary and beyond the law with a naked and lubricious female would find their principles a little strained. . . .

[I]t is plain that the present system of intensive farming cannot be defended. We can replace animal-protein by plant protein, even if we preserve some free-range beef herds and the like. We can reduce the amount of flesh we eat to the point where such whole-food farms can cope with the demand. We can always look for measures that will lessen distress in our animals rather than measures that will give us the least possible trouble.

Let us then be vegetarians, at least. For those who have recognized flesh-eating for what it is, the merest addiction, and one, as Shelley saw, to "kindle all putrid humours in [our] frame" ("Queen Mab" 8.215)—for such moralists the step is easy. It is not necessary, rather it is incompetent, to kill and torture animals to eat. Those who retain the end of flesh-eating but admit the iniquity of factory-farming and the need to reduce the demand for flesh, are in practice in no better state. Where so many eat so much flesh, there is no "moderate amount of flesh" that the moralist can decently eat. Until all have reduced their demands to whatever "reasonable compromise" between the passion for flesh and the distress of the animals the moralist has fixed, he must reduce his demand to zero. Again, he cannot in practice declare that he will eat only decently reared flesh—for he cannot tell what flesh has been decently reared, and if by chance he did he would, by buying it, be putting pressure on the farmer in question to increase his output by increasingly intensive methods. The open iniquity of factory farming has this merit, that it makes self-deception about the horrors caused to animals more difficult. It has this demerit, that by contrast the old ways seem courteous and kind. So the existence of concentration camps acclimatises us to slums.

There is a simple technique for evading responsibility for the things we cause to be done. In the popular morality of the Sherpas, "To kill a living creature is sin. . . . To kill yak and sheep is sin for the butchers, but not for those who eat the meat." The hypocrisy of this is revealed by the fact that though exorcizing spirits is also a sin, it is not the exorcizing lama, but the man who hires the lama, who is sinning. There is perhaps a certain sense in the casuistry: Buddhist monks, like Franciscan friars, thought it proper to eat what they were given. It was Brother Elias, the Judas of the Franciscan movement, who attempted a total ban on flesh-food, and was rebuked for it by God's angel. But however proper this may be for such, who would (in principle at least) surrender their own flesh to those in need, it hardly excuses the average irresponsibility of those who *require* other men to inflict suffering upon animals when, as they know, it is unnecessary. . . .

Honourable men may honourably disagree about some details of human treatment of the non-human, but vegetarianism is now as necessary a pledge of moral devotion as was the refusal of emperor-worship in the early Church. Those who have not made that pledge have no authority to speak against the most inanely conceived experiments, nor against hunting, nor against fur-trapping, nor bear-baiting, nor bull fights, nor pulling the wings off flies. Flesh-eating in our present circumstances is as empty a gluttony as any of these things. Those who still eat flesh when they could do otherwise have no claim to be serious moralists.

Notes

1. L. Ruland, *Foundations of Morality* (Tr. T. A. Ruttler), London 1936, pp. 373 ff.

2. H. S. Salt, *Animals' Rights*, London 1922, p. 7.

Like Driving a Cadillac

Frances Moore Lappé

Few individuals have done as much in this century to draw attention to the economic and ecological dangers of stock farming as Frances Moore Lappé. As author of Diet for a Small Planet *and other books as well as founder of the Institute for Food and Development Policy, Lappé has researched and written on the issues of diet and public policy for over twenty years. In this selection, taken from* Diet, *she argues that meat eating is a resource-costly habit. The agribusiness farming of food animals wastes enough protein to otherwise feed the world's population, consumes huge quantities of increasingly depleted ground-water reserves, and, in the United States alone, produces polluting animal waste equivalent to almost half the world's entire supply of human waste. While Lappé's essay is not an explicit defense of ethical vegetarianism, its discussion of the brutal social and environmental consequences of factory farming and mass flesh consumption has clear moral implications. As William A. Alcott said in the nineteenth century, "If . . . the adoption of the vegetable system by nations and individuals would greatly advance the happiness of all, in every known respect, and if, on this account, such a change in our flesh-eating countries would be sound policy, and good economy—then we have another moral argument in its favor."*

A few months ago a Brazilian friend, Mauro, passed through town. As he sat down to eat at a friend's house, his friend lifted a sizzling piece of prime beef off the stove. "You're eating that today," Mauro remarked, "but you won't be in ten years. Would you drive a Cadillac? Ten years from now you'll realize that eating that chunk of meat is as crazy as driving a Cadillac."

Mauro is right: a grain-fed-meat-centered diet *is* like driving a Cadillac. Yet many Americans who have reluctantly given up their gas-guzzling cars would never think of questioning the resource costs of their grain-fed-meat diet. So let me try to give you some sense of the enormity of the resources flowing into livestock production in the United States. The consequences of a grain-fed-meat diet may be as severe as those of a nation of Cadillac drivers.

A detailed 1978 study sponsored by the Departments of Interior and Commerce produced startling figures showing that *the value of raw materials consumed to produce food from livestock is greater than the value of all oil, gas, and coal consumed in this country.*[1] Expressed another way, one-third of the value of *all* raw materials consumed for all purposes in the United States is consumed in livestock foods.[2]

How can this be?

The Protein Factory in Reverse

Excluding exports, about one-half of our harvested acreage goes to feed livestock. Over the last forty years the amount of grain, soybeans, and special feeds going to American livestock has doubled. Now supposing 200 million tons, it is equal in volume to all the grain that is now imported throughout the world.[3] Today our livestock consume ten times the grain that we Americans eat directly[4] and they outweigh the human population of our country four to one.[5]

These staggering estimates reflect the revolution that has taken place in meat and poultry production and consumption since about 1950.

First, beef. Because cattle are ruminants, they don't need to consume protein sources like grain or soybeans to produce protein for us. Ruminants have the simplest nutritional requirements of any animal because of the unique fermentation "vat" in front of their true stomach. This vat, the rumen, is a protein factory. With the help of billions of bacteria and protozoa, the rumen produces microbial protein, which then passes on to the true stomach, where it is treated just like any other protein. Not only does the rumen enable the ruminant to thrive without dietary protein, B vitamins, or essential fatty acids, it also enables the animal to digest large quantities of fibrous foodstuffs inedible by humans.[6]

The ruminant can recycle a wide variety of waste products into high-protein foods. Successful animal feeds have come from orange juice squeeze remainders in Florida, cocoa residue in Ghana, coffee processing residue in Britain, and bananas (too ripe to export) in the Caribbean. Ruminants will thrive on single-celled protein, such as bacteria or yeast produced in special factories, and they can utilize some of the cellulose in waste products such as wood pulp, newsprint, and bark. In Marin County, near my home in San Francisco, ranchers are feeding apple pulp and cottonseed to their cattle. Such is the "hidden talent" of livestock.

Because of this "hidden talent," cattle have been prized for millennia as a means of transforming grazing land unsuited for cropping into a source of highly usable protein, meat. But in the last 40 years we in the United States have turned that equation on its head. Instead of just protein factories, we have turned cattle into protein disposal systems, too.

Yes, our cattle still graze. In fact, from one-third to one-half of the continental land mass is used for grazing. But since the 1940s we have developed a system of feeding grain to cattle that is unique in human history. Instead of going from pasture to slaughter, most cattle in the United States now first pass through feedlots where they are each fed over 2,500 pounds of grain and soybean products (about 22 pounds a day) plus hormones and antibiotics.[7]

Before 1950 relatively few cattle were fed grain before slaughter,[8] but by the early 1970s about three-quarters were grain-fed.[9] During this time, the number of cattle more than doubled. And we now feed one-third more grain to produce each pound of beef than we did in the early 1960s.[10] With grain cheap, more animals have been fed to heavier weights, at which it takes increasingly more grain to put on each additional pound.

In addition to cattle, poultry have also become a big consumer of our harvested crops. Poultry can't eat grass. Unlike cows, they need a source of protein. But it doesn't have to be grain. Although prepared feed played an important role in the past, chickens also scratched the barnyard for seeds, worms, and bits of organic matter. They also got scraps from the kitchen. But after 1950, when poultry moved from the barnyard into huge factorylike compounds, production leaped more than threefold, and the volume of grain fed to poultry climbed almost as much.

Hogs, too, are big grain consumers in the United States, taking almost a third of the total fed to livestock. Many countries, however, raise hogs exclusively on waste products and on plants which humans don't eat. When Nobel Prize winner Norman Borlaug heard that China had 250 million pigs, about four times the number here, he could hardly believe it. What could they possibly eat? He went to China and saw "pretty scrawny pigs." Their growth was slow, but by the time they reached maturity they were decent-looking hogs, he admitted in awe. And all on cotton leaves, corn stalks, rice husks, water hyacinths, and peanut shells.[11] In the United States, hogs are now fed about as much grain as is fed to cattle.

All told, each grain-consuming animal "unit" (as the Department of Agriculture calls our livestock) eats almost two and a half tons of grain, soy, and other feeds each year.[12]

What Do We Get Back?

For every 16 pounds of grain and soy fed to beef cattle in the United States we only get 1 pound back in meat on our plates.[13] The other 15 pounds are inaccessible to us, either used by the animal to produce energy or to make some part of its own body that we do not eat (like hair or bones) or excreted.

To give you some basis of comparison, 16 pounds of grain has twenty-one times more calories and eight times more protein—but only three times more fat—than a pound of hamburger.

Livestock other than cattle are markedly more efficient in converting grain to meat . . . ; hogs consume 6, turkeys 4, and chickens 3 pounds of grain and soy to produce 1 pound of meat.[14] Milk production is even more efficient, with less than 1 pound of grain fed for every pint of milk produced. (This is partly because we don't have to grow a new cow every time we milk one.)

Now let us put these two factors together: the large quantities of humanly edible plants fed to animals and their inefficient conversion into meat for us to eat. Some very startling statistics result. If we exclude dairy cows, the average ratio of all U.S. livestock is 7 pounds of grain and soy fed to produce 1 pound of edible food.[15] Thus, of the 145 million tons of grain and soy fed to our beef cattle, poultry, and hogs in 1979, only 21 million tons were returned to us in meat, poultry and eggs. *The rest, about 124 million tons of grain and soybeans, became inaccessible to human consumption.* (We also feed considerable quantities of wheat germ, milk products, and fishmeal to livestock, but here I am including only grain and soybeans.) To put this enormous quantity in some perspective, consider that 120 million tons is worth over $20 billion. If cooked, it is the equivalent of 1 cup of grain for every single human being on earth every day for a year. . . .[16]

Enough Water to Float a Destroyer

"We are in a crisis over our water that is every bit as important and deep as our energy crisis," says Fred Powledge, who has just written the first in-depth book on our national water crisis.[17]

According to food geographer Georg Borgstrom, to produce a 1–pound steak requires 2,500 gallons of water![18] The average U.S. diet requires 4,200 gallons of water a day for each person, and of this he estimates animal products account for over 80 percent.[19]

"The water that goes into a 1,000–pound steer would float a destroyer," *Newsweek* recently reported.[20] When I sat down with my calculator, I realized that the water used to produce just 10 pounds of steak equals the household consumption of my family for the entire year. . . .

Mining Our Water

Irrigation to grow food for livestock, including hay, corn, sorghum, and pasture, uses 50 out of every 100 gallons of water "consumed" in the United States. (Some of this production is exported, but not the major share, since close to half of the irrigated land used for livestock is for pasture and hay.[21]) Other farm uses—daily irrigation for food crops—add another 35 gallons, so agriculture's total use of water equals 85 out of every 100 gallons consumed. (Water is "consumed" when it doesn't return to our rivers and streams.)

Over the past fifteen years grain-fed-beef production has been shifting from the rain-fed Corn Belt to newly irrigated acres in the Great Plains. Just four Great Plains states, Nebraska, Kansas, Oklahoma, and Texas, have accounted for over three-fourths of the new irrigation since 1964, and most of that irrigation has been used to grow more feed. Today half of the grain-fed beef in the United States is produced in states that depend for irrigation on an enormous underground lake called the Ogallala Aquifer.[22]

But most of this irrigation just can't last.

Rainwater seeps into this underground lake so slowly in some areas that scientists consider parts of the aquifer a virtually non-renewable resource, much like oil deposits. With all the new irrigation, farmers now withdraw more water each year from the Ogallala Aquifer than the entire annual flow of the Colorado River. Pumping water at this rate is causing water tables to drop six inches a year in some areas, six feet a year in others. And lower water tables mean higher and higher costs to pump water. The Department of Agriculture predicts that in 40 years the number of irrigated acres in the Great Plains will have shrunk by 30 percent.[23]

In only two decades Texans have used up one-quarter of their groundwater.[24] Already some wells in northern Texas are running dry, and with rising fuel costs, farmers are unable to afford pumping from deeper wells. Why is this water being mined in Texas? Mostly to grow sorghum for the feedlots which have sprung up in the last decade.

When most of us think of California's irrigated acres, we visualize lush fields, growing tomatoes, artichokes, strawberries, and grapes. But in California, the biggest user of underground water, more irrigation water is used for feed crops and pasture than for all these specialty crops combined. In fact, 42 percent of California's irrigation goes to produce livestock.[25] Not only are water tables dropping, but in some parts of California the earth itself is sinking as groundwater is drawn out. According to a 1980 government survey, 5,000 square miles of the rich San Joaquin valley have already sunk, in some areas as much as 29 feet.[26]

The fact that water is free encourages this mammoth waste. Whoever has the $450 an acre needed to level the land and install pumping equipment can take groundwater for nothing. The replacement cost—the cost of an equal amount of water when present wells have run dry—is not taken into consideration. This no-price, no-plan policy leads to the rapid depletion of our resources, bringing the day closer when alternatives must be found—but at the same time postponing any search for alternatives.

Ironically, our tax laws actually entice farmers to mine groundwater. In Texas, Kansas, and New Mexico, landowners get a depletion allowance on the groundwater to compensate for the fact that their pumping costs rise as their groundwater mining lowers the water table. Moreover, the costs of buying the equipment and sinking the well are tax-deductible. Irrigation increases the value of the land enormously, but when the land is sold the profits from the sale are taxed according to the capital gains provisions; that is, only 40 percent of the difference between the original cost of the farm and its sale price is taxed as ordinary income. The rest is not taxed at all.

Few of us—and certainly not those whose wealth depends on the mining of nonrenewable resources—can face the fact that soon we will suffer for this waste of water. Donald Worster, author of *Dust Bowl: The Southern Plains in the 1930's* (New York: Oxford University Press, 1979), interviewed a landowner in Haskell County, Kansas, where $27.4 million in corn for feed is produced on about 100,000 acres of land irrigated with groundwater. He asked one of the groundwater-made millionaires, "What happens when the irrigation water runs out?"

"I don't think that in our time it can," the woman replied. "And if it does, we'll get more from someplace else. The Lord never intended us to do without water."[27]

Livestock Pollution

Some people believe that although we feed enormous quantities of high-grade plant food to livestock with relatively little return to us as food, there is really no loss. After all, we live in a closed system, don't we? Animal waste returns to the soil, providing nutrients for the crops that the animals themselves will eventually eat, thus completing a natural ecological cycle.

Unfortunately, it doesn't work that way anymore. Most manure is not returned to the land. Animal waste in the United

States amounts to 2 billion annually, equivalent to the waste of almost half of the world's human population.[28] Much of the nitrogen-containing waste from livestock is converted into ammonia and into nitrates, which leach into the groundwater beneath the soil or run directly into surface water, thus contributing to high nitrate levels in the rural wells which tap the groundwater. In streams and lakes, high levels of waste runoff contribute to oxygen depletion and algae overgrowth.[29] American livestock contribute five times more harmful organic waste to water pollution than do people, and twice that of industry, estimates food geographer Georg Borgstrom.[30]

A Fatal Blindness

[O]ur [meat] production system is ultimately self-destructive because it is self-deceptive; it can't incorporate the many costs I've outlined here. It can't look to the future. And it blinds those closest to it from even seeing what is happening. Thus, the task of opening our eyes lies more heavily with the rest of us—those less committed to protecting the status quo. As awakening stewards of this small planet, we have a lot to learn—and fast.

Notes

1. *Raw Materials in the United States Economy 1900–1977*; Technical paper 47, prepared under contract by Vivian Eberle Spencer, U.S. Department of Commerce, U.S. Department of Interior Bureau of Mines, p. 3.

2. Ibid. Table 2, p. 86.

3. U.S. Department of Agriculture, *Livestock Production Units, 1910–1961*, Statistical Bulletin No. 325, p. 18, and *Agricultural Statistics, 1980*, p. 56. Current world imports from *FAO at Work*, newsletter of the liaison office for North America of the Food and Agricultural Organization of the United Nations, May 1981.

4. David Pimentel et al., "The Potential for Grass-Fed Livestock: Resource Constraints," *Science*, February 22, 1980, volume 207, pp. 843 ff.

5. David Pimentel, "Energy and Land Constraints in Food Protein Production," *Science*, November 21, 1975, pp. 754 ff.

6. Robert R. Oltjen, "Tommorrow's Diets for Beef Cattle," *The Science Teacher*, vol. 38, no. 3, March 1970.

7. The amount varies depending on the price of grain, but 2,200 to 2,500 pounds is typical. See note 13 for more detailed explanation of grain feeding.

8. U.S. Department of Agriculture, Economic Research Service, *Cattle Feeding in the United States*, Agricultural Economics, Report No. 186, 1970, p. 5.

9. Ibid. p. iv.

10. U.S. Department of Agriculture, *Agricultural Statistics, 1979 and 1980*, Tables 76 and 77.

11. Norman Borlaug in conversation with Frances Moore Lappé, April 1974.

12. U.S. Department of Agriculture, *Agricultural Statistics, 1980*, Table 76.

13. How many pounds of grain and soy are consumed by the American steer to get 1 pound of edible meat?

(a) The total forage (hay, silage, grass) consumed: 12,000 pounds (10,000 pre-feedlot and 2,000 in feedlot). The total grain- and soy-type concentrate consumed: about 2,850 pounds (300 pounds grain and 50 pounds soy before feedlot, plus 2,200 pounds grain and 300 pounds soy in feedlot). Therefore, the actual percent of total feed units from grain and soy is about 25 percent.

(b) But experts estimate that the grain and soy contribute more to weight gain (and, therefore, to ultimate meat produced) than their actual proportion in the diet. They estimate that grain and soy contribute (instead of 25 percent) about 40 percent of weight put on over the life of the steer.

(c) To estimate what percent of edible meat is due to the grain and soy consumed, multiply that 40 percent (weight gain due to grain and soy) times the edible meat produced at slaughter, or 432 pounds: .4 x 432 = 172.8 pounds of edible portion contributed by grain and soy. (Those who state a 7:1 ratio use the entire 432 pounds edible meat in their computation.)

(d) To determine how many pounds of grain and soy it took to get this 172.8 pounds of edible meat, divide total grain and soy consumed, 2850 pounds, by 172.8 pounds of edible meat: 2850 divided by 172.8 = 16–17 pounds. (I have taken the lower figure, since the amount of grain being fed may be going down a small amount.) These estimates are based on several consultations with the USDA Economic Research Service and the USDA

Agricultural Research Service, Northeastern Division, plus current newspaper reports of actual grain and soy currently being fed.

14. U.S. Department of Agriculture, Economic Research Service and Agriculture Research Service, Northeastern Division, consultations with staff economists.

15. In 1975 I calculated this average ratio and the return to us in meat from *Livestock-Feed Relationships*, National and State Statistical Bulletin #530, June 1974, pp. 175–77. In 1980 I approached it differently and came out with the same answer. I took the total grain and soy fed to livestock (excluding dairy) from *Agricultural Statistics, 1980*. The total was about 145 million tons in 1979. I then took the meat and poultry and eggs consumed that year from *Food Consumption, Prices, and Expenditures*, USDA-ESS, Statistical Bulletin 656. (I excluded only the portion of total beef consumed that was put on by grain feeding, about 40 percent, and reduced the total poultry consumed to its edible portion; i.e., minus bones.) The total consumption was about 183.5 pounds per person or 20 million tons for the whole country. I then divided the 145 million tons of grain and soy fed by the 20 million tons of meat, poultry, and eggs produced by this feeding and came up with the ratio of 7 to 1. (Imports of meat are not large enough to affect this calculation appreciably.)

16. Calculated as follows: 124 million tons of grain "lost" annually in the United States x 2,000 pounds of grain in a ton = 248 billion pounds "lost" divided by 4.4 billion people = 56 pounds per capita divided by 365 days equals .153 pound per capita per day x 16 ounces in a pound—2.5 ounces per capita per day—1/3 cup of dry grain, or 1 cup cooked volume.

17. *Water: The Nature, Uses and Future of Our Most Precious and Abused Resource* (New York: Farrar, Straus & Giroux, 1981).

18. Georg Borgstrom, Michigan State University, presentation to the Annual Meeting of the American Association for the Advancement of Science (AAAS), 1981.

19. Ibid.

20. "The Browning of America," *Newsweek*, February 22, 1981, pp. 26ff.

21. To arrive at an estimate of 50 percent, I used *Soil Degradation: Effects on Agricultural Productivity*, Interim Report Number Four of the National Agricultural Lands Study, 1980, which estimates that 81 percent of all water consumed in the United States is for irrigation. And I used the *Fact Book of U.S. Agriculture*, U.S. Department of Agriculture, Misc. Publication No. 1065, November 1979, Table 3, which shows that about 64 per-

cent of irrigated land is used for feed crops, hay, and pasture. Sixty-four percent of 81 percent is 52 percent.

22. Philip M. Raup, "Competition for Land and the Future of American Agriculture," in *The Future of American Agriculture as a Strategic Resource*, edited by Sandra S. Batie and Robert G. Healy, A Conservation Foundation Conference, July 14, 1980, Washington, D.C., pp. 36–43. Also see William Franklin Lagrone, "The Great Plains," in *Another Revolution in U.S. Farming?*, Lyle Schertz and others, U.S. Department of Agriculture, ESCS, Agricultural Economic Report No. 441, December 1979, pp. 335–61. The estimate of grain-fed beef's dependence on the Ogallala is from a telephone interview with resource economist Joe Harris of the consulting firm Camp, Dresser, McKee (Austin, Texas), part of a four-year government-sponsored study: "The Six State High Plains Ogallala Aquifer Agricultural Regional Resource Study," May 1980.

23. William Franklin Lagrone, "The Great Plains," op. cit., pp. 356ff.

24. "Report: Nebraska's Water Wealth is Deceptive," *Omaha World-Herald*, May 28, 1981.

25. Giannini Foundation of Agricultural Economics, *Trends in California Livestock and Poultry Production, Consumption, and Feed Use: 1961–1978*, Information Series 80–5, Division of Agricultural Sciences, University of California Bulletin 1899, November 1980, pp. 30–33.

26. General Accounting Office, *Groundwater Overdrafting Must Be Controlled*, Report to the Congress of the United States by the Comptroller General, CED 80–96, September 12, 1980, p. 3.

27. Donald Worster, *Dust Bowl: The Southern Plains in the 1930's* (New York: Oxford University Press, 1979), p. 236.

28. *Environmental Science and Technology*, vol. 4, no. 12, 1970, p. 1098.

29. Barry Commoner, *The Closing Circle* (Knopf, 1971), p. 148.

30. Georg Borgstrom, *The Food and People Dilemma* (Duxberg Press, 1973), p. 103.

Images of Death and Life:
Food Animal Production
and the Vegetarian Option

Harriet Schleifer

In this selection, which originally appeared in 1985, social activist and co-founder of Quebec's Animal Liberation Collective Harriet Schleifer (1952–   ) touches on several issues. Writing with the passion of an activist, she discusses the meat industry's mega-marketing campaign to sell its product to consumers and points out that flesh eating is often touted by the industry as a status symbol. She then goes on to examine the ethical, ecological, and economic consequences of mass meat consumption, arguing that it is inhumane, destructive of natural resources, and a contributor to world hunger. In opposition to conventional cultural standards, she calls for "a basic shift in moral consciousness, a repudiation of human superiority over other species through force." Vegetarianism, she claims, "is both a fundamental and a personal means of affirming such a shift," offering as it does "the greatest potential for the radical transformation of our society." Schleifer concludes by advocating individual and collective boycotting of the food animal industry's products.

ystematic factual accounts of the meat industry's treatment of animals . . . [A]re almost numbing in the evidence they present of the needless exploitation and widespread abuse that our diet creates for other sensitive living beings. Surveying the problem on the broadest scale, they distract one's attention from the suffering of each individual and blur its unique significance.

Many people are overwhelmed by the extent of food animals' suffering. The rearing of livestock is commonplace in virtually every society on the planet, and there are billions of deaths every year. Indeed, in *The Hungry Planet* Georg Borgstrom has calculated that the global population of domestic food animals equals our own human population. When the number of fish caught and killed to feed us annually is added to this total, the death toll becomes staggering.

In the USA the meat industry is the second largest manufacturing and processing concern (the largest is the manufacture of cars) and worth approximately $50 billion a year. It plays a prominent role in other countries' economies as well. Large-scale fishing is of primary economic importance in much of the Third World, and significant in developed countries. Related industries, such as steel production and pharmaceutical manufacture, dramatically increase the meat and fish producers' influence and power. The steel industry supplies cages and machinery for factory farms, while more than half the world's production of antibiotics is used in medicated animal feeds.

But these statistics need not be disheartening. However great its size, the farm animal industry is extremely vulnerable to the threat posed to its continued existence by public compassion for the animals it victimizes. Well aware of this fact, meat producers go to extraordinary lengths to conceal and mystify the true nature of their activities. Factory farms and slaughterhouses are hidden from view, located away from urban cores and relatively isolated. Most prohibit all visitors. Our consciousness of what goes on in them is blurred by the way in which meat is typically sold, in neat, bloodless packets. Body parts which would identify meat as animal corpses—feet, tails, fur, eyes—are carefully removed, ostensibly for consumer convenience.

Slick and seductive advertising campaigns reinforce these illusions. Thoughts of living, suffering animals are virtually obliterated. Everyone is familiar with the smiling cows, dancing pigs, and laughing chickens depicted on meat, dairy, and egg industry packaging and vehicles, and which are also frequently used as restaurant logos. Wayne Swanson and George Schultz report in their book *Prime Rip,* which investigates fraud in the meat industry, that "the industry has always operated strong educational and public-relations programs to keep Americans thinking positive thoughts about meat." To cite just one example, culled from Dudley Giehl's *Vegetarianism: A Way of Life,* the California Beef Council routinely issues press releases to "some 500 newspapers and over 300 radio and television stations in California." Other animal exploiters, such as the dairy and egg industries, use similar tactics. Promotional handouts to supermarkets are common. These banners, posters, and literature are referred to as "consumer information" despite their industry source. Supermarkets themselves spend the largest proportion of their own advertising budgets on publicity for meat. Meat is a high profit margin product, with a mark-up of about 20 per cent, and they consider it a principal draw for customers.

Aside from their fraudulent use of animals in advertising, some meat industry advocates apparently have no qualms about manipulating public prejudices to sell their products. In *Vegetarianism: A Way of Life* Giehl describes a booklet called "The Story of Meat," published by the American Meat Institute. It asks the question, "Why couldn't the North American Indians living in a land teeming with natural resources lift themselves above their primitive stone age culture?" The answer? The Indians "failed to domesticate livestock for their principal food necessity—meat." Sexism is also condoned and encouraged. *Prime Rip* mentions a $4.6 million advertising and marketing campaign designed to sell "sensual beef": "'Sex sells everything else,' said a spokesman, 'so why not beef?'"

Special promotional efforts are directed at children, whose open and uninhibited appreciation of living animals presents the most dangerous challenge to a meat-centered diet. Giehl notes that a large proportion of meat industry propaganda is distributed in the public school system. This is confirmed by Swanson and Schultz. According to their research, "trade groups are a major provider of educational materials on nutrition (obviously stressing the importance of meat)." Such material contains not pictures of slaughterhouses but attractive portraits of living animals and commentary on what they "do for us." The MacDonald hamburger chain is a major producer of children's television commercials. In one of these Ronald McDonald explains that hamburgers "grow in little hamburger patches." Star-Kist has developed a series of ads in which Charlie the Tuna tries to be caught so he can be processed by the company. Perhaps the most outrageous example, however, is an Oscar Mayer commercial in which a group of children sing: "Oh, I wish I was an Oscar Mayer wiener, for that is what I'd really like to be." As Giehl wryly comments, "The old maxim that honesty is the best policy does not apply if you expect children to eat meat with compunction."

The food animal industry has largely succeeded in its attempt to make desirable practices that are inexcusable. A measure of its success is found in *Prime Rip*, whose authors state in all seriousness that "Many Americans would sooner give up their freedom than give up their meat." Unfortunately, meat has become a symbol of status. Preferences for specific kinds of meat vary widely, ranging from insects to frogs' legs, from buffalo steaks to pork chops, but it is universally related to wealth, and its absence from the diet is regarded as voluntary or involuntary privation. The problem becomes evident in the marketing of meat analogues, which the status-conscious meat eater rejects as "imitations," no matter how much they resemble the real thing.

Faced with the onslaught of propaganda and the fact that the consumption of animal products is a respected and entrenched custom in our society, it is little wonder that few people have the temerity to challenge the basis of the entire system. Still, nothing frightens the meat industry more than the idea of vegetarianism. They oppose its spread with aggressive vigor. Francis Moore Lappé's book *Diet for a Small Planet* was criticized as hysterical, unscientific faddism. Of course, significantly, it is the food animal industry that either funds or otherwise supports most research which claims to prove that its products are healthy and nutritionally sound. Its manipulation extends even to the most respected scientific bodies. The 1980 National Academy of Science report exonerating cholesterol as a factor in disease was prepared by paid consultants of the meat, dairy and egg industries. In 1976 intense lobbying by angry meat producers forced the American government to delete a recommendation in the McGovern report on nutrition,

"Decrease consumption of meat," and to change it to "Choose meats, poultry and fish which will reduce saturated fat intake." Such obsessive hostility towards the alternative of a vegetarian diet strongly suggests that its promotion may be a powerful weapon against the habit of meat consumption.

The animal liberation ethic demands a basic shift in moral consciousness, a repudiation of human superiority over other species through force. Our way of viewing the world becomes more compassionate, more respectful of the needs of other living beings. The vegetarian lifestyle is both a fundamental and a personal means of affirming such a shift. Confronting the oppression of food animals through vegetarianism lies at the heart of the animal liberation ethic and offers the greatest potential for the radical transformation of our society.

Killing, unless it is done as a merciful act, must involve a deliberate withholding of sympathy from the victim. Done repeatedly, it results in a hardening of the emotions. Thomas More, although not a vegetarian, recognized this when he wrote *Utopia* in 1518: "The Utopians feel that slaughtering our fellow creatures gradually destroys the sense of compassion, which is the finest sentiment of which our human nature is capable." The same theme has reappeared in countless writings, usually with a suggestion that heightened human sensitivity is a desirable goal.

The ethical argument for vegetarianism becomes even more persuasive when one considers the reasons for it that are not related directly to farm animal welfare. (I will not discuss any of the health considerations that make the vegetarian diet an attractive option, since they do not have an essentially moral basis.) Wildlife conservation is a popular concern for many people, though few know the extent to which domestic animals compete with wildlife for space and resources. Ninety per cent of agricultural land in the United States, more than half of the country's total land area, is presently used for meat, dairy and egg operations, making it unavailable as human or wildlife habitat. Nor do people realize that numerous species, among them the dodo and the passenger pigeon, became extinct because we chose to eat them and that other species are currently endangered for the same reason. Furthermore, the men who exploit animals for food do not take kindly to wildlife that interferes with their activities: American ranchers kill predators, antelope and prairie dogs, Australian sheep farmers kill kangaroos, and Japanese fishermen destroy dolphins—in each case because the animals are "pests." Other animals are "incidentally" exterminated; tuna and shrimp nets drown hundreds of porpoises and sea turtles.

Ecologically the production of animal products is wasteful and inefficient. According to Keith Akers' *A Vegetarian Sourcebook*, energy and water requirements are between ten and 1,000 times greater than they would be for an equal amount of plant food. Consequently, most soil erosion (90 percent), consumptive use of water (80 percent) and deforestation (70 percent) is the result of livestock agriculture. It is also responsible for most of our water pollution.

Meat consumption in Western countries is a primary cause of hunger, both at home and in the Third World. Only 42 percent of an animal's original weight becomes meat. In addition to this wastage, John McFarlane, Executive Director of the Council for Livestock Protection, has calculated that "the amount of meat lost each year through careless handling and brutality would be enough to feed a million Americans a year." Although the unfair distribution which characterizes international trade makes it an unlikely dream, it is also a fact that if everyone in the developed world became a vegetarian, it would be possible to give four tons of edible grain to every starving person.

Many studies have speculated on the connection between meat eating and inter-human violence, although none has been conclusive. Nevertheless, the links are suggestive. In *Fettered Kingdoms*, John Bryant mentions several sources which note that the rate of violent crime in communities is related to the presence of slaughter facilities. Certainly it is true that the slaughterer's occupation is grim and brutalizing. Few people work in stockyards by choice. Most are there because their families have worked in the business; many are illegal immigrants. Workers are forced to become indifferent to the vocal protests and struggling of the animals they kill. It is likely that the callousness they develop in order to endure the realities of their jobs will affect other areas of their lives.

The fact that most consumers try to ignore the horror of meat animals' lives and deny its moral importance suggests an underlying awareness of the unjustified cruelty involved. Human beings do not like to see themselves as killers, notwithstanding the exaggerated glamour we ascribe to the caveman and hunter. We are relieved to have animals killed for us by others, relieved that the distressing sights and sounds of death do not haunt our meals. Some of us repress the facts so well that we can hardly believe that suffering and death are part of meat production. In an interview published in the March/April issue of *Agenda*, Quebec animal rights activist Karen Urtnowski tells of a schoolmate who thought that steaks were surgically removed from cows, who then returned to a peaceful existence in their meadows. If such an example seems farfetched, consider the fact that a large percentage of intelligent, educated adults do not associate cow's milk with the animal's pregnancy. Nor do they realize that the unwanted calves become the raw material of the veal industry.

Whatever their level of awareness, it remains true that people eat meat because they are accustomed to its color, shape, texture and flavour, and have been conditioned to regard it as a highly desirable food. Their attitudes must be challenged, and changed. As Peter Singer has pointed out in *Animal Liberation*, "those who, by their purchases, require animals to be killed have no right to be shielded from this or any other aspects of the production of the meat they buy. If it is distasteful for humans to think about, what can it be like for the animals to experience it?"

The meaning of what we do to meat animals transcends hard statistics. The destructive impulses of the human spirit are grimly revealed in the suffering of these creatures, and most of us naturally recoil from the vision. As with the image of nuclear disaster, knowledge of the meat industry's exploitation of animals confronts us with the unthinkable, and demands a personal response we may feel unable to give. So we reassure ourselves with platitudes about the "necessity of meat" in human nutrition, arguments about our "dominion" over nature and the window-dressing provided by regulations designed to ensure humane slaughter.

Sadly, some elements within the animal rights movement itself have accepted these evasions. In despair at the apparent hopelessness of stopping the exploitation, or unwilling to face its reality, they attempt to be "reasonable" about the issue of food animals. The majority withdraw from the controversy altogether, on the grounds that the public is not ready to deal with it. They offer the myth of the "attainable goal" as a further rationalization. The idea behind this is to attack less widespread abuses, such as hunting or circuses, in the hope that smaller successes will build up the movement's credibility and popular support and allow the issue of food animals to be dealt with effectively later. The difficulty with this approach is that it tends to involve its proponents in lame excuses about their inaction on the larger problem or, worse, in deceit, actual denial that it has any significance. In effect, they reinforce the food animal industry's messages. The public comes to feel that the use of animals for food is in some way acceptable, since even the animal welfare people say so. This cannot help but make it much more difficult to eliminate the practice in the future. Far better to follow the strategy of union activists, who demand 20 percent in the hope of receiving at least 10 percent.

We cannot live in fear of making the public uncomfortable. Change that matters always involves initial doubt and pain, and it is our responsibility to guide that process in a constructive way, to ease the transition from a society that exploits to one that respects other species.

If it is true that once the public understands the immorality of other animal rights issues, it will be easy to convince them to become vegetarians, it is equally true that vegetarianism provides a consistent base for criticizing the lesser wrongs done to animals. Rejecting animal exploitation as ethical vegetarians saves us from the perilous acrobatics involved in dividing animals into two moral categories: animals that it is unequivocally wrong to abuse, and others that it is acceptable to exploit in a benevolent fashion.

Furthermore, the attitude that allows us to raise animals for food colours our treatment of all other creatures, from pets to laboratory animals and wildlife. Once we have accepted that we may utilize animals for so trivial a reason as our enjoyment of the taste of their flesh, it is easy to use them for any purpose which is equally frivolous, such as domesticating them as pets or confining them in zoos to amuse us, or for those which are more serious, such as using them in medical experiments that we believe will save human lives.

Other animal rights activists settle on the "compromise" solution of humane slaughter to ease their dilemma. The contradictions inherent in adopting such a position are evident. To begin with, sincere concern for living individuals leads such people to become, ironically, experts on the techniques of mass death-dealing. They learn to compare the speed, facility and cost of various devices and systems; the question of whether their use is justifiable at all never arises. The worst aspect of the humane slaughter option is that it focuses discussion on the least important consideration, the method of killing. By doing so, it suggests that the taking of life is not a problem, only the way it is done.

At the very core of the animal liberation philosophy is the idea that we should extend consideration to other species' needs and weigh them against our own. How is it possible to do that while denying, prima facie, that food animals should be free to live out their natural life spans and while killing them not even because it is desirable for them to die, for whatever reason, but simply because we enjoy the taste of their dead bodies? The falseness of advocating humane slaughter, while professing to believe in an animal rights ethic, is patently obvious. As John Bryant declares in *Unfettered Kingdoms*, the philosophy behind all food animal farming, whether traditional or intensive, is the same, "the arrogant stance that we can use animals for whatever purpose we wish."

To make matters worse, the notion of humane slaughter ignores the fact that the specific moment of death is only a fraction of a larger process. Even were we to agree that the death of food animals is acceptable, humane slaughter's preoccupation with the brief experience of dying is misleading. Some animal rights groups do demand that provisions made for animals prior to slaughter be humane, that they include adequate food, water and shelter. Yet few are willing to discuss regulations to minimize the terror of animals awaiting their deaths in stockyards. In fact such a goal is impossible to achieve. Death for meat animals does not come as a sudden, unexpected shock. Thousands of animals are assembled in a single location, close to a building that all of them must enter to die. They cannot remain unaware of their fate, and intense fear is the natural and inevitable result.

It sometimes seems as if advocates of meat eating understand the nature of the food animal industry better than we do. Adopting the view that killing is an unpleasant necessity, they are often more clear-sighted about their activities than are animal rights campaigners. The comments of Wayne Swanson and George Schultz, authors of *Prime Rip*, are particularly revealing, all the more so because of the complete absence of any empathy with the animals themselves. Evaluating the possibility of reducing corruption in the meat industry, they state:

No matter how much new technology is developed, and no matter how nicely meat is packaged, the central facts of the meat
business cannot be changed. This is an industry built around
noisy, foul-smelling animals whose fate is to have an eight-
inch-long-pin fired into their foreheads at point-blank range.
Their blood and guts will spill forth on the killing floor, and
their carcasses will be stripped and carved and chopped during
a process that, although it is governed by "humane slaughter"
laws, can be nothing other than gross and brutal.

In any event, exploitation is not just killing. It is also the manipulation of animals' genes to make them machines for our use, the
denial of freedom, the causing of pain and fear throughout their
lifetimes. Death can be a minor evil compared with these. People
who believe that the raising of food animals can be made humane
are deluding themselves. Meat is murder. If an animal does not
have the basic right to exist, any other rights become meaningless.
John Bryant says the "whole concept of 'marketing' living individuals is wrong." It cannot be improved by reforms, however liberal.

The rationale behind much animal abuse, the excuse that an
animal is going to die anyway, so it is all right to do x to it, is tempt-
ing and convenient and quickly erodes all other considerations. The
intensive systems in use today are only the logical and unavoidable
outcome of our general attitude towards farm animals as property.
The animals' welfare and our desire to have high-quality meat are
in direct conflict: well-exercised animals produce stringy meat;
their freedom to control their own sex lives makes births too unpre-
dictable and variable.

As long as a farm animal is perceived as an edible object, an "it"
to be put on our dinner plates, he or she will never have any meaningful rights. Domestication itself is an unnatural process, a method
of enslaving animals and subjecting their life processes to our will.
Animal liberation would return domestic animals to their wild ori-
gins, free to pursue their destinies without human interference.

Concrete individual and group action to promote vegetarianism can
be both simple and significant. All we need to do is boycott the food
animal industry's products. According to my calculations, which
are somewhat complicated and which I will not detail here, every

person who becomes a vegetarian is directly responsible for saving between forty and ninety-five creatures each year, depending on her or his level of meat consumption. It is the single most effective step one can take to assist individual animals.

Those who choose to take collective action as well increase their impact on the situation proportionally. The possibilities are endless. We can demystify meat through public education and pressure on governments. Perhaps a law requiring stores to sell only whole, intact animal bodies would be effective in emphasizing what meat is. We could confront those who promote meat directly. Suitable targets for such action might include single stores, restaurants or, for the more ambitious, nationwide chains. In *Big Mac: The Unauthorized Story of McDonald's* Max Boas and Steve Chain estimate that the corporation, whose hamburgers represent only 1 percent of the wholesale beef in the United States, accounts for the deaths of over 300,000 cattle annually. Closing them down would be a major triumph. We could publicize the vegetarian alternative, informing people about its potential and preparing meals for them to demonstrate its culinary attractiveness.

George Bernard Shaw wrote in his autobiography: "eating the scorched corpses of animals—cannibalism with its heroic dish omitted—becomes impossible the moment it becomes conscious instead of thoughtlessly habitual." As animal rights activists, it is our responsibility to stimulate the necessary thought to make such a transformation possible, both for ourselves and for others.

Dietethics:
Its Influence on
Future Farming Patterns

❧⊱✕⊰❧

Jon Wynne-Tyson

Jon Wynne-Tyson (1924–) is a British publisher and author of several books on vegetarianism and animal rights, including Food for Thought *and* The Extended Circle: A Commonplace Book of Animal Rights. *In this essay, originally delivered at a 1977 conference on The Ethical Aspects of Man's Relationships with Animals, Wynne-Tyson explores the ethics of diet, or "dietethics." The focus of dietethics, he says, extends to both "the animals we eat" and "the world's malnourished and starving human millions." Given the suffering and death inflicted upon animals by conventional husbandry, as well as the colossal amount of grain food fed to them which might otherwise be directly used in the struggle against world hunger, Wynne-Tyson argues that meat consumption and animal farming are ethically unsupportable. As an alternative — the only "feasible" one, in his estimation — he proposes that agriculture turn in the future to vegan farming, which is economically sound as well as ethically sensitive. Wynne-Tyson's brief for dietethics, then, is based upon a humane concern for the welfare of both humans and animals.*

cological studies now embrace considerations unthinkable in orthodox circles a few years ago. Not only our use for, but our treatment of, animals is at last being seen as a legitimate area for investigation.

But of all the ways in which we have exploited and ill-treated other species, their use for human food has until recently been the most overlooked. Now, however, enquiry into our ethical obligations to the many creatures we directly or indirectly consume has become so strong a concern that it perhaps deserves the label (and I fear we live in a labelled age) of Dietethics. That is, the study of the ethics of diet.

These ethics, let it be stressed, relate not only to the animals we eat, but also to the world's malnourished and starving human millions. In order that the affluent nations may enjoy the meat and dairy products that have long been the focal point of their dietary patterns, vast quantities of grain must be fed to cattle. It is not an over-simplification to say that if we abandoned the grossly wasteful habit of eating our plants via the bodies of animals, there need be no starving people in the world today.

Thankfully, such facts are being recognized, not only by previously unconcerned laymen but also in academic and scientific circles. What is more, there is a growing tendency to correlate these various realizations, rather than treat them in isolation.

Indeed, there appears to be increasing acceptance of the view that the science of ecology stands—or should stand—for a concept of life and values in which the practical, the ethical and the philosophical elements are given equal weight. Now that our exploitation of the natural world is at last being seen to be inextricably bound up with the exploitation of our fellow men and women, we are possibly entering a new age in which the understanding we term "ecology" may have an effect similar in many respects to that compound of wonder, knowledge and fierce inner need for an explanation, a sense of direction, and a framework of behavior, that in the past prompted notions of the Deity.

However, there are still many problems and mental blockages to be overcome. While convinced of the value of communication, and of the need to focus on points of accord rather than on our smaller differences, I think it relevant to warn that although ecological concerns have brought wider understanding of the inter-relationships of all species, progress—at least through what we now call the media—is being hampered and misdirected by those whose personal habit patterns influence them more strongly than any rational desire to accept scientific fact, or to arrive at an objective view of our obligations to other sentient life.

The current interest in self-sufficiency is in many respects very welcome, but among its more vociferous spokesmen are those whose concern seems to be more with scale than with any genuine reappraisal of our basic attitudes to other species. These spokesmen include both urban sentimentalizers and pastoral ecomystics, whose determination to cling to the basic diet that until now has been made so easily available by the meat and dairy industries, has provoked their hot defence of "backyard" stock-rearing. That such regression may be possible for some during a transitional period is not denied, but in the long term it is an unrealistic dream for any but a tiny minority; a compromise aimed at reducing rather than eliminating unnecessary cruelty; a measure motivated more by expediency than by compassion.

Perhaps a more dangerous viewpoint needing identification is that expressed by those who conduct anachronistic but popular campaigns to justify the behavioral deficiencies of the most miseducated members of our species. Commentators in this field would have us believe that the impulse to kill is an innate part of man's biological make-up, and that meat and many of its by-products are necessities, rather than mere wants for which there are ample alternatives. One comes across such nonsensical assertions as that "we should be doing something biologically unnatural if we all became herbivores" (Michael Crawford: *Earth in Danger*).

Most Aunt Sallies of this ilk are already flat on their backs. It is doubtful whether any balanced observer will leave this conference with the illusion that there can be any rational, scientific, aesthetic, instinctual, moral or philosophical justification for our treatment of the creatures we wish to eat. Nevertheless, we must identify and deal with the specious arguments of those who at heart seek no fundamental alteration in long-established patterns of habit.

To turn to practicalities, what feasible alternative is there to the present dominant stock-farming economy governing our eating patterns in the West? I suggest there is no doubt that the only alternative in the long term (and it is the long term we must keep constantly in mind) is vegan farming. This is not to suggest that it is practicable to bring orthodox farming policies to a halt overnight, as some of the more hysterically anti-progress lobbies seem to fear. Today's butchers and farmers need not fear for their livelihoods now or in the near future. Fundamental change invariably comes slowly. But they, with us, should face that the only ethical and lastingly workable future economy must be based on farming methods which are solely directed to the growing and consuming of plant foods. There can be no eventual place in such an economy for animals bred under man's control to satisfy his acquired taste for eating their bodies.

These are the first brush-strokes of a rather different picture to that painted by those dinosaurian pragmatists who continue to seek solutions based on animal exploitation. The don't-knock-meat lobby plans actually to *extend* our cruelties by massive programs for farming wild animals on top of a continuing policy of supporting domestic breeds on high protein foods that should go directly, and with far more responsible use of land resources, to humans. Such planning, if we take that vital long-term view, is the opposite of what conservation and ecological studies should be about. It is part and parcel of big agri-business that has spawned such recent developments as the production of protein for animal food from a derivative of natural gas, for the squalid purpose that intensively-reared livestock may continue to bring ever-greater profits to an industry still reluctant to read the writing on the wall.

Many people associate the term "conservationist" with a caring and concerned regard for our environment. But conservationists' pleas for the preservation of wild species need rigorous examination. Preservation for what? Too often, for man to crop them with no more pity than he feels lifting turnips. When I hear the word "conservation" I know that someone is reaching for his gun. If our only motive in conserving certain species is man's long-term benefit, then it would be more compassionate to encourage their earliest possible extinction.

I see no realistic long-term alternative to a world whose natural resources are regarded as factors with which we have to collaborate—not dominate—in order to take our proper place in the scheme of things. I suggest the reasons for this are not only expedient, but evolutionary. The cold arrogance of those who wish man to have self-interested mastery over everything he regards as beneath him is an out-of-date and short-sighted perversion of our responsibilities and potentialities.

However idealistic it may now seem to some, it is surely our role to envisage and work towards a world which is sanely and humanely controlled, not exploited, by those with the vision and humility to question established mores. I say "humility" because it is the arrogance born of long habit and entrenched prejudice that seeks to defend behavioral patterns that have long been a matter of comfortable acceptance for a privileged minority at the expense of the rest of the world.

It seems inevitable that sooner or later nations must collaborate to restrict populations to a size that will enable them to be fed on the many and adequate forms of plant life, while at the same time adopting those policies of deurbanization and deindustrialization that environmentalists are now recognizing to be essential. Indeed, although this is not the place to argue the matter, for it is hardly an arguable or neglected proposition, the fate of the whole world depends upon our species's success in controlling its numbers. No plague or pestilence is a greater threat than the infestation of humanity.

The symbiosis that could and should exist between man and his environment depends upon our adoption of a dietary system in keeping with our physiological structure. Whatever our spiritual potentialities may be (and I have no qualification to deny that they may be infinite), it is accepted fact that physically man is "by design" neither carnivorous nor omnivorous. He is a frugivore, "intended" to eat the fruits, nuts, shoots and other plant foods that form the basis of the normal diet of those great apes that are our nearest relatives. What habits some members of our species have got into since climatic and other factors supervened is neither here nor there. We know too much to suggest seriously that we can bring anything but benefit to ourselves and our environment by returning so far as is possible to that dietary system for which we are chemically and physiologically constituted.

In the gradual relinquishment of animal husbandry in favor of vegan farming methods, silviculture is an area of enormous potential. The important recent book *Forest Farming,* by J. Sholto Douglas and Robert A. de J. Hart, unfortunately failed to make clear that if we give up farming animals, a silvicultural/agricultural world economy could support even today's populations and provide such an abundance of land that a balanced and sane husbandry could be re-established, based on organic methods and bringing to an end the present vicious spiral of artificial fertilizers, herbicides and pesticides. Indeed, the book's findings may well be manipulated by those seeking ways of further prolonging an omnivorous economy by tapping sources of high plant protein for feeding to livestock. This is why the ethics of diet must lead, not be led by, the economics and expediences of the situation. Nevertheless, its findings confirm that the yields from farming food-bearing trees are far greater even than from conventional ground crops, and infinitely in excess of the meager returns from farming animals. Responsibly employed, such facts can herald an age as near to the elysian as anything that man in his present state of evolution has any right to expect.

Can the people who are thinking along these lines any longer be regarded as impractical cranks? I think not. Compare the following extract from literature put out by the Vegan Society of the U.K. with what is currently being stated (often as though it were some astonishing new discovery!) by respected orthodox nutritionists, ecologists and agriculturalists:

"The age of man the ruthless predator is coming to an end. He is wasting his resources and fouling his nest. It is imperative that those who are alive to the enormous challenge of the environmental crisis, go forward (not 'back to nature') to pioneer a way of life that is attainable by all the world's people and sustainable within natural cycles. Wise land use is of primary importance. What is required is a change from traditional agriculture to intensive horticulture, with careful composting of all wastes with plant materials to keep the land in good heart without animal manure or artificial fertilizers. The landscape of a vegan world would show small fields of cereals, fruits, vegetables and compost-producing plants surrounded by shelter-belts of fruit and nut-bearing trees. Hill slopes and other areas unsuitable for cultivation would be used for trees of all types, as a renewable source of fuel and raw material for many purposes, as well as for their function in maintaining the environment. One-sixth to one-third of an acre per head would be required for the vegan diet. Even in densely populated England, which has nearly an acre for each inhabitant, wide areas would be left for wild life and recreation."

Let us consider for a moment what the habit of meat-eating

involves in terms of the world's food supplies. It means the extensive growing of crops, notably grain, in order to feed them to animals from which, after an expensive interval, we take back in exchange an absurdly disproportionate quantity of food in a form that we hallow, quite incorrectly, as being superior to the plant life from which it was derived. In addition to being fed the corn that requires great tracts of the world's land supply, the animals themselves, even in these days of "factory-farming," still need further huge areas for pasture. About four-fifths of the world's agricultural land is used for feeding animals, and only about one-fifth for feeding man directly. Most of the fertile land devoted to cattle could show a much quicker and more economical return if used for crops suitable for direct feeding to human beings. On average, animals eat twenty pounds of protein for every pound they yield as meat. In comparing plant with animal food production in terms of yields per acre in less developed and more developed countries, it has been shown that:

"The plant protein production from cereals and pulses was three to six times the production of milk protein from the same area under the same conditions. For plant protein from leafy vegetables it was seven to twelve times. When these plant/animal ratios were measured against meat protein they were approximately doubled. On the average, about a fifth of the plant protein fed to animals becomes available for human consumption as milk, and about a tenth of it is turned into meat." (*Plant Foods for Human Nutrition*, Vol. I, No. 2, Pergamon Press).

The ratios and methods of calculation vary a good deal, and I have discussed them in more depth in my book *Food For a Future*. But the conclusion is always the same—that the world's human populations could more responsibly and economically be fed directly on plant life. Meat can be phased out (a process governed by demand) just as other forms of food and consumer goods have come and gone in obedience to fashion and the fluctuations of climate and natural resources. So, too, can the trades that depend on animal foods.

So far from vegetarianism springing from the anthropomorphism of predominantly urban dwellers, as has been suggested by its more superficial critics, it and its inevitable successor veganism are increasingly being recognized as a logical, even inescapable, process, essentially relevant, essentially practical, essentially compassionate to all species; the province no longer of the so-called crank, but of scientists and philosophers and clear-thinking laymen.

The practical details of a switch to a farming economy based on plants as the immediate source of mankind's food are well within our competence to grasp and implement. We are within sight of the day when crop rotation, multiple cropping, and adequate land for resting periods, for green manuring, for cover crops, and for the supply of composting materials will have placed the whole sad and shameful practice of stock-rearing, with all its attendant evils, in the annals of an extravagant and barbaric past. The changeover requires only—or, at least, above all—a change of heart and a conscious decision to rethink our educational priorities.

And therein lies the key. It is only by education that these fundamental changes can come about. This has been mentioned during the conference, but too little stressed. Those of us now in adult life must surely recognize that it is the rising generations who most need to be convinced of such basics as the paramount necessity for preventing the infestation of our own species, and for a truly and less selectively compassionate regard for our total environment. The answers lie always with the young. We must educate them away from becoming yet another generation of dinosaurs—a species which, let it be remembered, abandoned flesh-eating for a herbivorous diet too late in the day to avoid extinction!

Contextual Moral Vegetarianism

Deane Curtin

In this selection, excerpted from his "Toward an Ecological Ethic of Care," Deane Curtin (1951–   ), professor of philosophy at Gustavus Adolphus College, offers a defense of vegetarianism founded on an ethic of care, which he and other ecofeminists advocate instead of the rights-based vegetarianism propounded by people such as Tom Regan. Curtin calls himself a "contextual moral vegetarian" because he thinks that sometimes a caring response may entail the killing of animals for food. But in technologically well-off countries, he sees no excuse for meat eating.

In this [essay] I provide an example of a distinctively ecofeminist moral concern: our relations to what we are willing to count as food. Vegetarianism has been defended as a moral obligation that results from rights that nonhuman animals have in virtue of being sentient beings (Regan 1983, 330–53). However, a distinctively ecofeminist defense of moral vegetarianism is better expressed as a core concept in an ecofeminist ethic of care. One clear way of distinguishing the two approaches is that whereas the rights approach is not inherently contextual[1] (it is the response to the rights of all sentient beings), the caring-for approach responds to particular contexts and histories. It recognizes that the reasons for moral vegetarianism may differ by locale, by gender, as well as by class.

Moral vegetarianism is a fruitful issue for ecofeminists to explore in developing an ecological ethics because in judging the adequacy of an ethic by reference to its understanding of food one draws attention to precisely those aspects of daily experience that have often been regarded as "beneath" the interest of philosophy. Plato's remark in the *Gorgias* is typical of the dismissive attitude philosophers have usually had toward food. Pastry cooking, he says, is like rhetoric: both are mere "knacks" or "routines" designed to appeal to our bodily instincts rather than our intellects (Plato 1961, 245).

Plato's dismissive remark also points to something that feminists need to take very seriously, namely, that a distinctively feminist ethic, as Susan Bordo and others argue, should include the body as moral agent. Here too the experiences of women in patriarchal cultures are especially valuable because women, more then men, experience the effects of culturally sanctioned oppressive attitudes toward the appropriate shape of the body. Susan Bordo has argued that anorexia nervosa is a "psychopathology" made possible by Cartesian attitudes toward the body at a popular level. Anorexics typically feel alienation from their bodies and the hunger "it" feels. Bordo quotes one woman as saying she ate because "my stomach wanted it"; another dreamed of being "without a body." Anorexics want to achieve "absolute purity, hyperintellectuality and transcendence of the flesh" (Bordo 1988, 94, 95; also see Chernin 1981). These attitudes toward the body have served to distort the deep sense in which human beings are embodied creatures; they have therefore further distorted our being as animals. To be a person, as distinct from an "animal," is to be disembodied.

This dynamic is vividly exposed by Carol Adams in *The Sexual Politics of Meat* (Adams 1989, part 1). There are important connections through food between the oppression of women and the oppression of nonhuman animals. Typical of the wealth of evidence she presents are the following: the connection of women and animals through pornographic representations of women as "meat" ready to be carved up, for example in "snuff" films; the fact that language masks our true relationship with animals, making them "absent referents" by giving meat words positive connotations ("That's a meaty question;" "Where's the beef?") while disparaging nonflesh foods ("Don't watch so much TV! You'll turn into a vegetable"); men, athletes and soldiers in particular, are associated with red meat and activity ("To have muscle you need to eat muscle"), whereas women are associated with vegetables and passivity ("ladies' luncheons" typically offer dainty sandwiches with no red meat).

As a "contextual moral vegetarian," I cannot refer to an absolute moral rule that prohibits meat eating under all circumstances. There may be some contexts in which another response is appropriate. Though I am committed to moral vegetarianism, I cannot say that I would never kill an animal for food. Would I not kill an animal to provide food for my son if he were starving? Would I not generally prefer the death of a bear to the death of a loved one? I am sure I would. The point of a contextualist ethic is that one need not treat all interests equally as if one had no relationship to any of the parties.

Beyond personal contextual relations, geographical contexts may sometimes be relevant. The Ihalmiut, for example, whose frigid domain makes the growing of food impossible, do not have the option of vegetarian cuisine. The economy of their food practices, however, and their tradition of "thanking" the deer for giving its life are reflective of a serious, focused, compassionate attitude toward the "gift" of a meal.

In some cultures violence against nonhuman life is ritualized in such a way that one is present to the reality of one's food. The Japanese have a Shinto ceremony that pays respect to the insects that are killed during rice planting. Tibetans, who as Buddhists have not generally been drawn to vegetarianism, nevertheless give their own bodies back to the animals in an ultimate act of thanks by having their corpses hacked into pieces as food for the birds.[2] Cultures such as these have ways of expressing spiritually the idea "we are what we eat," even if they are not vegetarian.

If there is any context, on the other hand, in which moral vegetarianism is completely compelling as an expression of an ecological ethic of care, it is for economically well-off persons in technologically advanced countries. First, these are persons who have a choice of what food they want to eat; they have a choice of what they will count as food. Morality and ontology are closely connected here. It is one thing to inflict pain on animals when geography offers no other choice. But in the case of killing animals for human consumption where there is a choice, this practice inflicts pain that is completely unnecessary and avoidable. The injunction to care, considered as an issue of moral and political development, should be understood to include the injunction to eliminate needless suffering wherever possible, and particularly the suffering of those whose suffering is conceptually connected to one's own. It should not be understood as an injunction that includes the imperative to rethink what it means to be a person connected with the imperative to rethink the status of nonhuman animals. An ecofeminist perspective emphasizes that one's body is oneself, and that by inflicting violence needlessly, one's bodily self becomes a context for violence. One becomes violent by taking part in violent food practices. The ontological implication of a feminist ethic of care is that nonhuman animals should no longer count as food.

Second, most of the meat and dairy products in these countries do not come from mom-and-pop farms with little red barns. Factory farms are responsible for most of the 6 billion animals killed for food every year in the United States (Adams 1989, 6). It is curious that steriods are considered dangerous to athletes, but animals that have been genetically engineered and chemically induced to grow faster and come to market sooner are considered to be an entirely different issue. One would have to be hardened to know the conditions factory-farm animals live in and not feel disgust concerning their treatment.[3]

Third, much of the effect of the eating practices of persons in industrialized countries is felt in oppressed countries. Land owned by the wealthy that was once used to grow inexpensive crops for local people has been converted to the production of expensive products (beef) for export. Increased trade of food products with these countries is consistently the cause of increased starvation. In cultures where food preparation is primarily understood as women's work, starvation is primarily a women's issue. Food expresses who we are politically just as much as bodily. One need not be aware of the fact that one's food practices oppress others in order to be an oppressor.

From a woman's perspective, in particular, it makes sense to ask whether one should become a vegan, a vegetarian who, in addition to refraining from meat and fish, also refrains from eating eggs and dairy products. Since the consumption of eggs and milk have in common that they exploit the reproductive capacities of the female, vegetarianism is not a gender neutral issue.[4] To *choose one's diet* in a patriarchal culture is one way of politicizing an ethic of care. It marks a daily, bodily commitment to resist ideological pressures to conform to patriarchal standards, and to establishing contexts in which caring for can be nonabusive.

Just as there are gender-specific reasons for women's commitment to vegetarianism, for men in a patriarchal society moral vegetarianism can mark the decision to stand in solidarity with women. It also indicates a determination to resist ideological pressures to become a "real man." Real people do not need to eat "real food," as the American Beef Council would have us believe.

Notes

1. Regan calls the animal's right not to be killed a prima facie right that may be overridden. Nevertheless, his theory is not *inherently* contextualized.

2. This practice is also ecologically sound since it saves the enormous expense of firewood for cremation.

3. See John Robbins (1987). It should be noted that in response to such knowledge some reflective nonvegetarians commit to eating range-grown chickens but not those grown in factory farms.

4. I owe this point to a conversation with Colman McCarthy.

References

Adams, Carol J. 1989. *The sexual politics of meat: A feminist-vegetarian critical theory*. New York: Continuum.

Bordo, Susan R. Anorexia nervosa as the psychopathology of popular culture. In *Feminism and Foucault: Reflections on resistance*. Irene Diamond and Lee Quinby, eds. Boston: Northeastern University Press. Reprinted from *The Philosophical Forum* 17, 2 (Winter 1985–86).

Chernin, Kim. 1981. *The obsession: Reflections on the tyranny of slenderness*. New York: Harper and Row.

Plato. 1961. *Gorgias*. In *Plato: The collected dialogues*. Edith Hamilton and Huntington Cairns, eds. Princeton, NJ: Princeton University Press.

Regan, Tom. 1983. *The case for animal rights*. In *Animal rights and human obligations*. 2nd ed. Tom Regan and Peter Singer, eds., Englewood Cliffs, NJ: Prentice-Hall.

Robbins, John. 1987. *Diet for a new America*. Walpole, NH: Stillpoint Publishing.

The Social Construction of Edible Bodies and Humans as Predators

Carol J. Adams

No defenders of ethical vegetarianism have done more than Peter Singer and Carol Adams (1951–   ) to draw attention to the fact that the exploitation of animals bears a family resemblance to other patterns of oppression such as racism and sexism. In her groundbreaking book The Sexual Politics of Meat, *Adams argued that ideological structures redefine the objects of oppression in order to neutralize the possibility of moral condemnation. Living, sentient animals are transformed into antiseptically packaged "meat," for example, analogous to the way in which women are reduced to sexual objects. In this selection, taken from her essay "Ecofeminism and the Eating of Animals," Adams explains the ideological mechanism—what she calls "the structure of the absent referent"—responsible for the legitimation of animal eating.*

Are we predators or are we not? In an attempt to see ourselves as natural beings, some argue that humans are simply predators like some other animals. Vegetarianism is then seen to be unnatural while the carnivorism of other animals is made paradigmatic. Animal rights is criticized "for it does not understand that one species supporting or being supported by another is nature's way of sustaining life" (Ahlers 1990, 433). The deeper disanalogies with carnivorous animals remain unexamined because the notion of humans as predators is consonant with the idea that we need to eat meat. In fact, carnivorism is true for only about 20 percent of nonhuman animals. Can we really generalize from this experience and claim to know precisely what "nature's way" is, or can we extrapolate the role of humans according to this paradigm?

Some feminists have argued that the eating of animals is natural because we do not have the herbivore's double stomach or flat grinders and because chimpanzees eat meat and regard it as a treat (Kevles 1990). This argument from anatomy involves selective filtering. In fact, all primates are primarily herbivorous. Though some chimpanzees have been observed eating dead flesh—at the most, six times in a month—some never eat meat. Dead flesh constitutes less than 4 percent of chimpanzees' diet; many eat insects, and they do not eat dairy products (Barnard 1990). Does this sound like the diet of human beings?

Chimpanzees, like most carnivorous animals, are apparently far better suited to catching animals than are human beings. We are much slower than they. They have long-projecting canine teeth for tearing hide; all the hominoids lost their long-projecting canines 3.5 million years ago, apparently to allow more crushing action consistent with a diet of fruits, leaves, nuts, shoots, and legumes. If we do manage to get a hold of prey animals we cannot rip into their skin. It is true that chimpanzees act as if meat were a treat. When humans lived as foragers and when oil was rare, the flesh of dead animals was a good source of calories. It may be that the "treat" aspect of meat has to do with an ability to recognize dense sources of calories. However, we no longer have a need for such dense sources of calories as animal fat, since our problem is not lack of fat but rather too much fat.

When the argument is made that eating animals is natural, the presumption is that we must continue consuming animals because this is what we require to survive, to survive in a way consonant with living unimpeded by artificial cultural constraints that deprive us of the experience of our real selves. The paradigm of carnivorous animals provides the reassurance that eating animals is natural. But how do we know what is natural when it comes to eating, both because of the social construction of reality and the fact that our history indicates a very mixed message about eating animals? Some did; the majority did not, at least to any great degree.

The argument about what is natural—that is, according to one meaning of it, not culturally constructed, not artificial, but something that returns us to our true selves—appears in a different context that always arouses feminists' suspicions. It is often argued that women's subordination to men is natural. This argument attempts to deny social reality by appealing to the "natural." The "natural" predator argument ignores social construction as well. Since we eat corpses in a way quite differently from any other animals—dismembered, not freshly killed, not raw, and with other foods present—what makes it natural?

Meat is a cultural construct made to seem natural and inevitable. By the time the argument from analogy with carnivorous animals is made, the individual making such an argument has probably consumed animals since before the time she or he could talk. Rationalizations for consuming animals were probably offered when this individual at age four or five was discomfited upon discovering that meat came from dead animals. The taste of dead flesh preceded the rationalizations, and offered a strong foundation for believing the rationalizations to be true, and baby boomers faced the additional problem that as they grew up, meat and dairy products had been canonized as two of the four basic food groups. (This occurred in the 1950s and resulted from active lobbying by the dairy and beef industry. At the turn of the century there were twelve basic food groups.) Thus individuals have not only experienced the gratification of taste in eating animals but may truly believe what they have been told endlessly since childhood—that dead animals are necessary for human survival. The idea that meat eating is natural develops in this context. Ideology makes the artifact appear natural, predestined. In fact, the ideology itself disappears behind the facade that this is a "food" issue.

We interact with individual animals daily if we eat them. However, this statement and its implications are repositioned so that the animal disappears and it is said that we are interacting with a form of food that has been named "meat." In *The Sexual Politics of Meat*, I call this conceptual process in which the animal disappears the structure of the absent referent. Animals in name and body are made absent as animals for meat to exist. If animals are alive they cannot be meat. Thus a dead body replaces the live animal and animals become absent referents. Without animals there would be no meat eating, yet they are absent from the act of eating meat because they have been transformed into food.

Animals are made absent through language that renames dead bodies before consumers participate in eating them. The absent referent permits us to forget about the animal as an independent entity. The roast on the plate is disembodied from the pig who she or he once was. The absent referent also enables us to resist efforts to make animals present, perpetuating a means-ends hierarchy.

The absent referent results from and reinforces ideological captivity: partriarchal ideology establishes the cultural set of human/animal, creates criteria that posit the species difference as important in considering who may be means and who may be ends, and then indoctrinates us into believing that we need to eat animals. Simultaneously, the structure of the absent referent keeps animals absent from our understanding of patriarchal ideology and makes us resistant to having animals made present. This means that we continue to interpret animals from the perspective of human needs and interests: we see them as usable and consumable. Much of feminist discourse participates in this structure when failing to make animals visible.

Ontology recapitulates ideology. In other words, ideology creates what appears to be ontological: if women are ontologized as sexual beings (or rapeable, as some feminists argue), animals are ontologized as carriers of meat. In ontologizing women and animals as objects, our language simultaneously eliminates the fact that someone else is acting as a subject/agent/perpetrator of violence. Sarah Hoagland demonstrates how this works: "John beat Mary," becomes "Mary was beaten by John," then "Mary was beaten," and finally, "women beaten," and thus "battered women" (Hoagland 1988, 17–18). Regarding violence against women and the creation of the term "battered women," Hoagland observes that "now something *men do to women* has become instead something that is a part of *women's nature.* And we lose consideration of John entirely."

The notion of the animal's body as edible occurs in a similar way and removes the agency of humans who buy dead animals to consume them: "Someone kills animals so that I can eat their corpses as meat," becomes "animals are killed to be eaten as meat," then "animals are meat," and finally "meat animals," thus "meat."

Something we do to animals has become instead something that is a part of animals' nature, and we lose consideration of our role entirely.

References

Ahlers, Julia. Thinking like a mountain: Toward a sensible land ethic. *Christian Century* (April 25): 433–34.

Barnard, Neal. 1990. The evolution of the human diet. In *The power of your plate*. Summertown, TN: Book Publishing Co.

Hoagland, Sarah Lucia. 1988. *Lesbian ethics: Toward new values*. Palo Alto, CA: Institute for Lesbian Studies.

Kevles, Bettyann. 1990. Meat, morality and masculinity. *The Women's Review of Books* (May): 11–12.

Appendix I:
Arguments against Ethical Vegetarianism

A rguments dismissing, ridiculing, or seriously contending with ethical vegetarianism abound in contemporary writing on vegetarianism. Vegetarians have been charged with misguided sentimentality, have been viewed as fanatics, have been castigated as antiscience and antihumanist, and patronized as quaint. They are sometimes derided, even by fellow vegetarians, as concerned more with meatless cookbooks and yoga than with such larger issues as diminishing wild animal habitats, pollution, human overpopulation, and famine. Even at their most moderate, vegetarians struggle to express their philosophy in ways articulable to others for whom their beliefs seem quixotic. Yet such dialectic is not new, even if the killing of animals for food carries with it now, as it has in past centuries, the sweeping sanction of everyday habit and thought. In the history of philosophy several key figures have defended on various bases the subordination of animals to human beings and the rightful use of them for human purposes. Debate over ethical vegetarianism is not new.

Perhaps no argument has been more significant in opposing ethical vegetarianism than the argument represented by Aristotle in the selection that follows, and by those in later centuries who stress, like Aristotle, a hierarchy of being based on reason and language. In the *Politics* Aristotle argues for a natural hierarchy of relation between animals and men (women too are inferior to the rational element in men which makes right and proper their rule over subordinates.) The bodies of animals, as the bodies of slaves, properly "minister to the needs of life" because their nature is inferior and must be ruled by a master. It is difference rather than kindredness that Aristotle emphasized in the order of living things, and yet, unlike the more extreme view of Descartes centuries later, Aristotle acknowledged shared capacities in animals and human beings. In the shared capacity for nourishment, reproduction, sensory awareness, and feeling that animals and human beings possess, human beings also have the capacity to reason. Thus "the rational animal" rightfully enjoys the ministration to his life that slaves, women, and animals provide. Fascinating to ponder, and so far removed in spirit from Mill's sense of the imperfection of nature, is Aristotle's conviction that the order of nature is good and its provision proper for the continuation of animal and human life. "Now if nature makes nothing incomplete, and nothing in vain, the inference must be that she has made all animals for the sake of man. And so . . . the art of war is a natural art of acquisition, for the art of acquisition includes hunting, an art which we ought to practice against wild beasts, and against men who, though intended by nature to be governed, will not submit; for war of such a kind is naturally just." For Aristotle, the subordination of animals is justified by the same sweep of argument as the subordination of inferior men in war. The possession of "the rational principle" by superior men is the fundamental justification for the rule of the master. Any impulse to revolutionary resistance to the order of things is obviated by the assumption that what is is natural and therefore right and good. Animals exist in the hierarchy of nature for the sake of man.

Another emblematic defense of the killing of animals for food, and explicit absolution of those who kill animals, is René Descartes' seventeenth-century argument that neither thought nor understanding can be attributed to animals. The materiality of animals—their incapacity to speak, their incapacity to think, absolves human beings, Descartes argues, "from the suspicion of crime when they eat or kill animals." Animals act naturally and mechanically, he argues, as any machine created by the human hand acts. "Doubtless when the swallows come in spring, they operate like clocks. The actions of honeybees are of the same nature, and the discipline of cranes in flight and of apes in fighting. . . ." Interestingly, Descartes affirms the reasonability of thinking of animals as *automata* by contemplating human-made *automata*. "It seems reasonable, since art copies nature, and men can make various automata which move without thought, that nature should produce its own automata, much more splendid than artificial ones. These natural automata are the animals." Thus Descartes ascribes to animals only life and sensation, but it is life "consisting simply in the heat of the heart." We have no duties to animals; we have no need for conscience. Whatever intelligence, whatever pain we may seem to see cannot exist in creatures bereft of understanding and feeling. Thus ethical vegetarianism rests on a mistaken metaphysics—a mistaken attribution of mind to materiality.

Another philosophical defense of the use of animals for human ends is represented here by the eighteenth-century philosopher Immanuel Kant, who argued that only human beings have intrinsic moral worth. In the austere moral universe of Kant, human beings have no moral obligations to animals, no direct duties to animals at all. "Animals are not self-conscious and are there merely as a means to an end. That end is man," Kant writes in his *Lectures on Ethics*. Our care for animals is disciplined practice for the moral duties we have to human beings. "If he is not to stifle his human feelings, he must practice kindness towards animals, for he who is cruel to animals becomes hard also in his dealing with men. We can judge the heart of a man by his treatment of animals." Yet, oddly enough, when Kant argues that a man's cruelty to animals is not a failure in his duty to the dog but a failure in his duty to mankind, he remarks that "the more we come in contact with animals and observe their behavior, the more we love them, for we see how great is their care for their young. It is then difficult for us to be cruel in thought even to a wolf." It is natural, he goes on to argue, that a humane man have tender feelings toward dumb animals. Expressing repugnance at the cruelty toward animals in sport, or the master who turns out his dog when it is no longer of use, Kant nonetheless concludes that "our duties toward animals, then, are indirect duties towards mankind." If ever feeling were subordinated to philosophical position it must be here, in one who defends the view that only human beings can act according to the conception of laws and thus possess intrinsic value, while expressing admiration for Leibniz, who made use of a tiny worm for observation and put it back on its leaf careful not to have harmed it. Yet Kant's ascription of intrinsic moral worth to human beings alone, by virtue of their possession of rationality, free will, and autonomy, remains a central, if sometimes oblique, focus of debate today.

Contemporary arguments over ethical vegetarianism tend toward discussions of quite technical philosophical questions of animal rights, animal capacities, and animal pain, the perceived conflict by some between ecological concerns and animal rights advocacy, factory farming, world food supply, and the importance of the ends to which animal lives are sacrificed. Such debates frequently involve much larger issues than vegetarianism itself and frequently carry the passion of wider political and economic issues. In a long exchange of views in *Ethics* (1978), for example, Michael Fox critiques animal liberation arguments of the kind put forward by both Peter Singer and Tom Regan. Each replies in lengthy defense against Fox's contention that neither provides a solid philosophical foundation for animal liberation. Much of the philosophical debate concentrates on whether or not animals can be said to have the right to equal consideration of interests and the right to life. Fox questions why, if human beings are part of a larger ecological balance, they may not be viewed as part of the carnivorous as well as the herbivorous food chain. If we are part of nature, why isn't our meat eating natural and thus justifiable? And yet, amidst their argument and counterargument, the debate reveals deeper contemporary concerns, made explicit in Fox's argument, over modern methods of food production and animal exploitation, the world food crisis, the distribution of world food supplies, and increasing consumerism.

In one brief editorial in *The New York Times* (6/26/76) entitled *The Cruelty of Vegetarianism*, the author, Eldon W. Dickens, Jr., sounds a note frequently heard in contemporary critiques of vegetarianism. The note is ecological realism. Dickens claims that vegetarianism denies the immense source of cruelty, environmental destruction, and waste of life involved in the production of plants for food. What we ought to attend to rather than the shortsighted end of protecting animals is the protection of our environment—of flora endangered by overpopulation and over pollution. Neither eating plants nor eating animals, he argues, is in itself immoral or cruel. Each has its benefits and disadvantages. "Any effort to preserve populations of animals, without considering the relationships to other organisms, is futile and foolish," he argues. In this particularly modern argument—itself a rejoinder to vegetarians who claim meat production does ecological damage—the attention shifts to issues larger than the human relationship to animals. Much as ancient thinkers worried over moral purity and the kindred spirits of animals, so contemporary debates over vegetarianism reflect contemporary concerns over land, overpopulation, pollution, and our place in nature. Debates over vegetarianism interestingly mirror concerns of their time. Is it not evident that in the short selection from Aristotle, questions of the moral justification of slavery, oppression by the victors in war and the subordination of women all echo in what appears at first to be a discourse on the rule of the rational principle and the relationship between animals and men?

In the dialectic between ethical vegetarianism and anti-vegetarianism—beyond the rhetoric, the flamboyance, and the accusations of cruelty and environmental destruction—exist the deeper queries, metaphysical and moral, that have preoccupied anyone who meditates deeply upon nature and animal life. No matter what one finally concludes, whether one chooses a vegetarian diet or not, whether one adopts an ecological ethic that defends or opposes the killing of animals for food, whether one defends animal rights or not, decries factory farming as cruel or admires it as a technological marvel, there can be no doubt that at stake are some of the most fundamental philosophical questions that we ask.

Appendix II:
Animals and Slavery

Aristotle

I t is clear that the rule of the soul over the body, and of the mind and the rational element over the passionate, is natural and expedient; whereas the equality of the two or the rule of the inferior is always hurtful. The same holds good of animals in relation to men; for tame animals have a better nature than wild, and all tame animals are better off when they are ruled by man; for then they are preserved. Again, the male is by nature superior, and the female inferior; and the one rules, and the other is ruled; this principle, of necessity, extends to all mankind. Where then there is such a difference as that between soul and body, or between men and animals (as in the case of those whose business is to use their body, and who can do nothing better), the lower sort are by nature slaves, and it is better for them as for all inferiors that they should be under the rule of a master. For he who can be, and therefore is, another's and he who participates in rational principle enough to apprehend, but not to have, such a principle, is a slave by nature. Whereas the lower animals cannot even apprehend a principle; they obey their instincts. And indeed the use made of slaves and of tame animals is not very different; for both with their bodies minister to the needs of life. . . .

Aristotle, *Politics*, Book 1, Chapters 5 and 8.

Other modes of life are similarly combined in any way which the needs of men may require. Property, in the sense of a bare livelihood, seems to be given by nature herself to all, both when they are first born, and when they are grown up. For some animals bring forth, together with their offspring, so much food as will last until they are able to supply themselves; of this the viviparous or oviparous animals are an instance; and the viviparous animals have up to a certain time a supply of food for their young in themselves, which is called milk. In like manner we may infer that, after the birth of animals, plants exist for their sake, and that the other animals exist for the sake of man, the tame for use and food, the wild, if not all, at least the greater part of them, for food, and for the provision of clothing and various instruments. Now if nature makes nothing incomplete, and nothing in vain, the inference must be that she has made all animals for the sake of man. And so, in one point of view, the art of war is a natural art of acquisition, for the art of acquisition includes hunting, and art which we ought to practice against wild beasts, and against men who, though intended by nature to be governed, will not submit; for war of such a kind is naturally just.

Appendix III: Automatism of Brutes

René Descartes

Letter to the Marquis of Newcastle

. . . [A]s for the understanding or thought attributed by Montaigne and others to brutes, I cannot hold their opinion; not, however, because I am doubtful of the truth of what is commonly said, that men have absolute dominion over all the other animals; for while I allow that there are some which are stronger than we are, and I believe there may be some, also, which have natural cunning capable of deceiving the most sagacious men; yet I consider that they imitate or surpass us only in those of our actions which are not directed by thought; for it often happens that we walk and that we eat without thinking at all upon what we are doing; and it is so much without the use of our reason that we repel things which harm us, and ward off blows struck at us, that, although we might fully determine not to put our hands before our heads when falling, we could not help doing so. I believe, also, that we should eat as the brutes do, without having learned how, if we had no power of thought at all; and it is said that those who walk in their sleep sometimes swim across rivers,

---

The two letters are from *Descartes Selections*, ed. Ralph M. Eaton (New York: Charles Scribner & Sons, 1927).

where, had they been awake, they would have been drowned.

As for the movements of our passions, although in ourselves they are accompanied with thought, because we possess that faculty, it is, nevertheless, very evident that they do not depend upon it, because they often arise in spite of us, and, consequently, they may exist in brutes, and even be more violent than they are in the men, without warranting the conclusion that brutes can think; in fine there is no one of our external actions which can assure those who examine they that our body is any thing more than a machine which moves of itself, but which also has in it a mind which thinks—excepting words, or other signs made in regard to whatever subjects present themselves, without reference to any passion. I say words, or other signs, because mutes make use of signs in the same way as we do of the voice, and these signs are pertinent; but I exclude the talking of parrots, but not that of the insane, which may be apropos to the case in hand, although it is irrational; and I add that these words or signs are not to relate to any passion, in order to exclude, not only cries of joy or pain and the like, but, also, all that can be taught to any animal by art; for if a magpie be taught to say "good morning" to its mistress when it sees her coming, it may be that the utterance of these words is associated with the excitement of some one of its passions; for instance, there will be a stir of expectation of something to eat, if it has been the custom of the mistress to give it some dainty bit when it spoke those words; and in like manner all those things which dogs, horses, and monkeys are made to do are merely motions of their fear, their hope, or their joy, so that they might do them without any thought at all.

Now, it seems to me very remarkable that language, as thus defined, belongs to man alone; for although Montaigne and Charron have said that there is more difference between one man and another than between a man and a brute, nevertheless there has never yet been found a brute so perfect that it has made use of a sign to inform other animals of something which had no relation to their passions; while there is no man so imperfect as not to use such signs by which they express their thoughts, which seems to me a very strong argument to prove that the reason why brutes do not talk as we do is that they have no faculty of thought, and not at all that the organs for it are wanting. And it cannot be said that they talk among themselves, but we do not understand them; for, as

dogs and other animals express to us their passions, they would
express to us as well their thoughts, if they had them. I know,
indeed, that brutes do many things better than we do, but I am not
surprised at it; for that, also, goes to prove that they act by force of
nature and by springs, like a clock, which tells better what the hour
is than our judgment can inform us. And doubtless, when swallows
come in the spring, they act in that like clocks. All that honey-bees
do is of the same nature; and the order that cranes keep in flying,
or monkeys drawn up for battle, if it be true that they do observe
any order, and finally, the instinct of burying their dead is no more
surprising than that of dogs and cats, which scratch the ground to
bury their excrements, although they almost never do bury them,
which shows that they do it by instinct only, and not by thought. It
can only be said that, although the brutes do nothing which can
convince us that they think nevertheless, because their bodily
organs are not very different from ours, we might conjecture that
there was some faculty of thought joined to these organs, as we
experience in ourselves, although theirs be much less perfect, to
which I have nothing to reply, except that, if they could think as we
do, they would have an immortal soul as well as we, which is not
likely, because there is no reason for believing it of some animals
without believing it of all, and there are many of them too imperfect to make it possible to believe it of them, such as oysters,
sponges, etc.

Letter to Henry More, 1649

[B]ut the greatest of all the prejudices we have retained from
infancy is that of believing that brutes think. The source of our
error comes from having observed that many of the bodily members
of brutes are not very different from our own in shape and movements, and from the belief that our mind is the principle of the
motions which occur in us; that it imparts motion to the body and
is the cause of our thoughts. Assuming this, we find no difficulty in
believing that there is in brutes a mind similar to our own; but having made the discovery, after thinking well upon it, that two different principles of our movements are to be distinguished—the one
entirely mechanical and corporeal, which depends solely on the
force of the animal spirits and the configuration of the bodily parts,

and which may be called corporeal soul, and the other incorporeal, that is to say, mind or soul, which you may define a substance which thinks—I have inquired with great care whether the motions of animals proceed from these two principles or from one alone. Now, having clearly perceived that they can proceed from one only, I have held it demonstrated that we are not able in any manner to prove that there is in the animals a soul which thinks. I am not at all disturbed in my opinion by those doublings and cunning tricks of dogs and foxes, nor by all those things which animals do, either from fear, or to get something to eat, or just for sport. I engage to explain all that very easily, merely by the conformation of the parts of the animals. Nevertheless, although I regard it as a thing demonstrated that it cannot be proved that the brutes have thought, I do not think that it can be demonstrated that the contrary is not true, because the human mind cannot penetrate into the heart to know what goes on there; but, on examining into the probabilities of the case, I see no reason whatever to prove that brutes think, if it be not that having eyes, ears, a tongue, and other organs of sense like ours, it is likely that they have sensations as we do, and as thought is involved in the sensations which we have, a similar faculty of thought must be attributed to them. Now, since this argument is within the reach of everyone's capacity, it has held possession of all minds from infancy. But there are other stronger and more numerous arguments for the opposite opinion, which do not so readily present themselves to everybody's mind; as, for example, that it is more reasonable to make earthworms, flies, caterpillars, and the rest of the animals, move as machines do, than to endow them with immortal souls.

Because it is certain that in the body of animals, as in ours, there are bones, nerves, muscles, blood, animal spirits, and other organs, disposed in such a manner that they can produce themselves, without the aid of any thought, all the movements which we observe in the animals, as appears in convulsive movements, when, in spite of the mind itself, the machine of the body moves often with greater violence, and in more various ways than it is wont to do with the aid of the will; moreover, inasmuch as it is agreeable to reason that art should imitate nature, and that men should be able to construct divers *automata* in which there is movement without any thought, nature, on her part, might produce these *automata*, and far more excellent ones, as the brutes are, than those which come from the hand of man, seeing no reason anywhere why thought is to be found, wherever we perceive a conformation of bodily members like that of the animals, and that it is more surprising that there should be a soul in every human body than that there should be none at all in the brutes.

But the principal argument, to my mind, which may convince us that the brutes are devoid of reason, is that, although among those of the same species, some are more perfect than others, as among men, which is particularly noticeable in horses and dogs, some of which have more capacity than others to retain what is taught them, and although all of them make us clearly understand their natural movements of anger, of fear, of hunger, and others of like kind, either by the voice or by other bodily motions, it has never yet been observed that any animal has arrived as such a degree of perfection as to make use of a true language; that is to say, as to be able to indicate to us by the voice, or by other signs, anything which could be referred to thought alone, rather than to a movement of mere nature; for the word is the sole sign and the only certain mark of the presence of thought hidden and wrapped up in the body; now all men, the most stupid and the most foolish, those even who are deprived of the organs of speech, make use of signs, whereas the brutes never do anything of the kind; which may be taken for the true distinction between man and brute. . . . I omit, for the sake of brevity, the other arguments which deny thought to the brutes. It must, however, be observed that I speak of thought, not of life, nor of sensation; for I do not deny the life of any animal, making it to consist solely in the warmth of the heart. I do not refuse to them feeling even, in so far as it depends only on the bodily organs. Thus, my opinion is not so cruel to animals as it is favorable to men; I speak to those who are not committed to the extravagances of Pythagoras, which attached to those who ate or killed them the suspicion even of a crime.

Appendix IV: We Have Only Indirect Duties to Animals

Immanuel Kant

I. Second Formulation of the Categorical Imperative: Humanity as an End in Itself

The will is conceived as a faculty of determining oneself to action *in accordance with the conception of certain laws*. And such a faculty can be found only in rational beings. Now that which serves the will as the objective ground of its self-determination is the end, and if this is assigned by reason alone, it must hold for all rational beings. On the other hand, that which merely contains the ground of possibility of the action of which the effect is the end, this is called the *means*. The subjective ground of the desire is the *spring*, the objective ground of the volition is the *motive*; hence the distinction between subjective ends which rest on springs, and objective ends which depend on motives valid for every rational being. Practical principles are *formal* when they abstract from all subjective ends; they are *material* when they assume these, and therefore particular springs of action. The ends which a rational being proposes to

The first section is from Kant's *Foundations of the Metaphysics of Morals* (1873), trans. T. K. Abbott. The second section is from Kant's *Lectures on Ethics*, trans. Louis Infield (New York: Harper & Row, 1963.

himself at pleasure as *effects* of his actions (material ends) are all only relative, for it is only their relation to the particular desires of the subject that gives them their worth, which therefore cannot furnish principles universal and necessary for all rational beings and for every volition, that is to say practical laws. Hence all these relative ends can give rise only to hypothetical imperatives.

Supposing, however, that there were something whose existence has in itself an absolute worth, something which, being an end in itself, could be a source of definite laws, then in this and this alone would lie the source of a possible categorical imperative, i.e. a practical law.

Now I say: man and generally any rational being *exists* as an end in himself, *not merely as a means* to be arbitrarily used by this or that will, but in all his actions, whether they concern himself or other rational beings, must be always regarded at the same time as an end. All objects of the inclinations have only a conditional worth; for if the inclinations and the wants founded on them did not exist, then their object would be without value. But the inclinations themselves being sources of want are so far from having an absolute worth for which they should be desired, that, on the contrary, it must be the universal wish of every rational being to be wholly free from them. Thus the worth of any object which is *to be acquired* by our action is always conditional. Beings whose existence depends not on our will but on nature's, have nevertheless, if they are nonrational beings, only a relative value as means, and are therefore called *things*; rational beings, on the contrary, are called *persons*, because their very nature points them out as ends in themselves, that is as something which must not be used merely as means, and so far therefore restricts freedom of action (and is an object of respect). These, therefore, are not merely subjective ends whose existence has a worth *for us* as an effect of our action, but *objective ends*, that is things whose existence is an end in itself: an end moreover for which no other can be substituted, which they should subserve *merely* as means, for otherwise nothing whatever would possess *absolute worth*; but if all worth were conditioned and therefore contingent, then there would be no supreme practical principle of reason whatever.

If then there is a supreme practical principle or, in respect of the human will, a categorical imperative, it must be one which, being drawn from the conception of that which is necessarily an end for everyone because it is *an end in itself*, constitutes an *objective* principle of will, and can therefore serve a universal practical law. The foundation of this principle is: *rational nature exists as an end in itself*. Man necessarily conceives his own existence as being so: so far then this is a *subjective* principle of human actions. But every other rational being regards its existence similarly, just on the same rational principle that holds for me: so that it is at the same time an objective principle, from which as a supreme practical law all laws of the will must be capable of being deduced. Accordingly the practical imperative will be as follows: *So act as to treat humanity, whether in thine own person or in that of any other, in every case as an end withal, never as means only*. We will now inquire whether this can be practically carried out.

II.

Baumgarten speaks of duties towards beings which are beneath us and beings which are above us. But so far as animals are concerned, we have no direct duties. Animals are not self-conscious and are there merely as a means to an end. That end is man. We can ask, "Why do animals exist?" But to ask, "Why does man exist?" is a meaningless question. Our duties towards animals are merely indirect duties towards humanity. Animal nature has analogies to human nature, and by doing our duties to animals in respect of manifestations of human nature, we indirectly do our duty towards humanity. Thus, if a dog has served his master long and faithfully, his service, on the analogy of human service, deserves reward, and when the dog has grown too old to serve, his master ought to keep him until he dies. Such action helps to support us in our duties towards human beings, where they are bounden duties. If then any acts of animals are analogous to human acts and spring from the same principles, we have duties towards the animals because thus we cultivate the corresponding duties toward human beings. If a man shoots his dog because the animal is no longer capable of service, he does not fail in his duty to the dog, for the dog cannot judge, but his act is inhuman and damages in himself that humanity which it is his duty to show toward mankind. If he is not to stifle his human feeling, he must practice kindness towards animals, for he who is cruel to animals becomes hard also in his dealing with men. We can judge the heart of a man by his treatment of animals. Hogarth depicts this in his engravings. He shows how cruelty grows and develops. He shows the child's cruelty to animals, pinch the tail of a dog or a cat; he then depicts the grown man in his cart running over a child; and lastly, the culmination of cruelty in murder. He thus brings home to us in a terrible fashion the rewards of cruelty, and this should be an impressive lesson to children. The more we come in contact with animals and observe their behavior, the more we love them, for we see how great is their care for their young. It is then difficult for us to be cruel in thought even to a wolf. Leibnitz used a tiny worm for purposes of observation, and then carefully replaced it with its leaf on the tree so that it should not come to harm through any act of his. He would have been sorry—a natural feeling for a humane man—to destroy such a creature for no reason. Tender feelings towards dumb animals develop humane feelings towards mankind. In England butchers and doctors do not sit on a jury because they are accustomed to the sight of death and hardened. Vivisectionists, who use living animals for their experiments, certainly act cruelly, although their aim is praiseworthy, and they can justify their cruelty, since animals must be regarded as man's instruments; but any such cruelty for sport cannot be justified. A master who turns out his ass or his dog because the animal can no longer earn its keep manifests a small mind. The Greeks' ideas in this respect were highminded, as can be seen from the fable of the ass and the bell of ingratitude. Our duties towards animals, then, are indirect duties towards mankind.

Appendix V:
Bibliography of
Antivegetarian Sources

David, William H. "Man-eating Aliens." *Journal of Value Inquiry* 10 (Fall 1976)): 178–85.

Devine, Philip E. "The Moral Basis of Vegetarianism." *Philosophy* 53 (October 1978): 481–505.

Diamond, Cora. "Eating meat and eating people." *Philosophy* 53 (October 1978): 465–79.

Dickens, Eldon W., Jr. "Cruelty in Vegetarianism." *New York Times* (June 26, 1976): 23.

Ewbank, Roger. "The Trouble with Being a Farm Animal." *New Scientist* (October 18, 1973): 172–73.

Fager, Charles E. "Vegetarianism: A Force Against Famine?" *Christian Century* 92/35 (October 29, 1975): 971–72.

Ferré, Frederick. "Moderation, Morals, and Meat." *Inquiry.* (December 1986): 391–406.

————. "Animal Liberation: A Critique." *Ethics* 88 (January 1978): 106–118.

Fox, Michael. "Animal Suffering and Rights: A Reply to Singer and Regan." *Ethics* 88 (January 1978): 134–38.

Francis, Leslie Pickering, and Norman, Richard. "Some Animals are More Equal Than Others." *Philosophy* 53 (October 1978): 507–27.

Frey, R. G. "Rights, Interest, Desires and Beliefs." *American Philosophical Quarterly* 16/3 (July 1979): 233–39.

———. *Rights, Killing and Suffering: Moral Vegetarianism and Applied Ethics*. London: Basil Blackwell, 1983.

George, Kathryn Paxton. "Discrimination and Bias in the Vegan Ideal." *Journal of Agricultural Ethics* (1994): 19–28.

George, Kathryn Paxton. "So Animal a Human . . . , or The Moral Relevance of Being an Omnivore." *Journal of Agricultural Ethics* (1990): 172–86.

Lehman, H. S., and Hurnik, J. F. "On an Alleged Moral Basis of Vegetarianism." *Applied Animal Ethology* 6/3 (July 1980): 205–29.

Levin, Michael. "All in a Stew About Animals: A Reply to Singer." *Humanist* 37/5 (September–October 1977): 58.

———. "Philosophical Vegetarianism: Con and Pro; Animals Rights Evaluated." *Humanist* 37/4 (July–August 1977): 12, 14–15.

Martin, Michael. "A Critique of Moral Vegetarianism." *Reason Papers* 3 (1976): 13–43.

———. "Vegetarianism, the Right to Life and Fellow Creaturehood." *Animal Regulation Studies* 2/3 (August 1980): 205–14.

Nielsen, Kai, "Persons, Morals and the Animal Kingdom." *Man and World* 11 (1978): 231–56.

Pluhar, Evelyn. "Who Can Be Morally Obligated to be a Vegetarian?" *Journal of Agricultural Ethics* (1992): 189–215.

Weir, Jack. "Unnecessary Pain, Nutrition, and Vegetarianism." *Between Species* (Winter 1991): 13–26.

Young, Thomas. "The Morality of Killing Animals: Four Arguments" *Ethics Animals* (December 1984): 88–101.

For Further Reading

The literature of ethical vegetarianism is rich and ancient, stretching in the West at least as far back as the pre-Socratics. Unfortunately, it is also widely scattered and frequently difficult to find outside of specialized libraries or the collections of research universities. The selections collected in this anthology are some of the most important and representative, but they are really only the tip of the iceberg.

Essential tools for further exploration are bibliographies—preferably annotated ones—of the available literature. Fortunately, there are several that may be consulted, although none of them is either exhaustive or completely up-to-date. The most comprehensive is Judith C. Dyer's *Vegetarianism: An Annotated Bibliography* (Metuchen, N.J.: Scarecrow Press, 1982). Although the bibliography is not devoted exclusively to ethical treatments of vegetarianism, there are a couple of pertinent sections in it. The listings for literature prior to the twentieth century are rather sparse. The section on vegetarianism in Charles R. Magel's *Keyguide to Information Resources in Animal Rights* (Jefferson, N.C.: McFarland, 1989) is also worth consulting. A quite good bibliography, partially annotated, which lists twentieth-century works up to 1980 is included as an appendix (170–225) to a recent reprint of Henry S. Salt's 1892 *Animal Rights: Considered in Relation to Social Progress* (Clarks Summit, Pa.: Society for Animal Rights, 1980). The bibliography was compiled by Charles R. Magel. In that same reprinted volume can be found a useful annotated bibliography (137–69) compiled by

273

Salt himself of pertinent works published between 1723 to 1921.

A historical study that has become an indispensable resource is Howard Williams's *The Ethics of Diet: A Catena of Authorities Deprecatory of the Habit of Flesh-eating* (London: Richard J. James and Manchester: Albert Broadbest, 1883). In his book, Williams provides analyses of a number of ethical defenses of vegetarianism, ranging from Hesiod through the nineteenth century. Although the original edition is a bit difficult to locate, the book was reprinted numerous times in the subsequent fifty years, particularly in an abridged version. Many good libraries contain copies.

While Williams's study is probably the single best historical overview of ethical vegetarianism, Dudley Giehl's *Vegetarianism: A Way of Life* (N.Y.: Harper & Row, 1979) and John Lawrence Hill's *The Case for Vegetarianism: Philosophy for a Small Planet* (Lanham, Md.: Rowman & Littlefield, 1996) are the two best analyses of vegetarianism as a deliberate way of life. Giehl's study goes beyond the ethical aspects of vegetarianism to examine its nutritional advantages as well. His book is also forwarded by Isaac Bashevis Singer. Hill's book provides an excellent survey of the major philosophical defenses of ethical vegetarianism. Although philosophically rigorous, it is accessible to the lay reader. Also worth examining is Mark Matthew Braunstein's fine *Radical Vegetarianism: A Dialectic of Diet and Ethic* (Los Angeles, Calif.: Panjandrum Books, 1988).

Because there is such an intimate connection between defenses of ethical vegetarianism and discussions of animal rights, many fine discussions of the former have made their way into collections devoted to the latter. Five of the best of these anthologies are the following: Stanley and Roslind Godlovitch and John Harris, ed., *Animals, Men and Morals: An Inquiry into the Maltreatment of Nonhumans* (London: Gollancz, 1972); Harlan B. Miller and William H. Williams, eds., *Ethics and Animals* (Clifton, N.J.: Humana, 1983); Richard Knowles Morris and Michael W. Fox, eds., *On the Fifth Day: Animal Rights and Human Ethics* (Washington, D.C.: Acropolis Press, 1978); Tom Regan and Peter Singer, eds., *Animal Rights and Human Obligations* (Englewood Cliffs, N.J.: Prentice-Hall, 1976); and Jon Wynne-Tyson, ed., *The Extended Circle: A Commonplace Book of Animal Rights* (N.Y.: Paragon House, 1989).

Three book-length philosophical studies that discuss ethical vegetarianism have become classics. Peter Singer's *Animal Libera-*

tion: A New Ethics for our Treatment of Animals (New York: Avon, 1975) is a pioneering work which argued that human practices such as carnivorism and animal research are speciesistic. Tom Regan's *The Case for Animal Rights* (Berkeley, Calif.: University of California Press, 1983) is by far the most rigorous defense of animal rights and ethical vegetarianism. While Singer's book is easily accessible to the general reader, Regan's is not. A third work, one that argues that carnivorism is of a kind with sexism and racism, is Carol J. Adams's *The Sexual Politics of Meat: A Feminist-Vegetarian Critical Theory* (New York: Continuum, 1989).

Daniel Dombrowski's *The Philosophy of Vegetarianism* (Amherst: University of Massachusetts Press, 1984) is an excellent analysis of ethical vegetarianism in the Hellenistic world. His *Charles Hartshorne and the Metaphysics of Animal Rights* (Albany: SUNY Press, 1988) also has an interesting defense of vegetarianism.

Many contemporary defenses of ethical vegetarianism build their cases on the devastating ecological and economic consequences of factory farming and carnivorism. The ground-breaking study in this area is Ruth Harrison's *Animal Machines* (London: Stuart, 1964). Although somewhat dated, it is still useful. A more recent study is Jim Mason and Peter Singer, *Animal Factories* (New York: Crown, 1980). In addition to Frances Moore Lappé's pioneering *Diet for a Small Planet*, other studies of ethical vegetarianism that focus on economic and ecological concerns are Patricia Kutzner *World Hunger* (Santa Barbara, Calif.: ABC-Clio, 1991); Francis Moore Lappé and Joseph Collins, *Food First: Beyond the Myth of Scarcity* (Boston: Houghton Mifflin, 1977); Radha Sinha, *Food and Poverty* (London: Croom Helm, 1976); and Jon Wynne-Tyson, *Food for a Future: The Ecological Priority of a Humane Diet* (London: Davis-Poynter, 1975). Most of the primary studies as well as the essay collections cited here have excellent bibliographies.

Finally, a recent historical study of vegetarianism is both fulsome and entertaining: Colin Spencer's *The Heretic's Feast: A History of Vegetarianism* (Hanover, N.H.: University Press of New England, 1995).

Sources and Acknowledgments

Pythagoras

Iamblichus. "On the Pythagorean Life." In *The Pythagorean Sourcebook and Library*. Edited and translated by Kenneth Sylvan Guthrie. (Grand Rapids, Mich.: Phanes Press, 1987), 84. Reprinted by permission of the publisher.

Diogenes Laertius. "The Life of Pythagoras." In *The Pythagorean Sourcebook and Library*. Edited and translated by Kenneth Sylvan Guthrie. (Grand Rapids, Mich.: Phanes Press, 1987), 144–45. Reprinted by permission of the publisher.

Ovid. *Metamorphosis*. Translated by Rolfe Humphries. (Bloomington, Ind.: Indiana University Press, 1963), 367–69. [book 15, lines 59–477] Reprinted by permission of the publisher.

Seneca

Lucius Annaeus Seneca. *Lucilium Epistulae Morales*. Translated by Richard M. Gummere. (New York: G. P. Putnam's, 1925), vol. 3, 241–45. [Epistle 58]

Plutarch

Plutarch. *Moralia*. Translated by Harold Cherniss and William C. Helmbold. (Cambridge, Mass.: Harvard University Press, 1927), vol. 12, 541–79.

Porphyry

Porphyry. *On Abstinence from Animal Food*. Translated by Thomas Taylor, edited by Esme Wynne-Tyson. (London: Centaur Press, 1965), 109–11, 116–17, 118–22, 123, 126–31, 137–41. Reprinted by permission of the publisher.

Bernard Mandeville

Bernard Mandeville. *The Fable of the Bees; or, Private Vices, Publick Benefits*, vol. 1. (Oxford, 1705), 172–81.

David Hartley

David Hartley. *Observations on Man, His Frame, His Duty, and His Expectations*, vol. 2. (London: Richard Cruttwell, 1810), 230–32.

Oliver Goldsmith

Oliver Goldsmith. *Letters from a Citizen of the World to His Friends in the East*. In *The Miscellaneous Works of Oliver Goldsmith*. Edited by Washington Irving. (Philadelphia: Crissy & Markley, n.d.), 263–64.

William Paley

William Paley. *The Principles of Moral and Political Philosophy*. (Boston: Richardson & Lord, 1825), pp. 76–78.

Percy Bysshe Shelley

Percy Bysshe Shelley. "A Vindication of Natural Diet." In *Shelley's Prose, or The Trumpet of a Prophecy*. Edited by David Lee Clark. (Albuquerque, N.M.: University of New Mexico Press, 1954), 83–84, 85–88, 90.

Alphonse de Lamartine

Alphonse de Lamartine. *Les Confidences*. Translated by Eugene Plunkett. (New York: Appleton & Co., 1865), 59–61 [note 8]

William A. Alcott

William A. Alcott. *Vegetable Diet.* (New York: Fowlers & Wells, 1848), 263–65, 276–83.

Richard Wagner

Richard Wagner. "Against Vivisection." In *Richard Wagner's Prose Works.* Translated by William Ashton Ellis, volume 6: *Religion and Art.* (London: Routledge & Kegan Paul, Ltd., 1897), 201–7. Reprinted by permission of publisher.

Selected Letters of Richard Wagner. Translated and edited by Stewart Spencer and Barry Millington. (New York: W. W. Norton & Company, 1987), 422–24. Reprinted by permission of publisher.

Leo Tolstoy

Leo Tolstoy. "The First Step" (Preface to Howard Williams' *The Ethics of Diet.*) In Leo Tolstoy, *Essays and Letters.* Trans. Aylmer Maude. (New York: H. Frowde, 1909), 82–91.

Anna Kingsford

Anna Kingsford and Edward Maitland. *Addresses and Essays on Vegetarianism.* (London: John M. Watkins, 1912), 145–50.

Henry S. Salt

Henry S. Salt. *The Humanities of Diet.* (Manchester: The Vegetarian Society, 1914).

J. Howard Moore

J. Howard Moore. *The New Ethics.* (London, 1907).

J. Howard Moore. *The Universal Kinship.* (London, 1906).

Romain Rolland

Romain Rolland. *Jean-Christophe.* Translated by Gilbert Cannan. (New York: Random House Modern Library, 1938), 326–28.

Mohandas Gandhi

Mohandas Gandhi. *Diet and Diet Reform*. (Ahmedabad, India: Navajivan Publishing House, 1949), 8–12, 35–36.

Albert Schweitzer

Albert Schweitzer. *Civilization and Ethics. The Philosophy of Civilization, Part II.* Translated by John Nash. (London: A. & C. Black, 1923), 254–58, 264–65.

Tom Regan

Tom Regan. "The Moral Basis of Vegetarianism." *The Canadian Journal of Philosophy* (October 1975), 205–13. Reprinted by permission of publisher and author.

Peter Singer

Peter Singer. "All Animals Are Equal." *Philosophic Exchange* 1 (summer 1974), 103–9. Reprinted by permission of publisher and author.

Thomas Auxter

Thomas Auxter. "The Right Not to be Eaten." *Inquiry* 22 (summer 1974), 221–30. Reprinted by permission of publisher and author.

Peter Wenz

Peter S. Wenz. "An Ecological Argument for Vegetarianism." *Ethics and Animals* 5 (March 1984), 2–9. Reprinted by permission of publisher and author.

Stephen Clark

Stephen R. L. Clark. *The Moral Status of Animals.* (Oxford: Clarendon Press, 1977), 42–45, 46–47. Reprinted by permission of publisher.

Frances Moore Lappé

Frances Moore Lappé, *Diet for a Small Planet.* (New York: Ballantine Books, 1982), 66–69, 71, 76, 78–79, 84, 462–65, 466–67, 468. Reprinted by permission of author.

Harriet Schleifer

Harriet Schleifer. "Images of Death and Life: Food Animal Production and the Vegetarian Option." In *In Defense of Animals*. Edited by Peter Singer. (New York: Harper & Row, 1985), 62–73. Reprinted by permission of the publisher.

Jon Wynne-Tyson

Jon Wynne-Tyson. "Dietethics: Its Influence on Future Farming Patterns." In *Animals' Rights: A Symposium*. Edited by Richard Ryder and David Paterson. (London: Centaur Press, 1979). Reprinted by permission of the publisher and author.

Deane Curtin

"Toward an Ecological Ethic of Care." *Hypatia* 6 (spring 1991), 68–71. Reprinted by permission of the publisher and author.

Carol J. Adams

"Ecofeminism and the Eating of Animals." *Hypatia* 6 (spring 1991), 134–37.

Index